A

Wuthering Heights

HANDBOOK

D1264537

A
Wuthering Heights
HANDBOOK

RICHARD LETTIS • WILLIAM E. MORRIS

C. W. Post College   *Ohio University*

THE ODYSSEY PRESS • INC.

NEW YORK

Introduction

The things we do demonstrate our character; in our approach to tasks our personality is revealed. This is especially true of the manner of our reading. For example, our need for relaxation is often expressed in the choice of a novel that we can read with ease: we turn on television, begin a crossword puzzle, peel a banana, and devote what is left of our attention to a good story. Our need for excitement may be similarly demonstrated by our reading a detective story or a Western, our interest in the past may guide us to historical novels, or our delight in the unusual may lead us to science fiction or ghost tales. Sometimes our reading becomes merely an attempt to escape for a moment from where and what we are; this too tells us something about ourselves.

There is probably nothing wrong with any of the above reasons for reading; indeed, each provides us with some of our happiest contacts with literature. But many readers find that the most rewarding experience of all is to approach a novel as they would pursue a hobby; that is, they expect to enjoy it by working at it. In this they pay a novel the same deference that the hi-fi enthusiast pays to his tweeters and woofers, the golfer gives to his five iron, and the hot rodder confers upon his four-barreled carburetor. They decide that there will be as much pleasure in mastering a book as there is in becoming proficient in any challenging field of endeavor. And they are aware that real proficiency always requires great concentration, careful attention, acute perception, and plenty of work.

Your reasons for reading are, of course, your own. But as you undertake the study of *Wuthering Heights* for the purpose of writing a research paper, you find yourself with an excellent opportunity for deciding just how much pleasure can be derived from working at a novel—a great one. You will find that such work is indeed challenging: a writer of considerable ability dares you to go beyond the mere assimilation of facts, the easy noting of "what happened," to the more stimulating and rewarding business of finding meaning in the facts, of deciding *why* it happened, and of determining what it all means and how successful and good and true it all is. The writer is not interested in making this work easy for you: it is not

your need for relaxation that she intends to meet. Indeed, she probably believed making all that her novel holds easily available to
you would destroy the artistry of her work and seriously impair
your ability to enjoy it (just as you would soon lose interest in
playing tennis when the net is lowered, or in working on a crossword puzzle when the answers are provided on the next page). Certainly you will want to note the facts, and it is hoped that you will
enjoy finding out "what happens," but to this you will add the
pleasure derived from coming to grips with other aspects of the
novel: the theme, characterization, structure, atmosphere, point of
view, style, and so on.

This text should convince you that you are not alone in seeking
such pleasure from *Wuthering Heights*. For the essays you will read
here are written by people who also decided to give some effort to
the novel, and were so delighted or disturbed or disgusted by the
result that they had to tell somebody about it. Now they are telling
you. And whatever pleasure comes from your own reading of the
novel, chances are that you will find your response enriched by
joining theirs to it.

Naturally, you will want to read and experience the novel before
you read the criticism, so that you can take your own approach,
make your own response to the challenges, and establish your own
relationship with Heathcliff, Catherine, and the rest. But then you
can go on to tap the approaches and responses of others, extending
your perceptions, correcting your misreadings, and deepening your
penetration (remember, those who are helping you have themselves been helped). If you give your energies to all this, you will
finish your reading with enough material for several research
papers, any of which will be the record of a full and satisfying
learning experience, and will command the respect and attention
of your instructor.

The criticism presented here should help you to a study of
Wuthering Heights from almost any interpretive or evaluative
standpoint you may select. The characters, for example, offer a
serious challenge. What are they like? Who are the good people,
and the bad? Has the author made them seem real, believable—for
example, do they act consistently throughout, or do they change
unnaturally, or seem to act without proper motive, or appear rather
to represent human qualities than to be human beings? Answering
these questions will lead you to other considerations—for example,
the plot, or action of the story. Is the structure of the plot confusing? Does the action take you away from the main line of develop-

ment of the novel? Is there significant conflict, and is it probable?
Does the plot progress, or does it just wander, or appear to repeat
itself? Does the action reach an acceptable climax (a point, not
necessarily the biggest or most violent in the story, where the complications end and the story begins to move to its conclusion)?
How much exposition (background of the characters and the action) does the reader need? Has the author worked it into the story
deftly, or awkwardly?

Many other problems offer themselves. You may consider the
point of view (the selection of a narrator to tell the story—the author himself, for example, or, as in *Wuthering Heights,* one or more
characters within the novel). You may evaluate the style—its effectiveness as communication, its suitability to the subject matter, its
polish or its clumsiness. The study of symbolism and imagery will
be of particular importance to your understanding of *Wuthering
Heights,* for Emily Brontë constantly shapes her materials so that
they stand for ideas and concepts beyond themselves. For instance
Wuthering Heights itself is at first just a house, and a very real one;
but as the reader contrasts it with Thrushcross Grange, and considers what happens in each house, who lives there, and so on, he
comes to feel that the weather-beaten building represents something, and he needs to decide what that something is. He may feel
the same way about Heathcliff, about Lockwood's dreams, and even
about the countryside. And he will find his understanding of such
symbols augmented and enriched by the powerful imagery—the
metaphors and similes and personifications—which pervades the
novel and helps the reader respond to the events of the story with
his senses and with the memory of his own human experience.

We have only begun to suggest approaches. And we have only
briefly mentioned terms and tools of criticism which you will want
to familiarize yourself with at greater length in class discussion, so
that you can meet your problem with as solid a foundation as you
can acquire. As you continue to equip yourself to treat *Wuthering
Heights,* keep in mind the kinds of approach you can take to such
a novel. You can examine the criticism of the novel historically, deciding how the evaluation and interpretation of *Wuthering
Heights* has changed. You can present your own interpretation or
evaluation, using such criticism as seems most useful. Or you can
combine the historical and interpretive approaches in the study of
a particular problem such as the changing interpretations of the
character of Heathcliff. Depending on the size of your paper, and
the depth of your study, you can choose as broad or as narrow a

a field of interest as you wish—the significance of a broken window or a hanged puppy, for instance, or the nature of Brontë's attitude toward good and evil, life and death.

The editors of this text have tried to help you in your work in two ways. First, we have presented the essays in a form as close to the original as possible. You will find that the pages of the articles are given (in slash marks: /21/) just as they occur in the periodical or book from which they are taken. Any errors, misprints, or omissions which appeared there are reproduced here,* so that you are virtually placed in a library, on your own, with a book spread out before you. It will be your task to note pages correctly, to check the form of bibliographical entries, and to proofread quotations for accuracy, just as it will be your job to read and understand and use the novel and its criticism. Second, we have added to each article suggestions for discussion and writing, have listed more comprehensive topics for research at the end of the articles, and have supplied topics and a bibliography which will enable you to pursue your study of *Wuthering Heights* beyond the limitations of this text, if your instructor so desires. You will note that our suggestions are essentially of three kinds: they raise problems concerning the article they follow, problems concerning the article in relation to the novel, and problems concerning the article in comparison to other articles. It is hoped that these suggestions will afford you with many lines of approach to the material before you. On the other hand, it is hoped that you will not let yourself be limited by the suggestions, but will pursue your own interest toward those areas of research which satisfy you and your instructor.

It is not possible to name all the individuals who have helped to prepare this text, but the authors wish at least to thank Priscilla Lettis and Florence Morris for their help in preparing the manuscript, proofreading the copy, and keeping the children quiet.

R. L.
W. E. M.

* There are two exceptions to this. At the request of Professors Worth and Hafley, and of *Nineteenth-Century Fiction,* we have corrected typographical errors which impaired the sense of the articles by these two authors.

Contents

Jane Eyre and *Wuthering Heights*

VIRGINIA WOOLF

The meaning of a book, which lies so often apart from what happens and what is said and consists rather in some connection which things in themselves different have had for the writer, is necessarily hard /224/ to grasp. Especially this is so when, like the Brontës, the writer is poetic, and his meaning inseparable from his language, and itself rather a mood than a particular observation. *Wuthering Heights* is a more difficult book to understand than *Jane Eyre*, because Emily was a greater poet than Charlotte. When Charlotte wrote she said with eloquence and splendour and passion "I love", "I hate", "I suffer". Her experience, though more intense, is on a level with our own. But there is no "I" in *Wuthering Heights*. There are no governesses. There are no employers. There is love, but it is not the love of men and women. Emily was inspired by some more general conception. The impulse which urged her to create was not her own suffering or her own injuries. She looked out upon a world cleft into gigantic disorder and felt within her the power to unite it in a book. That gigantic ambition is to be felt throughout the novel—a struggle, half thwarted but of superb conviction, to say something through the mouths of her characters which is not merely "I love" or "I hate", but "we, the whole human race" and "you, the eternal powers . . ." the sentence remains unfinished. It is not strange that it should be so; rather it is astonishing that she can make us feel what she had it in her to say at all. It surges up in the half-articulate words of Catherine Earnshaw,

"If all else perished and *he* remained, I should still continue to be; and if all else remained and he were annihilated, the universe would turn to a mighty stranger; I should not seem part of /225/ it". It breaks out again in the presence of the dead. "I see a repose that neither earth nor hell can break, and I feel an assurance of the endless and shadowless hereafter—the eternity they have entered—where life is boundless in its duration, and love in its sympathy and joy in its fulness." It is this suggestion of power underlying the apparitions of human nature, and lifting them up into the presence of greatness that gives the book its huge stature among other novels. But it was not enough for Emily Brontë to write a few lyrics, to utter a cry, to express a creed. In her poems she did this once and for all, and her poems will perhaps outlast her novel. But she was novelist as well as poet. She must take upon herself a more laborious and a more ungrateful task. She must face the fact of other existences, grapple with the mechanism of external things, build up, in recognisable shape, farms and houses and report the speeches of men and women who existed independently of herself. And so we reach these summits of emotion not by rant or rhapsody but by hearing a girl sing old songs to herself as she rocks in the branches of a tree; by watching the moor sheep crop the turf; by listening to the soft wind breathing through the grass. The life at the farm with all its absurdities and its improbability is laid open to us. We are given every opportunity of comparing *Wuthering Heights* with a real farm and Heathcliff with a real man. How, we are allowed to ask, can there be truth or insight or the finer shades of emotion in men and women who so little resemble /226/ what we have seen ourselves? But even as we ask it we see in Heathcliff the brother that a sister of genius might have seen; he is impossible we say, but nevertheless no boy in literature has so vivid an existence as his. So it is with the two Catherines; never could women feel as they do or act in their manner, we say. All the same, they are the most lovable women in English fiction. It is as if she could tear up all that we know human beings by, and fill these unrecognisable transparences with such a gust of life that they transcend reality. Hers, then, is the rarest of all powers. She could free life from its dependence on facts; with a few touches indicate the spirit of a face so that it needs no body; by speaking of the moor make the wind blow and the thunder roar. /227/

Questions for Discussion and Writing

1. What does Mrs. Woolf mean when she says, "There is no 'I' in *Wuthering Heights*"? (page 225) What have other critics said about this?

2. What does Mrs. Woolf mean by saying that the love in *Wuthering Heights* "is not the love of men and women"? (page 225)

3. Express in your own words what you think Mrs. Woolf is saying about Emily Brontë's genius on pages 226-227. Support or attack the criticism with evidence from the novel.

4. Starting with Mrs. Woolf's statements on Emily Brontë as a person and as an author, discuss portraits which critics have drawn of the writer of *Wuthering Heights*.

The Structure of
Wuthering Heights

C. P. SANGER

By common consent *Wuthering Heights* is a remarkable book. I do not propose to discuss its literary merits, but to confine myself to the humbler task of investigating its structure, which presents certain peculiarities. Whether this is worth doing I do not know, but I found that it added to my interest in the book and made the tale much more vivid for me.

The main theme is how a sort of human cuckoo, called Heathcliff, sets out with success to acquire all the property of two families, the Earnshaws and the Lintons. The tale is a fairly complicated one, and the incidents extend over a period of more than thirty years. Stated as baldly and shortly as I can, the plot is as follows: Mr and Mrs Earnshaw live at Wuthering Heights, a farm-house on a Yorkshire moor. They have two children, a son called Hindley and a daughter Catherine. One day Mr Earnshaw, who has been to Liverpool on business, brings home a waif he has picked up there. This waif, Heathcliff, is brought up at Wuthering Heights. Not long after, Mrs Earnshaw dies. Heathcliff is Mr Earnshaw's favourite; he is also great friends with /5/ Catherine, but Hindley, who is older, bullies him. At last, Hindley is sent off to college. When Mr Earnshaw dies, Hindley returns for the funeral, bringing with him a young wife. He takes possession, ill-treats Heathcliff, thrusts him into the position of a mere servant, and allows him no more education. But Catherine and Heathcliff have remained great friends, and one Sunday they go for a walk, and out of curiosity look at Thrushcross Grange, a gentleman's house in a park four

A paper read to the Heretics, Cambridge, England. By permission of Hogarth Press, Ltd., London, 1926.

miles off where Mr and Mrs Linton live. Catherine and Heathcliff peep in through the drawing-room window and see the two
Linton children—Edgar and Isabella. The Lintons, hearing Heathcliff and Catherine and taking them for robbers, let the bulldog
loose on them; the dog seizes Catherine and hurts her ankle badly.
She is taken in and looked after at Thrushcross Grange for five
weeks, and returns to Wuthering Heights elegantly dressed. Heathcliff, who is very dirty and untidy, is ashamed. The next day the two
Lintons come to dinner; Heathcliff behaves ill and is punished by
Hindley. The next year Hindley's wife gives birth to a son—Hareton. She, however, is consumptive and does not survive long. In
despair at her death Hindley takes to drink. When Catherine is
fifteen Edgar Linton proposes to her. She accepts him, feeling all
the time that she is doing wrong because she loves Heathcliff. She
tells Hareton's nurse, Ellen Dean, about it; Heathcliff overhears
part of the conversation, runs off and vanishes. Catherine is distracted by this, gets fever, and when convalescent goes to stay at
Thrushcross Grange. Her host and hostess, Mr /6/ and Mrs Linton,
both catch the fever and die. This may be considered the end of the
first stage of the story. The elder generation are all dead. The next
generation are all alive—Hindley and Catherine at Wuthering
Heights, Edgar and Isabella at Thrushcross Grange. Hindley's
wife is dead, but his son Hareton—the only representative of the
third generation—is alive. Heathcliff has disappeared. His passion
for Catherine and his revenge is the main theme of the root of the
story.

Catherine in due course marries Edgar and goes to live at Thrushcross Grange. After six months of happiness, Heathcliff, who has
meanwhile mysteriously got some education and money, reappears.
He sets himself to ruin Hindley, who gambles and drinks. He also
finds that Isabella is in love with him, and decides to marry her to
get her money. One day, after a violent scene between Heathcliff
and Edgar, Catherine goes on hunger strike and gets brain fever.
Isabella elopes with Heathcliff, who treats her abominably, and finally brings her back to Wuthering Heights. One Sunday while
Edgar is at church, Heathcliff comes to see Catherine. There is a
passionate scene. That night Catherine gives birth to a daughter
and dies. On the night after the funeral, Hindley tries to kill
Heathcliff but is nearly killed by him. Isabella escapes from Wuthering Heights and goes to the South of England, where she gives
birth to a sickly child named Linton Heathcliff. Soon after this
Hindley dies of drink, and Heathcliff is left in possession of Wuth-

ering Heights with Hareton, whom, out of revenge for the way he was treated as a boy, he brings up as a mere brute. /7/ At this stage there is a long gap in the story. Edgar's daughter, who is also called Catherine, lives with him at Thrushcross Grange; Isabella's son, Linton, lives in the South of England with her. Catherine is kept in ignorance of both her cousins Linton and Hareton.

Edgar hears that Isabella is dying and goes to see her. Catherine in his absence goes to Penistone Crags, and in doing so has to pass Wuthering Heights, where she sees Hareton. On Isabella's death, Edgar comes home with Linton, but Heathcliff claims him, and he is taken to Wuthering Heights. Catherine is not allowed by Edgar, her father, to go there. One day, after some time, Catherine on a walk meets Heathcliff and Hareton and goes to Wuthering Heights, where she sees her cousin, Linton. Catherine and Linton correspond secretly. The correspondence is detected and stopped. Catherine's father, Edgar, becomes ill. Heathcliff meets Catherine and tells her that Linton is seriously ill. She goes to see him, and many times visits him secretly. One day, just before her father dies, she is kidnapped by Heathcliff and forced to marry Linton. Soon after Linton dies, having made a will leaving all his personal property to his father, Heathcliff. Heathcliff takes possession of Thrushcross Grange, and lets it to Mr Lockwood, who tells the story. But Heathcliff dies soon after, and Hareton and Catherine marry.

How is a long story like this to be told? How is the reader's interest to be excited? How is the tale to be kept together? How are we to be made to feel the lapse of time without being pestered by dates? How far /8/ did the authoress accurately visualise the ages of the characters in the different incidents, the topography, and so on? And how did Heathcliff succeed in getting the property? These are the questions I attempt to answer.

The most obvious thing about the structure of the story which deals with three generations is the symmetry of the pedigree. Mr and Mrs Earnshaw at Wuthering Heights and Mr and Mrs Linton at Thrushcross Grange each have one son and one daughter. Mr Linton's son marries Mr Earnshaw's daughter, and their only child Catherine marries successively her two cousins—Mr Linton's grandson and Mr. Earnshaw's grandson. See the pedigree given on the next page.

In actual life I have never come across a pedigree of such absolute symmetry. I shall have to refer to this pedigree again later. It is a remarkable piece of symmetry in a tempestuous book.

The method adopted to arouse the reader's interest and /9/ to

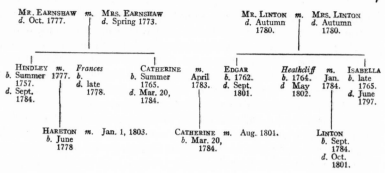

give vividness and reality to the tale is one which has been used with great success by Joseph Conrad. But it requires great skill.

After Edgar Linton's death, Mr Lockwood, the narrator, takes Thrushcross Grange for a year. He goes to call on his landlord, Heathcliff, at Wuthering Heights, and is puzzled to find there a *farouche* young woman and an awkward boor. At first he supposes Catherine to be Heathcliff's wife; when told she is his daughter-in-law, he then supposes that Hareton is Heathcliff's son, and has again to be corrected. He, and the reader, are naturally puzzled at this strange trio. Lockwood calls again, and is forced to spend the night because of a heavy fall of snow. In his room he finds some books with the name Catherine Earnshaw and Catherine Linton, and a sort of diary of Catherine's in a childish hand which gives a vivid picture of the situation just after her father's death. Mr Lockwood has a nightmare in which Catherine's spirit comes to the window, and he also witnesses a strange scene of Heathcliff imploring Catherine's spirit. Our interest cannot fail now to be excited. What is this strange man and this strange menage? Who was this Catherine who died years before? What were her relations with Heathcliff? Naturally, Lockwood is much intrigued. On his way back next day he catches a chill and becomes ill. To pass the time he asks Ellen Dean, the housekeeper at Thrushcross Grange, what she knows about the family at Wuthering Heights. She, who was first Hareton's nurse and then the younger Catherine's, tells him the story of the past thirty years in considerable detail. So that /10/ during the major part of the book Mr Lockwood is telling us what Ellen Dean told him, but sometimes, also, what Ellen Dean told him that someone else—for instance, Isabella—had told her. Only a small part, perhaps one-tenth of the book, consists of direct narrative by Lockwood from his own knowledge. But such a scheme may be confusing, and it is easy to muddle the time. Did Emily Brontë realise and let us know the dates when each event happened? She did, but not by giving them directly. Look again at the pedigree. The dates there have all been derived from the book, yet only one is directly stated. What first brought me to study the book more closely was when I noticed that the first word in the book was a date—1801. I thought this must have some significance. Similarly, the first word of Chapter XXXII is 1802. Apart from this, only one other date is given directly. In the last sentence of Chapter VII, Ellen Dean says, "I will be content to pass on to the next summer— the summer of 1778, that is, nearly twenty-three years ago." This gives no further information, as 1801 is twenty-three years after 1778, but in the first sentence of the next chapter she tells us that Hareton was born in June. This is how I get June 1778 for Hareton's birth in the pedigree. But what about the rest of the dates, not only those in the pedigree but of all the incidents in the story? There are a considerable number (perhaps nearly a hundred) indications of various kinds to help us—intervals of time, ages of characters, the months, the harvest moon, the last grouse, and so forth, and we learn, incidentally, that the younger Catherine's birthday was on 20th March. Some- /11/ times, too, we know the day of the week—thus Ellen Dean will remember something which happened on a Sunday, or on a Christmas Eve. Taking all these indications, it is, I think, possible to ascertain the year, and, in most cases, the month of the year in which every event takes place—also the ages of the various characters, except, naturally, there is a slight doubt as to Heathcliff, because no one knows his exact age when he was found by Mr Earnshaw. But one has to go warily and consider all the indications together, for there is a curious subtlety that sometimes the characters are described as *looking* some ages which are not exact. Thus Lockwood when he first describes them says that Heathcliff was about forty and Catherine did not look seventeen. In fact, Catherine was seventeen and three-quarters and Heathcliff cannot have been more than thirty-eight. It would be too tedious to state the process by which I have discovered each date (see Appendix). But I will give one or two illustrations. We already know that Hareton was born in June 1778; we are told that he was nearly five when Catherine Earnshaw married Edgar Linton, so that the marriage was before June 1783. But Heathcliff returned in September after they had been happily married for six months. Thus the marriage was in April 1783. We are told that the scene that led to Catherine's death was a Sunday in the March after

Heathcliff's return, and that her daughter, Catherine, was born about midnight, and the mother died two hours after. Later on we learn that Catherine's birthday was the 20th (and that this was also treated as the day of her mother's death). Hence /12/ Catherine died at 2 a.m. on Monday, 20th March 1784.

I will give only one other instance. Lockwood begins his account in 1801; it is snowy weather, which might be in January or February or in November or December. But he returns in 1802 before his year's tenancy is out. Hence the story begins at the end of 1801. A Michaelmas tenancy begins on the 10th October—not on 29th September—because when the calendar was reformed eleven days were left out. Therefore, the story begins after 10th October 1801. Now after Lockwood has been ill three weeks Heathcliff sends him some grouse, the last of the season. Since the Game Act, 1831, grouse may not be shot after 10th December, so we may take this as about the date for the last grouse. Thus the story begins about the middle of November, and this fits pretty well with the later indications. That is sufficient to illustrate the process. Sometimes it is only by fitting together several indications, each rather vague, that one can find the month. There is, however, one curious fact. We can ascertain Hindley's age. Now Ellen Dean was of the same age. She was his foster sister, and the doctor also refers to her as being of the same age as Hindley. Yet she makes two mistakes about her own age. Middle-aged people do, of course, make mistakes about their age, and these slips may have been intentional on the part of Emily Brontë, but if so, it seems to me a little over-subtle.

The topography is equally precise. On going from Thrushcross Grange to the village of Gimmerton a high- /13/ way branches off to the moor on the left. There is a stone pillar there. Thrushcross Grange lies to the south-west, Gimmerton to the east, and Wuthering Heights to the north. The distance from Thrushcross Grange to Wuthering Heights is four miles, and Penistone Crags lie a mile and a half farther on. It was half an hour from Gimmerton to Thrushcross Grange.

The botany is sure to be correct. Emily Brontë loved the country. I was a little surprised to find an ash tree in bud as early as 20th March, but then I realised that it was not on the moor but in the park at Thrushcross Grange, which lay low and was no doubt sheltered.

I now come to the final problem. Heathcliff schemed to get all the property of both the Earnshaws and the Lintons. How did he do it? Emily Brontë clearly had a considerable knowledge of the law. We know the source of George Eliot's use of a base fee for the plot of Felix Holt. We do not know the source of Jane Austen's unerring grasp of the law of real property; but she lived among people who had settled estates and could easily have obtained it. But how Emily Brontë acquired her knowledge I cannot guess. There is also this difficulty. *Wuthering Heights* was written in the eighteen-forties. It was published in 1847. But the period of the tale is from 1771 to 1803. The Inheritance Act of 1834, the Wills Act of 1837, and, I think, the Game Act of 1831, had changed the law. Did Emily Brontë apply the law at the time she wrote or that at the period of the tale? In one case, as we shall see, she used the earlier law.

Novelists sometimes make their plots depend on the /14/ law and use legal terms. But they frequently make mistakes and sometimes are absurd as Trollope is in *Orley Farm*. What is remarkable about *Wuthering Heights* is that the ten or twelve legal references are, I think, sufficient to enable us to ascertain the various legal processes by which Heathcliff obtained the property. It is not a simple matter. There was a fundamental difference between the law of land (real property) and that of money and goods (personal property).

Let us begin with Wuthering Heights. The Earnshaws were farmers and not likely to have their estate settled. The property had been in their family since 1500. We may take it then that Mr Earnshaw was owner in fee-simple, that is in effect absolute owner, of Wuthering Heights, and was not likely to have possessed any investments. It is more likely that there was a mortgage on the house and farm. On Mr Earnshaw's death the land descended to Hindley as his heir-at-law. There is no mention of a will. The personal property, which, probably, was only the farming stock and the furniture, would go equally to his children, Hindley and Catherine, subject to the payment of his debts out of it. On Catherine's marriage Edgar would have become entitled to her personal property. Now Hindley drinks and gambles away all he has, and at his death the property is mortgaged up to the hilt. Heathcliff we find is the mortgagee. The personal property would also be liable to the debts. So that Heathcliff is mortgagee in possession and for practical purposes, owner of all the Earnshaw property except any personalty that had gone to Catherine. This /15/ is all fairly simple; but it is more difficult when we come to the Linton property. They were landed gentry; they had a park, they had tenants. Mr Linton, and Edgar after him, was a magistrate. Such people, generally, had a settlement of their land, and we find, in fact, that Mr Linton had settled it by his will. To understand what happens it is necessary to go into the intricacies of real property law and to look at the pedigree.

I must explain very shortly the law of entails. What is called an estate tail is an estate which descends according to the following rules: (1) Males are preferred to females; (2) males take in order according to seniority of birth, but females take equally; (3) descendants represent their ancestor. In case of a conflict between them, rule (3) prevails. A tenant in tail of full age in possession could by means of a fictitious action (for which a deed was substituted by the Fines and Recoveries Act, 1833) bar the entail and obtain the fee-simple, which practically amounts to absolute ownership. By his will a testator could settle his land on living persons for life, but could not give life estates to the children of such persons who were not alive at the testator's death. Consequently, if he wanted to tie up his estate as long as possible, he gave life estates to such of his descendants as were living at his death, followed by estates tail to their children.

Now the settlement made by Mr Linton's will must have been as follows: The estate was devised to Edgar, his only son, for life, then to Edgar's sons in tail; Edgar's daughters were passed over in favour of Mr Linton's daughter, Isabella, who, presumably, had a life interest with /16/ remainder to her sons in tail. This is the usual form. Thus on Edgar Linton's death, Linton Heathcliff became tenant in tail in possession during the few weeks he survived his uncle. As a minor he could not bar the entail. It is most improbable that he had an estate in fee-simple; that would have been too unusual. Isabella might have had an estate tail instead of a life interest. This is most improbable, but if she did, her son, Linton Heathcliff, would have become tenant in tail by descent, so the result is the same. Heathcliff claims the property—by what right? Ellen Dean says that he claimed and kept the Thrushcross Grange estate in his wife's right and in his son's also. She adds: "I suppose, legally at any rate, Catherine, destitute of cash and friends, cannot disturb his possession." She is quite right in her suspicions. Even if Isabella had had an estate tail, or even an estate in fee-simple, Heathcliff would not have had any right as husband to an estate for life—the estate known as an estate by courtesy—because Isabella was never in possession. And even if, which to my mind is not possible, Linton Heathcliff had had an estate in fee-simple, his father would not have been his heir before the Inheritance Act, 1833, because it was considered unnatural that an inheritance should ascend

directly; and, as Ellen Dean knows and states, Linton Heathcliff as
a minor could not dispose of his land by will. There is no difficulty
as to the personal property. Whatever Isabella had Heathcliff got
by marrying her. There was no Married Women's Property Act in
these days. They eloped, so there was no question of a marriage
settlement. /17/ Edgar Linton had saved out of his rents to make
a provision for his daughter, Catherine. When dying he decides, in
order to prevent Heathcliff getting at them, to alter his will so as to
settle them on Catherine for life and then for her children. The attorney for whom he sends is, however, kept from going by Heathcliff, and Edgar dies before his will is altered, so the money passes
to Catherine and then to her husband, Linton. He, though a minor,
could (before the year 1838) make a will of personalty. He is induced or forced to do so, and leaves it all to Heathcliff.

Thus, at Heathcliff's death, the position seems to be that he has
acquired all the personal property of both families: he is mortgagee
in possession of Wuthering Heights, and is, though wrongfully, in
possession of Thrushcross Grange, which he has let to Lockwood.
He thinks of making a will but does not do so. What then happens
on his death? He has no relations, so that his real property will
escheat, and his personal property will go to the Crown as *bona
vacantia*. What then becomes of Hareton and Catherine who, when
the tale ends, are to be happily married on New Year's Day, 1803?
At one time I thought this was the climax to the tragedy. These
young people, ill-educated and incompetent, were to be left destitute. But that would be going too far. Catherine, as you will see
from the pedigree, is the sole living descendant of Mr Linton. In
some way or other, I need not go through the various alternatives,
she must have become entitled to Thrushcross Grange, which is
plainly by far the most valuable property. Heathcliff /18/ had been
mortgagee in possession of Wuthering Heights for eighteen years,
but this was not long enough to obtain an absolute title by adverse
possession. Hareton, as Hindley's heir, would be entitled to the
equity of redemption. Now if Heathcliff, who managed well, properly accounted for his profits during the eighteen years as he could
be made to do, it may well be that they were sufficient, if he was
charged a proper occupation rent, to pay off the mortgage. So that
Hareton would get the house and land unincumbered or, at any
rate, only slightly burdened. The personal property was comparatively unimportant, and we can only hope that the Crown did not
insist on its rights, if it knew of them, or that if it did insist, the
happy couple could buy out the Crown's claim out of the rent
which Lockwood, as we know, paid.

There is, so far as I know, no other novel in the world which it is possible to subject to an analysis of the kind I have tried to make. This in itself makes the book very unusual. Did the authoress carry all the dates in her head, or did she work with a calendar? Was 20th March 1784, for example, on a Monday? According to my calculations it was not, it was a Saturday, but I should like to have this confirmed by some competent chronologist; for if I am right, it shows that Emily Brontë did not use a calendar, and that nothing will be gained by finding out, for instance, the date of Easter in 1803.

However dull and technical the above details may be, they do, I believe, throw a light on the character of Emily Brontë and her book. German romances can hardly have been the source of her knowledge of English /19/ law. A great critic has spoken of the passionate chastity of the book; but the extreme care in realising the ages of the characters at the time of each incident which is described seems to me a more unusual characteristic of a novel. It demonstrates the vividness of the author's imagination. /20/

APPENDIX

CHRONOLOGY OF WUTHERING HEIGHTS

CHAP.			
	1757,	before September.	Hindley Earnshaw born.
	1762,	"	Edgar Linton born.
	1764,	"	Heathcliff born.
	1765,	summer.	Catherine Earnshaw born.
	"	late.	Isabella Linton born.
IV.	1771,	summer, beginning of harvest.	Heathcliff brought to Wuthering Heights.
	1773,	spring or early summer.	Mrs. Earnshaw dies.
V.	1774,	October.	Hindley sent to college.
	1777,		Hindley marries.
	"	"	Mr. Earnshaw dies.
VI.	"	"	Hindley returns with his wife.
III.	"	October or November.	The scene described by Catherine.
VI.	"	November, third week, Sunday.	Catherine and Heathcliff go to Thrushcross Grange.
VII.	"	Christmas Eve.	Catherine returns to W. H.
	"	Christmas Day.	The Lintons visit W. H.
VIII.	1778,	June.	Hareton Earnshaw born.
	"	late.	Frances Earnshaw dies.

CHAP.			
	1780,	summer.	Edgar Linton calls at W. H. and proposes to Catherine.
IV.	"	"	Hindley returns drunk.
	"	"	Catherine tells Ellen about Edgar.
	"	"	Heathcliff goes off. /21/
IV.	1780,	summer.	Catherine gets wet through and catches fever.
	"	autumn.	Catherine, convalescent, goes to Thrushcross Grange, Mr. and Mrs. Linton catch the fever and die.
	1783,	April.	Edgar marries Catherine.
X.	"	September.	Heathcliff returns and sees Catherine.
	"	autumn.	Isabella falls in love with Heathcliff, who visits Thrushcross Grange from time to time.
XI.	"	December.	Ellen Dean sees Hareton. Heathcliff kisses Isabella.
	1784,	January 6, Monday.	Violent scene at Thrushcross Grange. Heathcliff is turned out and Catherine goes on hunger strike.
XII.	"	January 10, Friday.	Catherine delirious.
	"	" " 2 a.m.	Isabella elopes with Heathcliff.
XIII.	"	March 13, Monday.	The Heathcliffs return to W. H.
XIV.	"	March 15, Wednesday.	Ellen Dean goes to W. H.
XV.	"	March 19, Sunday.	Heathcliff sees Catherine: violent scene.
XVI.	"	" midnight.	Catherine Linton born.
	"	March 20, Monday, 2 a.m.	Catherine (the elder) dies.
	"	March 21, Tuesday.	Heathcliff puts a lock of hair in Catherine's locket.
	"	March 24, Friday.	Catherine's funeral.
XVII.	"	same day, midnight.	Heathcliff nearly kills Hindley, who tried to kill him.
	"	March 25, Saturday. /22/	Isabella runs off.
XVII.	1784,	September.	Linton Heathcliff born.
	"	September or October.	Hindley Earnshaw dies. All his property is mortgaged to Heathcliff.

CHAP.

X.	"	three weeks later.	Heathcliff sends grouse.
	"	one week later.	Heathcliff calls.
XV.	1802.	January, one week later.	Lockwood continues his account.
XXXI.	"	January, 2nd week.	Lockwood calls at W. H.
XXXII.	"	beginning of February.	Ellen goes to live at W. H.
	"	March.	Hareton has an accident.
	"	Easter Monday.	Catherine is nice to Hareton.
XXXIII.	"	Easter Tuesday.	Scene about altering garden.
	"	(after March 18.)	Heathcliff getting odd.
XXXIV.	"	April.	Heathcliff goes on hunger strike.
	"	May.	Heathcliff dies.
	"	September.	Lockwood visits Thrushcross Grange and Wuthering Heights.
XXXIV.	1803,	January 1.	Catherine and Hareton marry. /24/

Questions for Discussion and Writing

1. Do you find that the discussion of structure of *Wuthering Heights* adds to your interest in the book? Does the novel become more vivid? If yes, in what ways? If not, why not?

2. Look up (in a good dictionary) the meaning of "cuckoo," and decide what the author means by applying it to Heathcliff.

3. Evaluate the author's summary of the plot. Has he included too much? Not enough? Is this summary useful or necessary to his paper? (Your instructor has probably suggested to you that mere summary generally hurts a critical paper.)

4. The "symmetry of the pedigree" (page 9) which Sanger brings to our attention might be thought to hurt the novel on the grounds of improbability: life does not order things so neatly. If you agree, write a complete statement of the way in which symmetry weakens *Wuthering Heights*. If you disagree, defend the novel against this attack.

5. See if you can discover the process by which Sanger determined one or two of the dates listed in the appendix. (Consult page 12f., where he illustrates this process for two of the dates.)

6. How much of the topography, as Sanger arranges it, can you find evidence for?

7. Sanger believes that his investigations "throw a light on the character of Emily Brontë and her book." Can you suggest, beyond the one or two illustrations of this at the end of his article, the significance of his investigations?

8. Either as a supplement to the above, or as an individual study, write a paper on the extent to which later criticism is indebted, directly or indirectly, to C. P. Sanger.

Wuthering Heights

E. F. BENSON

To turn then to the book itself, which is among the greatest works of fiction the world has ever seen, the composition and construction are inconceivably awkward, and this awkwardness is entirely due to the manner in which it begins. It opens—dated 1801—with the first-hand narrative of Mr. Lockwood, the tenant of Thrushcross Grange, who goes to visit his landlord Heathcliff at Wuthering Heights, and it is clear that the intention of the writer was to make him a personage in the story. He pays a second visit next day and is immensely struck with the younger Catherine, whom he has not seen before. He pities her for being buried alive with these savages: he thinks she is Hareton's wife.

> She has thrown herself away on that boor [he reflects] from sheer ignorance that better individuals existed! A sad pity—I must beware how I cause her to regret her choice. The last reflection may seem conceited: it was not. My neighbour struck me as bordering on repulsive; I knew through experience that I was tolerably attractive. . . .

It is impossible to imagine a clearer indication of the writer's intention to make a *motif* out of Catherine's beauty and Lockwood's complacent susceptibility. But nothing happens; the intention was scrapped. Lockwood returns to Thrushcross Grange next morning, after some bitter nocturnal experiences, and asks his housekeeper Nellie Dean to tell him more about this strange family. Thereupon she becomes the narrator, and talks to him that day for eighty pages. Next day he falls ill, and is a month in bed. When he gets better, she resumes her narrative, he merely listening. She began it from her earliest years and now completes it up to the date at which the story opens, giving him the entire history of the Earnshaws, of the Lintons, and of Heathcliff. We lose sight of Lockwood

From *Charlotte Brontë* (London and New York: Longmans, Green and Company, 1932).

altogether; he only listens to Nellie Dean as she repeats verbatim /174/ long conversations, telling this voluminous history at first hand as she witnessed it. She reads him a letter of eleven pages, which Lockwood reproduces word for word; she oversees, she over-hears, and it is not till page 367, quite near the end of the book, that the original narrator appears again to tell us that Mrs. Dean's story, which has lasted for twenty-seven chapters, is over. Then Lockwood narrates one chapter, describing his third visit to Wuthering Heights, and leaves the district. After a break he dates his next chapter 1802, and when he visits the Heights once more, Nellie Dean again tells him what has happened while he has been away. From first page to last he has had nothing whatever to do with the story to which, instead of narrating it himself, as he began to do, he is merely audience, and writes down what Nellie Dean has told him. He has no more to do with it than the occupant of a stall in the theatre has to do with the action on the stage.

No single author could have planned a book in so topsy-turvy a manner. It begins, in point of time, nearly at the end, the original narrator drops completely out, and the actual narrator, whose story forms the bulk of the book, tells it to him. But supposing that, for some reason, the first few chapters had to be retained, this com-plete change of plan, though productive of endless awkwardnesses, was necessary in order to tell the story at all. Lockwood, the newly arrived tenant who autobiographically opens the book, could not know the previous history of Heathcliff and the rest. So Nellie Dean must recount it to him, and it takes so long that he must needs fall ill so that his convalescence may be beguiled with it. Nobody plan-ning a story from the first could have begun with an episode so mis-placed that such an awkward device must be resorted to. Moreover, though from first to last Lockwood has nothing to do with the story at all, there are those sure indications in the early /175/ chapters that he was meant to play a part in it. He warns himself that he must not make himself *too* attractive, and cause the enchanting Catherine (married, so he fancies, to the boorish Hareton) to fall in love with him. /176/

Questions for Discussion and Writing

1. Use the comments on construction here as a beginning for an evaluation of the preponderance of critical opinion on this aspect of the novel.

2. Justify the retaining of the first few chapters.

3. What does Benson mean by "the writer's intention to make a *motif* out of Catherine's beauty"? (page 174) What have other critics said of Catherine's beauty that supports or conflicts with Benson's idea of her beauty as a *motif?*

4. Identify those qualities in Lockwood which lead Benson to believe that the character "was meant to play a part" in the novel much more important than the one he now plays.

5. Benson questions the organization of *Wuthering Heights* and Emily Brontë's handling of time in the novel. With the use of recent critical opinion, make a case for the organization and time sequence of *Wuthering Heights.*

Emily Brontë and
Wuthering Heights

DAVID CECIL

I

Wuthering Heights—the very name is enough to set the imagination vibrating. We hear it perhaps spoken in a London street, for a moment the intricate roar of traffic and chattering people fades into stillness, and instead our mental ear is filled by the rush of streams, the shock and reverberation of thunder, the whistling of the wind over the moors. Nor is the sound fainter to us than it was to its contemporaries. Alone of Victorian novels *Wuthering Heights* is undimmed, even partially, by the dust of time. Alone it stirs us as freshly today as the day it was written.

Yet Emily Brontë has never been generally appreciated as she deserved. In her own time she was hardly appreciated at all, and though since she has slowly pushed her way to the front rank of Victorian novelists, she is still regarded, even by admirers, as an unequal genius, revealing some flashes of extraordinary imagination, but remote from the central interests of human life, often clumsy and exaggerated, and incapable of expressing her inspiration in a coherent form.

As a matter of fact she is a great deal more than that. /157/ Yet it is not odd that people should have failed to realize it. We tend to judge a work of art by a preconceived standard drawn from the masterpieces of the form and school of which it is representative. We take for granted that an author writing a novel in the Victorian age is trying to write an orthodox Victorian novel; and we estimate it accordingly. Now by any such criterion there is no doubt that Emily Brontë is a very imperfect novelist indeed. If *Wuthering*

Heights was meant to be the same sort of novel as *Vanity Fair* or *David Copperfield,* it is a lamentable failure.

But it was never meant to be anything of the kind. The first fact to be realized about Emily Brontë, if we are ever to appreciate her properly, is that her achievement is of an intrinsically different kind from that of any of her contemporaries. Like that of Dickens, indeed, it is specially distinguished by the power of its imagination. And like his, hers is an English imagination. There is nothing exotic about Emily Brontë. *Wuthering Heights* is not like *Esther Waters,* a French novel written in English, in accordance with French ideals and with French limitations. The imagination that informs it is characteristically English, violent, unself-conscious, spiritual. And the mode in which it expresses itself is wholly the product of native influences. Its every fiber smells of the northern soil where it had its root. But though Emily Brontë is characteristic of England, she is not characteristic of Victorian England. No generalization that is true of Thackeray and Dickens, Trollope and Mrs. Gaskell, is true of her. She writes about different subjects in a different manner /158/ and from a different point of view. She stands outside the main current of nineteenth-century fiction as markedly as Blake stands outside the main current of eighteenth-century poetry.

For one thing she writes about a different world from the other novelists of her age. She spent her short tense aloof life almost entirely in her father's parsonage in Yorkshire. And Yorkshire, in those days of slow infrequent communications and before the industrial revolution, was pretty well cut off from the influence of those forces that shaped the main trend of the time. Its life remained essentially the same as it had been in the days of Queen Elizabeth; a life as rugged and unchanging as the fells and storm-scarred moors and lonely valleys which were its setting; a primitive life of confined interests and unbridled passions, of simple earthly activities and complex demon-haunted imaginings, where feuds endured for generations, and a whole existence could concentrate itself with fanatical frenzy upon a single object.

Nor did she, like her sister Charlotte, ever turn from this life to contemplate the world outside. She drew mankind only from the grim race who inhabited the land of her childhood and from her own grimmer relations. So that if we are accustomed to the picture presented by Dickens or Thackeray, hers seems, to say the least of it, odd. That bustling, prosaic, progressive world of nineteenth-century middle-class England, which is the background of their whole picture, simply does not come into her view at all. Finally,

since she was unconscious of this world, she did not, as all the
/159/ other Victorians did, write to please it. So that its conventions and preoccupations and moral preferences left as little mark
on the world of her creation as if she had lived and died in China.

But even if she had lived and died at Brighton, her books would
still have been essentially unlike those of Dickens or Thackeray.
For she looked at the human life which was their common subject
from a different point of view. I have said that she stood outside
her age as Blake stood outside his. It is for the same reason. Like
Blake, Emily Brontë is concerned solely with those primary aspects
of life which are unaffected by time and place. Looking at the
world, she asks herself not, how does it work? what are its variations?—but what does it mean? None of the other Victorian novelists are concerned with such a question. And the fact that she is so
occupied makes Emily Brontë's view of life essentially different
from theirs. For it means that she sees human beings, not as they do
in relation to other human beings, or to human civilizations and
societies and codes of conduct, but only in relation to the cosmic
scheme of which they form a part. Mrs. Brown appears not as to
Jane Austen in relation to Mr. Brown, or as to Scott in relation to
her ancestors, or as to Trollope in relation to her place in the social
structure, or as to Proust in relation to herself; but in relation to
time and eternity, to death and fate and the nature of things.
Nature plays a much larger part in Emily Brontë's books than it
does in most novelists'. On the other hand those individual and
social aspects of life which fill their canvasses do /160/ not appear
on hers. Her great characters exist in virtue of the reality of their
attitude to the universe; they loom before us in the simple epic
outline which is all that we see of man when revealed against the
huge landscape of the cosmic scheme.

This does not make her unique even in English literature;
Hardy is primarily interested in man's relation to the universe. And,
as a matter of fact, she is more like Hardy than anyone else. But she
is not very like him. Essentially, her view of human nature is more
unlike his than his is unlike that of Thackeray or Dickens. For
though she was concerned with the same aspects of it as he was,
she looked at them from a different angle. Hardy sees man and nature in a different proportion to one another from Thackeray and
Dickens, but they have the same significance for him. Hardy's heroes
were concerned with fate and free will, Dickens' with their marriages
and their careers; but fate and free will meant much the same thing

to them as they would have to Dickens' heroes if they had happened
to consider them.

Not so the heroes and heroines of Emily Brontë. It is here we
come to the determining factor in her personality. She was—once
more like Blake—a mystic. She had on certain occasions in her life
known moments of vision—far and away the most profound of her
experiences—in which her eyes seemed opened to behold a tran-
scendental reality usually hidden from mortal sight. And it is in the
light of these moments of vision that she envisages the world of mortal things; they endow it with a new significance; they are the foundation of /161/ the philosophy on which her picture of life rests.
What precisely this philosophy was she never tells us in explicit
terms. She was an artist, not a professor. Moreover, founded as it
was on sporadic flashes of vision, she seems never to have made it
wholly clear even to herself. And any attempt to state it explicitly
reveals it as full of dark places and baffling inconsistencies of detail.
However, its main features are clear enough.

The first is that the whole created cosmos, animate and inanimate, mental and physical alike, is the expression of certain living
spiritual principles—on the one hand what may be called the principle of storm—of the harsh, the ruthless, the wild, the dynamic; and
on the other the principle of calm—of the gentle, the merciful, the
passive and the tame.

Secondly, in spite of their apparent opposition these principles
are not conflicting. Either—Emily Brontë does not make clear
which she thinks—each is the expression of a different aspect of a
single prevading spirit; or they are the component parts of a harmony. They may not seem so to us. The world of our experience is,
on the face of it, full of discord. But that is only because in the
cramped condition of their earthly incarnation these principles are
diverted from following the course that their nature dictates, and
get in each other's way. They are changed from positive into negative forces; the calm becomes a source of weakness, not of harmony,
in the natural scheme, the storm a source not of fruitful vigor, but
of disturbance. But when they are free from fleshly bonds they flow
unimpeded and uncon- /162/ flicting; and even in this world their
discords are transitory. The single principle that ultimately directs
them sooner or later imposes an equilibrium.

Such convictions inevitably set Emily Brontë's view of human
life in a perspective fundamentally different from that presented to
us by other English novelists. For they do away with those antith-

eses which are the basis of these novelists' conceptions. The antithesis between man and nature to begin with: Emily Brontë does not see animate man revealed against inanimate nature, as Mrs. Gaskell does. She does not even see suffering, pitiful, individual man in conflict with unfeeling, impersonal, ruthless natural forces, like Hardy. Men and nature to her are equally living and in the same way. To her an angry man and an angry sky are not just metaphorically alike, they are actually alike in kind; different manifestations of a single spiritual reality.

" 'One time, however,' "—it is Catherine Linton speaking of Linton Heathcliff—" 'we were near quarrelling. He said the pleasantest manner of spending a hot July day was lying from morning till evening on a bank of heath in the middle of the moors, with the bees humming dreamily about among the bloom, and the larks singing high up overhead, and the blue sky and bright sun shining steadily and cloudlessly. That was his most perfect idea of heaven's happiness: mine was rocking in a rustling green tree, with a west wind blowing, and bright white clouds flitting rapidly above; and not only larks, but throstles, and blackbirds, and linnets, and cuckoos pouring music on every side and the /163/ moors seen at a distance, broken into cool dusky dells; but close by great swells of long grass undulating in waves to the breeze; and woods and sounding water, and the whole world awake and wild with joy. He wanted all to lie in an ecstasy of peace; I wanted all to sparkle and dance in a glorious jubilee. I said his heaven would be only half alive; and he said mine would be drunk; I said I should fall asleep in his; and he said he could not breathe in mine.' "

In this passage Linton's and Catherine's choices represent no chance preference, but the fundamental bias of their different natures. Each is expressing his or her instinctively felt kinship with that aspect of nature of which he or she is the human counterpart. When Linton says that he could not "breathe" in Catherine's heaven he is stating a profound truth. He draws the breath of his life from a different spiritual principle.

Again, and more important, Emily Brontë's vision of life does away with the ordinary antithesis between good and evil. To call some aspects of life good and some evil is to accept some experiences and to reject others. But it is an essential trait of Emily Brontë's attitude that it accepts all experience. Not that she is an optimist who believes that the pleasant parts of life are its only real aspects. The storm is as much part of her universe as the calm. Indeed, she is peculiarly aware of the storm; she makes out the

harsh elements of life to be as harsh as they can be. Her characters
set no bridle on their destructive passions; nor do they repent of
their destructive deeds. But since these deeds and passions do not
spring from essentially destructive /164/ impulses, but impulses
only destructive because they are diverted from pursuing their natural course, they are not "bad." Further, their fierceness and ruthlessness have, when confined to their true sphere, a necessary part to
play in the cosmic scheme, and as such are to be accepted. Emily
Brontë's outlook is not immoral, but it is pre-moral. It concerns
itself not with moral standards, but with those conditioning forces
of life on which the naïve erections of the human mind that we
call moral standards are built up.

In consequence that conflict between right and wrong which is
the distinguishing feature in the Victorian view of life does not
come into her view. Human nature, to her, is not a mixture of good
and bad elements, as it is to Thackeray. It cannot be grouped into
the virtuous and the wicked, as it is by Charlotte Brontë or Dickens.
The conflict in her books is not between right and wrong, but between like and unlike. No doubt she herself did find some characters more sympathetic than others. But this did not lead her to
think them "better," in the strict sense of the word. Sympathetic and
unsympathetic alike, they act only according to the dictates of the
principle of which they are the manifestation; and are not, therefore, to be blamed or praised. Even when one of her characters undergoes a change of heart, she never represents this as a moral
process. Catherine Linton is first cruel to Hareton, and then kind:
but she shows no remorse for her cruelty; nor does her creator give
any sign that she thinks she ought to have.

Emily Brontë's attitude to human emotion is /165/ equally different from that of her contemporaries. Her characters have extremely intense emotions, the most intense in English fiction. They
are implacable and irresistible as the elemental forces they resemble;
unchanging as the hills, fierce as the lightning; beside them, even
Mr. Rochester's passions seem tame and tea-party affairs. But they
are not awakened by the same causes as the emotions in other Victorian novels. Emily Brontë's heroes and heroines do not love
each other because they find each other's personalities pleasant, or
because they admire each other's characters. They may be super-
ficially attracted for such reasons, as Catherine Earnshaw is attracted
to Edgar Linton. But their deeper feelings are only roused for someone for whom they feel a sense of affinity, that comes from the fact
that they are both expressions of the same spiritual principle. Cath-

erine does not "like" Heathcliff, but she loves him with all the strength of her being. For he, like her, is a child of the storm; and this makes a bond between them, which interweaves itself with the very nature of their existence. In a sublime passage she tells Nelly Deans that she loves him—" 'not because he's handsome, Nelly, but because he's more myself than I am. Whatever our souls are made of, his and mine are the same, and Linton's is as different as a moonbeam from lightning, or frost from fire. . . . My great miseries in this world have been Heathcliff's miseries, and I watched and felt each from the beginning: my great thought in living is himself. If all else perished, and *he* remained, *I* should still continue to be; and if all else remained, and he were an- /166/ nihilated, the universe would turn to a mighty stranger: I should not seem a part of it. My love for Linton is like the foliage in the woods: time will change it, I'm well aware, as winter changes the trees. My love for Heathcliff resembles the eternal rocks beneath: a source of little visible delight, but necessary. Nelly, I *am* Heathcliff! He's always, always in my mind; not as a pleasure, any more than I am always a pleasure to myself, but as my own being.' "

The quality of these emotions is as remote from that of the ordinary lover's passion as its origin. For all its intensity, Catherine's love is sexless; as devoid of sensuality as the attraction that draws the tide to the moon, the steel to the magnet; and it is as little tender as if it were hate itself. Catherine does not care whether her death will make Heathcliff unhappy or not. She fears only lest it may break the bond between them. If inconsolable anguish will keep him faithful to her, she is glad of it.

" 'You and Edgar have broken my heart, Heathcliff! And you both come to bewail the deed to me, as if *you* were the people to be pitied! I shall not pity you, not I. You have killed me—and thriven on it, I think. How strong you are! How many years do you mean to live after I am gone? . . . I wish I could hold you till we were both dead! I shouldn't care what you suffered. I care nothing for your sufferings. Why shouldn't *you* suffer? I do! Will you forget me? Will you be happy when I am in the earth? Will you say twenty years hence, "That's the grave of Catherine Earnshaw? I loved her long ago, and was wretched to /167/ lose her; but it is past. I've loved many others since: my children are dearer to me than she was; and, at death, I shall not rejoice that I am going to her: I shall be sorry that I must leave them!" ' "

Finally, Emily Brontë does away with the most universally accepted of all antitheses—the antithesis between life and death.

She believes in the immortality of the soul. If the individual life be the expression of a spiritual principle, it is clear that the mere dissolution of its fleshly integument will not destroy it. But she does more than believe in the immortality of the soul in the orthodox Christian sense. She believes in the immortality of the soul *in this world*. The spiritual principle of which the soul is a manifestation is active in this life; therefore, the disembodied soul continues to be active in this life. Its ruling preoccupations remain the same after death as before. Here she is different from other Victorian novelists, and, as far as I know, from any novelists of any time. Emily Brontë does not see human conflict as ending with death. Catherine Earnshaw dreams that she goes to heaven, but is miserable there because she is homesick for Wuthering Heights, the native country of her spirit. Nor is this a parable: it is a sort of prophecy. For when in fact she comes to die, her spirit does take up its abode at Wuthering Heights. And not just as an ineffective ghost: as much as in life she exerts an active influence over Heathcliff, besieges him with her passion.

Thus the supernatural plays a different part in *Wuthering Heights* from that which it does in other /168/ novels. Most novelists, intent on trying to give a picture of life as they know it, do not bring in the supernatural at all. Those who do, either use it as a symbol, not to be believed literally, like Nathaniel Hawthorne—or like Scott, as an extraneous anomaly at variance with the laws of nature. With Emily Brontë it is an expression of those laws. It is, in truth, misleading to call it supernatural: it is a natural feature of the world as she sees it.

Her characters hold this view of death as much as she does. They may regret dying, but it is only because death means a temporary separation from those with whom they feel an affinity. For themselves they welcome it as a gateway to a condition in which at last their natures will be able to flow out unhampered and at peace; a peace not of annihilation, but of fulfillment.

" 'And,' " cries the dying Catherine, " 'the thing that irks me most is this shattered prison, after all. I'm tired of being enclosed here. I'm wearying to escape into that glorious world, and to be always there: not seeing it dimly through tears, and yearning for it through the walls of an aching heart: but really with it, and in it. Nelly, you think you are better and more fortunate than I; in full health and strength: you are sorry for me—very soon that will be altered. I shall be sorry for *you*. I shall be incomparably beyond and above you all.' " And Nelly, gazing on her dead body, has the same thought. " 'I see a repose that neither earth nor hell can break, and I feel an assurance of the endless and shadowless hereafter—the Eternity they have /169/ entered—where life is boundless in its duration, and love in its sympathy, and joy in its fulness.' "

II

So different a conception of the universe from that of Dickens or Trollope inspires a different sort of novel. *Wuthering Heights,* unlike *David Copperfield* or *Pendennis* or *Jane Eyre,* is a spiritual drama. And this means that its characters and incidents are displayed in a different focus from theirs. If we do not realize this, if we try to see them in the same focus, we shall inevitably find it baffling and confusing.

Consider the plot. Earnshaw, a squire, living in the remote wilds of eighteenth-century Yorkshire, with a daughter, Catherine, and a son, Hindley, brings home a foundling boy, whom he calls Heathcliff. Heathcliff supplants the heir, Hindley, in the affections both of his sister and his father. After a year or two the father dies, and Hindley, in revenge, degrades Heathcliff to the position of a servant. Further, Catherine—though fundamentally she cares for Heathcliff more than anyone else—is seduced by a superficial attraction to marry a handsome young man, Edgar Linton, living at Thrushcross Grange in the valley below. Heathcliff runs away and returns five years later, rich, to revenge himself on the two men who have injured him. He gets Hindley into his clutches, wins his property from him by gambling, and finally drives him to drink himself to death: he also persuades Isabella, Edgar Linton's sister, to marry him. Under the double shock of these events, and also the conflict stirred in her by her re- /170/ awakened love for Heathcliff, Catherine dies giving birth to a child. Heathcliff is overcome with grief, for he still loves her; but his grief only feeds his revenge. He torments Isabella until she leaves him.

Fifteen years now elapse, during which Hareton, child of Hindley, Catherine, child of Edgar, and Linton, child of Heathcliff, all grow to maturity. Heathcliff now proceeds to wreak his revenge on the second generation. He conspires to marry Catherine the second to his sickly son, Linton, so that he may obtain ultimate possession of both the Linton and the Earnshaw properties. His plot succeeds: they marry. Edgar Linton dies. So does young Linton Heathcliff. Heathcliff is left in complete control of the two children of his enemies to torment at his pleasure. But at this, the climax of his revenge, events suddenly take another turn. Ever since her death he had been haunted by memories of the first Catherine, and now sixteen years after he begins one day actually to see her ghost. He forgets his schemes, he forgets even to sleep and eat; with eyes fixed on his supernatural visitant he slowly starves to death. Meanwhile, Hareton and the second Catherine have fallen in love. At Heathcliff's death they retire to dwell happily at Thrushcross Grange; while the spirits of Heathcliff and the first Catherine, united at last, remain in possession of Wuthering Heights.

Now if this extraordinary story is what it is generally assumed to be, an orthodox Victorian tale of ordinary human beings, involving conflict between the heroes, Edgar Linton and Hareton, on the one hand, and /171/ the villain, Heathcliff, on the other, and ending in the discomfiture of the villain and a happy marriage, it is certainly a terrible muddle. It is fantastically improbable, for one thing, with its ghost and disappearances and sudden, timely deaths. And for another, it is very badly constructed. Why have two heroes and one villain for one drama? Why kill off half the characters in the middle of the book and start again with a new batch who play much the same rôle in the action as the first? Why work up the story to a tragic climax and then in the last few chapters contrive a happy ending by so grotesque a device as a ghost, the sight of which drives a man to self-starvation? Besides, the characters do not fill their rôles properly. Edgar, the first hero, is a poor creature—one can well understand Catherine's preference for Heathcliff—Hareton, the second, is a sketch: neither is a proper counterpart for the tremendous Heathcliff. Alike in form and detail Emily Brontë fails consistently to make her book conform to the model she is assumed to have chosen.

However, a closer examination of it conclusively shows that she did not choose such a model at all. Elements in the story, clearly of the first importance, make any such hypothesis impossible. The character of the first Catherine, for one thing: what rôle can she be supposed to play in a conventional conflict between heroes and villain? She is all the way through on the side of the villain, and dies committed to him and alienated from her husband. Yet she feels no remorse for this; nor does her creator seem to blame her. Again, the conclusion of a conflict between good /172/ and evil, if it is to be happy, should entail either the discomfiture of the villain or his repentance. In *Wuthering Heights* neither happens. Heathcliff is not discomfited: the love between Hareton and Catherine, which gives the book its happy ending, is made possible only by his own tacit relinquishment of his plans. Yet this is due to no change of heart on his part. He never shows a sign of regret for his wrongdoing; he only stops tormenting Catherine and Hareton because he is otherwise occupied. Finally—and oddest of all—after his death it is he who is rewarded by spiritual union with the first Catherine, not Edgar, her lawful husband and the supposed hero of the story.

Nor, wild as the plot may be by conventional standards, does careful examination of it support the view that this wildness is unintentional. It is not a clumsy improvisation, like the plot of *Bleak House*. The author calling himself "C. B. S." in his remarkable essay, *The Structure of Wuthering Heights,* has shown how carefully the concrete facts with which the action deals are worked out and documented; the accuracy of its elaborate legal processes, its intricate family relationships, its complex time system. It is impossible to believe that an author so careful of the factual structure of her story as Emily Brontë shows herself to be, should be careless of its artistic structure. And, indeed, if we can manage to read her book with a mind unprejudiced by preconceived ideas, we do not feel it to be carelessly constructed. The impression it leaves on us is not the unsatisfying impression of confused magnificence left by *Bleak House*. It is the /173/ harmonious complete impression left by the formal masterpieces of fiction, by *Persuasion, Fathers and Children,* and *Madame Bovary*.

And rightly. If *Wuthering Heights* gives a confused impression the confusion lies only in our own minds—and not Emily Brontë's. We are trying to see it in the wrong focus. When we shift our focus to reconsider *Wuthering Heights* in the light of her particular vision, its apparent confusion vanishes. From a murky tangle lighted by inexplicable flashes, it falls into a coherent order.

The setting is a microcosm of the universal scheme as Emily Brontë conceived it. On the one hand, we have Wuthering Heights, the land of storm; high on the barren moorland, naked to the shock of the elements, the natural home of the Earnshaw family, fiery, untamed children of the storm. On the other, sheltered in the leafy valley below, stands Thrushcross Grange, the appropriate home of the children of calm, the gentle, passive, timid Lintons. Together each group, following its own nature in its own sphere, combines to compose a cosmic harmony. It is the destruction and re-establishment of this harmony which is the theme of the story. It opens with the arrival at Wuthering Heights of an extraneous element—Heathcliff. He, too, is a child of the storm; and the affinity between him and Catherine Earnshaw makes them fall in love with each other. But since he is an extraneous element, he is a source of discord, inevitably disrupting the working of the natural order. He drives the father, Earnshaw, into conflict with the son, Hindley, and as a /174/ result Hindley into conflict with himself, Heathcliff. The order is still further dislocated by Catherine, who is seduced into uniting herself in an "unnatural" marriage with Linton, the child of calm. The shock of her infidelity and Hindley's ill-treatment of him now, in its turn, disturbs the natural harmony of Heathcliff's nature, and turns him from an alien element in the established order, into a force active for its destruction. He is not therefore, as usually supposed, a wicked man voluntarily yielding to his wicked impulses. Like all Emily Brontë's characters, he is a manifestation of natural forces acting involuntarily under the pressure of his own nature. But he is a natural force which has been frustrated of its natural outlet, so that it inevitably becomes destructive; like a mountain torrent diverted from its channel, which flows out on the surrounding country, laying waste whatever may happen to lie in its way. Nor can it stop doing so, until the obstacles which kept it from its natural channel are removed.

Heathcliff's first destructive act is to drive Hindley to death. Secondly, as a counterblast to Catherine's marriage, and actuated not by love, but by hatred of the Lintons, he himself makes another "unnatural" marriage with Isabella. This, coupled with the conflict induced in her by her own violation of her nature, is too much for Catherine; and she dies. Heathcliff, further maddened by the loss of his life's object, becomes yet more destructive, and proceeds to wreak his revenge on the next generation, Hareton Earnshaw, Catherine Linton and Linton Heathcliff. These—for /175/ Hindley, like Heathcliff and Catherine, had married a child of calm—cannot be divided as their parents were into children of calm or storm; they are the offspring of both and partake of both natures. But there is a difference between them. Hareton and Catherine are the children of love, and so combine the positive "good" qualities of their respective parents: the kindness and constancy of calm, the strength and courage of storm. Linton, on the other hand, is a child of hate, and combines the negative "bad" qualities of his two parents—the cowardice and weakness of calm, the cruelty and ruthlessness of storm.* Heathcliff obtains power over all three children. Catherine is married to her natural antipathy, Linton; so that her

* Of course, this is true only in a broad sense. Emily Brontë has too great a sense of reality to create unmitigated villains or impeccable heroes. Moreover, all three children springing as they do from "unnatural" unions are not perfectly homogeneous characters. Hareton can be surly, Catherine wilful. And Linton—for his mother loved his father at first, if only with a physical passion—is touched at times with a /176/ redeeming gleam of pathos.

own nature, diverted from its purpose, grows antagonistic to her
natural affinity—Hareton. The natural order is for the time being
wholly subverted: the destructive principle reigns supreme. But
at this, its high-water mark, the tide turns. From this moment the
single purpose that directs the universe begins to reassert itself, to
impose order once more. First of all Linton Heathcliff dies. Negative as his nature is, it has not the seed of life within it. Then, freed
from the incubus of his presence, the affinity between Hareton and
Catherine begins to override the superficial antagonism that Heathcliff's actions have raised between them; they fall in love. The only
obstacle left to the re-establishment /176/ of harmony is Heathcliff's antagonism; finally this, too, changes. His nature could never
find fulfillment in destruction; for it was not—as we have seen—primarily destructive, and has become so only because it was frustrated of its true fulfillment—union with its affinity, Catherine Earnshaw. Heathcliff's desire for this union never ceased to torment
him. Even at his most destructive, her magnetic power dragged at
his heart, depriving him of any sense of satisfaction his revenge
might have obtained for him. Now it grows so strong that it breaks
through the veil of mortality to manifest itself to his physical eye
in the shape of her ghost. The actual sight of her gives him strength
at last to defeat the forces that had upset his equilibrium; with a
prodigious effort the stream breaks through the obstacles that had
so long stood in its way, and flows at last in a torrent down its rightful channel. He forgets his rage, he forgets even to satisfy the wants
of physical nature; he wants only to unite himself with Catherine.
Within two days his wish is satisfied. He dies. His death removes the
last impediment to the re-establishment of harmony. Hareton and
Catherine settle down happy and united at Thrushcross Grange.
Wuthering Heights is left to its rightful possessors, the spirits of
Heathcliff and the first Catherine. The wheel has come full circle;
at length the alien element that has so long disturbed it has been
assimilated to the body of nature; the cosmic order has been established once more.

   This analysis is enough to show how wide of the mark the usual
criticisms of *Wuthering Heights* are. /177/ It is not incoherent.
On the contrary, its general outline is as logical as that of a fugue.
Nor is it an improbable story. On the plane on which it is composed
its every incident is the inevitable outcome of the situation. Still
less is it remote from the central issues of human life. It may seem
so, because it presents the world from an angle in which the aspects
which bulk biggest to most novelists are hidden from its view. But

those aspects with which it is concerned are nearer to the heart of life than those explored by any other Victorian novelist. Even the varied world-panorama of *Vanity Fair* seems trivial beside this picture of a sparsely populated country village, revealed, as it is, against the background of the eternal verities. For in it Emily Brontë has penetrated beneath those outward shows of experience which are the subject matter of Thackeray and his contemporaries, to the ultimate issues which are generally looked on as the subject matter of tragedy or epic. Like *Hamlet* and the *Divine Comedy, Wuthering Heights* is concerned with the primary problems of men and destiny. Like *Paradise Lost* it sets out "to justify the ways of God to Man." No novel in the world has a grander theme.

However, it is not the grandeur of its theme that makes *Wuthering Heights* a great novel. After all, the theme is only a skeleton. It has to be clothed with flesh and blood before it acquires that breathing, individual life which distinguishes a work of creative art from a work of the intellect. Very few writers have an imagination powerful enough so to clothe a story on the scale of *Wuthering Heights.* /178/

But Emily Brontë had it. Her imagination is built on the same tremendous scale as her subject. Of course, it has the limitations imposed by her angle of vision. It does not take in the complex or the microscopic. It does not assimilate a mass of heterogeneous material, like Balzac's or Tolstoy's: it never insinuates itself into the crannies of the coastline of personality, like that of Dickens; or explores the cobwebby intricacies of the inner soul, like Henry James's; it passes by those details of appearance and character that give life to the world of Mrs. Gaskell; never sparkles in a crystalline stream over the slight, the homely and the trivial, like Jane Austen's. It confines itself to the elemental, and presents it in an elemental way. No more than Charlotte Brontë's does Emily Brontë's imagination know moods of relaxation and uncertainty. There are no half-shades in it, no whimsical interweaving of smiles and tears; Emily Brontë never casts a sidelong glance; she is innocent of irony. All the same she has the most extraordinary imagination that ever applied itself to English fiction.

Apart from anything else it is so original. For all that Emily Brontë concentrates only on elements, she does not present them as anyone else would. Nor is this merely due to the peculiar angle from which she looks at them. Charlotte looked at life from a peculiar angle, but she expressed her vision largely through the accepted formulas of her day; in bulk, the impression made by her work is

unique, in detail it often recalls the work of others. Emily Brontë's
mode of expression shows almost as little mark of outside influence
/179/ as her view of life. Only in a few minor aspects does she ever
recall other writers. The effect she makes would be the same, one
feels, if she had never read a book at all. To express her new vision,
she set herself to invent new formulas. And she succeeded. On every
aspect of her work she has put the fire-new stamp of her own imagination.

Its individuality comes from a combination of three qualities.
First of all its intensity. Emily Brontë's imagination is as intense as
that of Dickens. Like him, she can sweep us with a stroke of the
pen into a world more living than the one we know. But her
achievement is more wonderful than that of Dickens. For her world
was harder to vitalize. Dickens had all the solid, sappy, recognizable
life of Victorian London to set his bonfire blazing and crackling.
Hers was composed in great part of the improbable and the imma-
terial, of superhuman passions and supernatural happenings. Yet it
burns with an equal heat. Her genius is all fire and air; it can set
the pulse of life throbbing in incredible vagaries of feeling, give the
most aerial conception a local habitation and a name. If any other
novelist had described a man as embracing a woman so passionately
that those who watched him wondered if she would come out alive,
we should only have thought it comic. Emotion in *Wuthering
Heights* is keyed up to such a pitch of intensity, that such an em-
brace seems its only adequate expression. Again, if another
novelist had described a man as dying of starvation because he was
occupied in looking at a ghost, we simply should not have believed
it. But /180/ Emily Brontë not only makes us believe it; she makes
us believe it without any difficulty. We accept it effortlessly, as we
accept Jane Austen's statement that Mr. Collins was a clergyman.

Effortlessness, indeed, is a distinguishing mark of her intensity.
Though she is concerned with the most violent emotions in any
English novel, she always manages to seem to have something in reserve, to be writing within her strength. She never raves: she
makes an effect quietly and in a single sentence. " 'Oh! Cathy! Oh,
my life! How can I bear it?' " says Heathcliff, confronted with his
dying love. But these ten words have a force behind them that
makes all the rhetoric of Lucy Snowe weak by comparison. Emily
Brontë's magnificently agile imagination enables her to take the
most fantastic leaps in her stride, and without showing a sign of
strain.

Yet for all that it is so extreme and so unearthly, Emily Brontë's imagination is not unsubstantial. This brings us to its second distinguishing characteristic, its solidity. Most writers who are at home with dreams—Edgar Allan Poe, for instance, or Mr. Walter de la Mare—tend to invest their whole world with a dreamlike quality. It is a place of half-lights and phantoms; its figures loom before us as through the lurid, blurred atmosphere of a magician's laboratory. One gleam of ordinary daylight one feels would be enough to dissipate the illusion of their reality forever. And it does. If for a moment these writers do attempt to describe a scene of everyday life, their figures either fade into shadows or stand exposed as stiff and sawdust dummies. This is /181/ not true of *Wuthering Heights*. So far from breathing a confined atmosphere, its every word reads as if it had been written out-of-doors. Thrushcross Grange is no shifting cloud-palace of fairy-tale, but solid stone and masonry: Catherine Earnshaw, tearing her frock as a little girl, is as real as Catherine Earnshaw haunting Heathcliff's dreams. Nor do the two realities differ in kind. We are conscious of no jolt, experience no need to readjust our focus, as we pass from the supernatural to the natural plane. The ardor of Emily Brontë's imagination fuses them in a glowing homogeneous actuality.

Its intensity does not mean that Emily Brontë's imagination is forced, any more than it means that it is unsubstantial. On the contrary, the third ingredient in its peculiar flavor, is its spontaneity. Here it is like those of Charlotte Brontë and Mrs. Gaskell, and for the same reason. Like them, Emily Brontë lived a simple existence, which prevented her taste for life growing satiated or sophisticated. But her freshness is different from theirs. Charlotte Brontë's freshness is that of an immature and inexperienced girl; Mrs. Gaskell's that of a candid disposition, unsullied by contact with a sordid world; Emily Brontë's is the more incorrigible freshness of a bird or an animal. There is nothing cloistered about her imagination. It roves over the world as fearless and unconfined as the young eagle, and it has the young eagle's unspoilt, unhesitating, zestful responsiveness to life. It may often concern itself with the wild and the grim. But that is because the wild and the grim are part of its native /182/ element. Eagle-like, it is at home amid the buffetings of the storm, yields itself with an instinctive joy to the fierce exhilaration of the hunt. But it can respond with the same spontaneity to the gentle as to the savage. When for a moment the clouds part, it relaxes with an equal zest in the genial warmth of the sunshine, yields itself with equal abandon to its enjoyment of the aromatic sweetness of the gorse-flowers.

No other English writer expresses so well man's primitive joy in the earth as Emily Brontë does—the joy of Catherine Earnshaw, exultant in the shrill night wind; of Catherine Linton, half-drugged with the luxury of a summer's day spent in the rocking branches of an elm tree. This unjaded responsiveness gives *Wuthering Heights* a quality odd in conjunction with its subject matter. For all that its story is so somber, there is nothing morbid about it. On the contrary, its atmosphere breathes a wild exhilarating health. A pure clear morning light irradiates it; a wind keen with the tang of virgin snow blows through its pages. Nor, though the passions it describes are so violent, is there anything fevered or sultry about them; their heat is the white heat of a cleansing vestal flame. Finally, for all that the characters are so harsh, the impression left on us by their story is not forbidding. On the contrary, round its every page hovers a youthful, a tameless, an irresistible charm.

Substance, intensity, freshness—these then are the three elements that give its individuality to Emily Brontë's imagination. They reveal themselves in every aspect of her world. Emily Brontë's is the most telling /183/ landscape of any in English fiction. As might be expected her observation is not minute or precise. She does not distinguish between the different sounds made by the wind as it blows through oak trees or larch, as Hardy does, nor convey with the exact violence of D. H. Lawrence its impact on the physical senses. She sketches in the main features of her scene—sky, trees, heath—in general terms, and briefly. There is not a single set-piece of landscape painting in her book. Yet its background pervades her every chapter. For her intensity enabled her to convey in a way no other English novelist does the vitality of nature. She felt nature to be the expression of a living force, and she makes us feel it too. Her background is no still-life composition: it is a moving picture of an animate being. The moor luxuriates in the sun like an animal; the wind howls and hushes with a human voice; the last flowers droop in apprehensive melancholy at the fading of autumn. The changes of the seasons are presented to us not as the shiftings of static stage scenery, but as acts in a dynamic drama. Like the adherents of some primitive religion we watch the Earth God stiffen in the death of winter; rise with youth mysteriously renewed to blossom in the spring. It is to be noted that Emily Brontë's most memorable bits of description always represent nature in motion; racing clouds, fluttering leaves: "Sky and hills muffled in one bitter whirl of wind and suffocating snow." The rippling of the brook in Thrushcross valley, which "always sounded on quiet days following a great thaw or a season of steady rain." /184/

Yet though she makes landscape living, she never makes it un-naturally human; her world is unmistakably the world we ourselves live in. The solidity of her imagination keeps it as true to fact as it is vivid. Indeed, no other writer gives us such a feeling of naked contact with actual earth and water, presents them to us so little bedizened by the artificial flowers of the literary fancy. To read Emily Brontë's descriptions after those of most authors, is like leav-ing an exhibition of landscape paintings to step into the open air.

Her characters are as vivid as their setting. Not all of them; the servants, old Joseph and Nelly Dean, indeed, are one of the few features of her work which show outside influence. They are char-acter parts in the regular English tradition of Fielding, drawn in the flat rather than the round, made individual by a few strongly marked, personal idiosyncrasies. Nor are they the greatest of their kind. They do not step living from the page, like Squire Western: they are more like the comic rustics of Hardy. But they are quite as good as his; massive, racy bits of rural life, drawn with that touch of genial humor which is the mark of their type.

And they are essential to the effect of the plot. The weight of their everyday solidity helps to anchor it to the world of reality. Further, once more like Hardy's rustics—and Shakespeare's, too, for that matter—they provide a standard of normality which shows up in vivid relief the thrilling strangeness of the protagonists.

It is in these protagonists that Emily Brontë's true genius ap-pears. They, also, show her limitations. Her /185/ imagination, as we have seen, was oblivious of the homely, the trivial and the minute. And since poor human nature is compounded largely of these ele-ments, a picture of it that omits them will necessarily be a little summary and a little remote. Portrayed as she is without any of those vivifying accidents of individuality that caught the eye of Tolstoy, Catherine Linton never achieves the intimate reality of Natasha Rostov. She exists rather on the generalized plane of a heroine of ballad or epic. On this plane, however, she is as living as possible. With her limitations, Emily Brontë's characters reveal also all her extraordinary talents. They have their solidness. They are never brilliant façades of personality masking a confused psycho-logical structure like so many of Dickens'. They are always true to themselves, they do not suddenly act in a manner inconsistent with the fundamental bent of their natures. For the fact that they are each the expression of a spiritual principle or conjunction of prin-ciples knits their varying aspects into a logical unity.

Yet they are never too logical to be human. It is here that Emily Brontë's intensity and freshness comes to her aid. For all that they represent spiritual principles, they are not allegorical characters like those of Bunyan or Mr. Bernard Shaw. Indeed, they are clothed so convincingly in flesh and blood that most readers fail to notice that they represent spiritual principles at all. We never feel that their acts are the mechanical movements of puppets, but always the spontaneous expression of free and living personalities. Moreover, they are very individual personalities. Wild, /186/ wilful, lovable Catherine Linton; fierce, capricious, enchanting Catherine Earnshaw; Linton, the wretched child of sin, cowardly and ruthless, soft and heartless; above all, black-browed Heathcliff, with his brusque manner and his burning eloquence—all these are as unmistakable as people we have met. We should know them if they came into the room.

Indeed, Emily Brontë illustrates some aspects of human nature more fully than the other Victorians. Its hereditary character, for one thing; her story turns largely on the transmission of hereditary traits. And her experience, formed as it was in great part on the observation of one family—her own—taught her to take advantage of it. Her characters are all obviously members of the particular family to which they belong. Isabella and Edgar Linton share a family temperament as pronounced as a family nose; so do Catherine and Hindley Earnshaw. In every action and word of Linton Heathcliff and Catherine Linton we can trace, slightly modified, the typical idiosyncrasies of their respective parents: "How like his father," we find ourselves saying. "It might be her mother speaking."

No other novelist before Emily Brontë brings out hereditary characteristics in this way. Even Jane Austen, impeccable realist as she is, has created children that have nothing in common with their parents. By what improbable miracle did Mr. and Mrs. Bennet produce a child like Jane?

Emily Brontë, too, shows, better than her contemporaries, how people mature. During a great part of *Wuthering Heights*, the characters are children, and /187/ very realistically drawn children. For since Emily Brontë drew direct from her own experience, she never sentimentalized or conventionalized. The children in her book are fighting, laughing, squalling, untamed little animals, like real children. There are no impossible, intolerable little angels of virtue among them; even the courteous Edgar Linton can tease and whine and lose his temper. But although they are convincing children, they are also convincing embryos of their maturer selves. In addition to the characteristics common to childhood, they are each marked by traits special to themselves. And her grasp of those traits makes Emily Brontë able to show how the personality develops, how the embryo matures. We recognize Heathcliff, the child, in Heathcliff, the man. But we see how age and experience have altered him. He is Heathcliff the child divested of the typical traits of childhood, his character no longer fluid and implicit, but fully expressed, set into its final mold.

Above all, Emily Brontë's intensity gives her the power to describe one aspect of human nature which never appears in the works of her contemporaries at all. She can present man at the climax of his spiritual crises—in spiritual ecstasy, in the turmoils of spiritual hatred and despair, at the moment of death. None of the other Victorians can successfully describe a death scene. Awestruck at so tremendous a task, they lose their creative nerve; their imaginations boggle and fail, and they fill up the gaps left by its absence with conventional formulas. A stagey light of false tragic emotion floods the scene; the figures become puppets, /188/ squeaking out appropriately touching or noble sentiments. But Emily Brontë's eagle imagination gazed with as undaunted an eye on death, as on everything else. The light she sheds on it is the same light that prevades her whole scene, and it is the light of day. Mr. Earnshaw's last moments are described as realistically and calmly as his arrival from a journey. Nor do Emily Brontë's characters lose individuality in moments of intense emotion. Catherine Earnshaw is not less, but more herself when declaring her sense of spiritual union with Heathcliff. The intensity of the emotion which animates her seems to break through the irrelevant dross with which the happenings of everyday life have damped down her personality so that it jets up to heaven in a pure and dazzling flame.

This power of expressing intensity of emotion is connected with the third mode in which Emily Brontë's imagination expresses itself—her poetry. She is the most poetical of all our novelists. She is not the only poetical one. Poetry, the most concentrated expression of the imagination, is generated when the imagination is at its intensest; and Charlotte Brontë and Dickens, to name no others, achieve it frequently. But Emily Brontë's genius is more consistently intense, so that she achieves poetry more continuously and more variously. A great deal of it is the same kind as theirs. Her moorland landscapes, checkered with fleeting storm and sunshine; the lyrical emotion that trembles round Catherine Linton wander-

ing with her lover through the scented summer twilight—these are
poetical in the same way as the sullen marshes of *Great Expecta-*
/189/ *tions,* or Mr. Rochester's lovemaking in the nightingale-
haunted garden of Thornfield Hall. But in the fullest flood of her
inspiration Emily Brontë rises to poetry of a rarer kind. The poetry
of Dickens is the poetry of atmosphere, that of Charlotte Brontë
is the poetry of mood. Both appear in the setting of their dramas,
rather than in the drama itself. The poetry heightens the situation
with which it is connected; it is not intrinsic to it; you could take
it out, and the scene, though poorer, would still exist in its essentials. It is its dress, not its blood and bone.

Emily Brontë's highest flights, on the other hand, are inherent in
the structure of her drama. They express themselves in the turn
which the plot takes; their images are the necessary actions and
words of the characters.

Examine the wonderful scene where Catherine Earnshaw, yearning for Heathcliff and Wuthering Heights, rendered desperate by
disappointment and three days of starvation, goes into delirious
raving. Emily Brontë does not, like most novelists, state the facts
and then suggest their poetical aspect by description and comment.
The poetry expresses itself through the actual turn of Catherine's
thought, the form and current of her impulses.

"Tossing about, she increased her feverish bewilderment to madness, and tore the pillow with her teeth; then raising herself up all
burning, desired that I would open the window. We were in the
middle of winter, the wind blew strong from the north-west, and
I objected. Both the expressions flitting over her face, and the
changes of her moods, began to alarm me terribly; /190/ and
brought to my recollection her former illness, and the doctor's injunction that she should not be crossed. A minute previously she
was violent; now, supported on one arm, and not noticing my refusal to obey her, she seemed to find childish diversion in pulling
the feathers from the rents she had just made, and ranging them
on the sheet according to their different species: her mind had
strayed to other associations.

"'That's a turkey's,' she murmured to herself; 'and this is a wild
duck's; and this is a pigeon's. Ah, they put pigeon's feathers in the
pillows—no wonder I couldn't die! Let me take care to throw it on
the floor when I lie down. And here is a moor-cock's; and this—I
should know it among a thousand—it's a lapwing's. Bonny bird;
wheeling over heads in the middle of the moor. It wanted to get to
its nest, for the clouds had touched the swells, and it felt rain com-

ing. This feather was picked up from the heath, the bird was not shot: we saw its nest in the winter, full of little skeletons. Heathcliff set a trap over it, and the old ones dared not come. I made him promise he'd never shoot a lapwing after that, and he didn't. Yes, here are more! Did he shoot my lapwings, Nelly? Are they red, any of them? Let me look.'

" 'Give over with that baby-work!' I interrupted, dragging the pillow away, and turning the holes towards the mattress, for she was removing its contents by handfuls. 'Lie down and shut your eyes: you're wandering. There's a mess! The down in flying about like snow.'

"I went here and there collecting it. /191/

" 'I see in you, Nelly,' she continued, dreamily, 'an aged woman: you have grey hair and bent shoulders. This bed is the fairy cave under Penistone Crags, and you are gathering elf-bolts to hurt our heifers; pretending while I am near, that they are only locks of wool. That's what you'll come to fifty years hence: I know you are not so now. I'm not wandering: you're mistaken, or else I should believe you really *were* that withered hag, and I should think I *was* under Penistone Crags; and I'm conscious it's night, and there are two candles on the table making the black press shine like jet.'

" 'The black press? where is that?' I asked. 'You are talking in your sleep!'

" 'It's against the wall, as it always is,' she replied. 'It *does* appear odd—I see a face in it!'

" 'There's no press in the room, and never was,' said I, resuming my seat, and looping up the curtain that I might watch her.

" 'Don't *you* see that face?' she inquired, gazing earnestly at the mirror.

"And say what I could, I was incapable of making her comprehend it to be her own; so I rose and covered it with a shawl.

" 'It's behind there still!' she pursued, anxiously. 'And it stirred. Who is it? I hope it will not come out when you are gone! Oh! Nelly, the room is haunted! I'm afraid of being alone!' "

Again, Catherine's spirit, sighing at Heathcliff's window in the snowy night; Linton and Catherine the second, prone on the sunburnt heath, whispering to /192/ each other their dreams of heaven; these episodes are intrinsically poetical, their root conception shows that concentrated activity of the imagination which generally reveals itself only in a brilliant metaphor or a passionate melodious cadence. It is as though Emily Brontë's plot, gathering momentum from the passion stored within it, suddenly leaves the ground in an astonishing flight of poetical invention. This kind of poetry, pure dramatic poetry, is very rare among novelists; only Dostoievski has it to anything like the same degree. To find a parallel in English we must leave the novel and go to Shakespeare himself; to Lady Macbeth's blood-haunted sleep-walking, to Desdemona singing the songs of her childhood as she undresses for death.

Certainly Emily Brontë's imagination is the most extraordinary that ever applied itself to English fiction. It is also an imagination appropriate to the material on which she chose to work. The theme of *Wuthering Heights* to be successfully realized needs just the qualities Emily Brontë is best able to supply. Because it conceives nature as informed by a vital spirit, it needs an imaginative apprehension of landscape. Because it involves an acute dramatic conflict, it needs the power to express violent emotion. Because it invests this emotion with a spiritual significance that could not be conveyed by a mere literal realism, it neeeds the power of poetic invention. Finally, because it expresses a view of the world remote from ordinary experience, it needs an imagination at once intense and substantial. *Wuthering Heights,* for all that it illustrates a transcen- /193/ dental philosophy, is first and foremost a novel. By a prodigious feat of creative imagination, Emily Brontë has contrived to incarnate an interplay of ultimate principles in a drama of human beings.

Nor is her success impaired by her limitations. Here we come to the second distinguishing feature of her genius. She had not only an imagination of the first order, she was also a consummate artist. In addition to the creator's, she had the craftsman's qualities. Of these, the first is artistic integrity, the power to keep within her true imaginative range. Emily Brontë's imagination, like that of Dickens and Charlotte Brontë, was limited; but unlike them, she never went outside its limits. It did not matter that she was not inspired by the homely, the trivial and the minute, by family life or social distinctions. Her chosen theme did not entail any of these subjects. So that she was never forced, as Dickens and Charlotte Brontë were, for the sake of the plot to intersperse her inspired passages with uninspired pieces of machinery. Her living Catherines and Heathcliffs are not set off by lifeless Miss Ingrams and Agnes Wickfields. She writes only of what stimulated her creative imagination, so that her book is continuously imaginative.

She had the other craftsman's qualities, too; she had the sense of form. We have seen how consistently the ideas behind *Wuthering*

Heights show themselves in its structure. And it is as well-constructed artistically as it is intellectually. It is designed, that is, not only strictly in relation to the general ideas that inspire it, but also in the form best fitted to convey those ideas /194/ effectively to the reader. This was not the customary novel form of the day. Emily Brontë was as independent artistically as she was intellectually. She did not take her form from other authors: she made it up herself, as she made up her philosophy of life. With the result that, judged by the standards established by other authors, her form is hard to follow. *Wuthering Heights* is usually considered as artistically confused, just as it is considered intellectually confused. But it is no more the one than it is the other. Its form fits the subject like a glove. There is not a loose thread in it. So far from being crude, it is far more sophisticated than the narrative method employed by Dickens and Trollope. To find anything so complex we must go forward eighty years, to Henry James and Conrad. As a matter of fact, the form of *Wuthering Heights* is very like that of a Conrad novel. Just as in *Lord Jim*, the story is shown to us through the eyes of a character, and a character not involved in its central drama, so in *Wuthering Heights* it is told partly by Nelly Deans, the servant of the Lintons, and partly by Mr. Lockwood, who takes Thrushcross Grange after Edgar Linton's death. Such a method serves two objects. First, it insures that we see the drama in all the fresh reality in which it would have shown itself to its spectators; and secondly, since these spectators are detached and normal, we see it as it really was, undistorted by the emotions of those actors who were involved in it.

Again as in *Lord Jim*, Emily Brontë begins her story in the middle. The book opens with Mr. Lockwood's first visit to Wuthering Heights at the climax of /195/ Heathcliff's revenge when he has at last obtained complete power over Catherine and Hareton, before the forces of harmony have begun to make themselves felt. Mr. Lockwood sees Heathcliff triumphant, Catherine and Hareton miserable: beleaguered for the night by a storm, he is kept awake by the first Catherine's spirit calling at the window. Such an opening serves three purposes.

To begin with it introduces us in the best way possible to the scene and the characters. We see Heathcliff and Wuthering Heights for the first time in all the fresh vivid detail in which they would appear to the curious stranger. In the second place it enables Emily Brontë to set the story from the first in its right perspective, to put the reader in a place of vantage where his eye is directed to the contrast on which the interest of the action turns, the contrast between a world of discord and a world of harmony. Straight away we are shown a "close-up" of the discord at its height; so that our interest is immediately directed to learn whence it arises and how it is to be resolved.

Such an opening, finally, strikes the right emotional key. This is very important. For the plot of *Wuthering Heights* is so remote from our ordinary experience that unless we approach it from the start with a mind tuned to its key, we are bound to find it unconvincing. If Emily Brontë had started off with the relatively credible incidents of Heathcliff's and Catherine's childhood, she would have found it very hard to maintain the reader's belief in the story when the time came to tell him of its extraordinary catastrophe. But with supreme dar- /196/ ing she storms the very citadel of the reader's skepticism at the outset. She begins with ghosts and infernal passions; and this induces in us a heightened, inflamed mood of the imagination that makes us accept without any difficulty the most sensational events of its climax.

Having set the stage, Emily Brontë now goes back twenty years, and in the person of Nelly Deans tells the story of the beginning. She continues until she has reached that point in the plot to which we are introduced in the first chapter. Then once more darkness descends on the story for a period; and when it dissipates, Mr. Lockwood, not Nelly Deans, is the narrator. He has returned after nine months' absence to find Wuthering Heights steeped in an evening peace. He asks Nelly Deans what has happened; she resumes and finishes the story; Mr. Lockwood takes a last look at the place, and leaves.

This second break in the narrative is also carefully calculated to reinvigorate the reader's interest. More important, like the opening, it sets the story in a perspective from which its essential significant trend is visible. As at first we are shown a close-up of Wuthering Heights at the climax of discord, so now we are shown a close-up of it in the fullness of harmony; and, as before, with the added actuality which would invest it in the eyes of a stranger from the outside world. The artistic scheme of the book is worked out with the same rigid symmetry as is the intellectual.

The detail of the narrative is as technically brilliant as the design. Emily Brontë—here for once she is typically Victorian—was a mistress of the art of telling /197/ a story. Her method may be defined as the dramatic-pictorial. The plot is arranged in a series of set scenes linked together by the briefest possible passages of narrative. These separate scenes, too, are composed, like those in a play, of words and action, helped by only a minimum of explanatory comment. But Emily Brontë seeks to make us see her characters as well as hear them; and she succeeds in both. Her ability to make a character live, her power to express emotion, makes her scenes highly dramatic; while the intensity and substance of her imagination gives her an extraordinary power of visualization. She brings her scenes before our mental eye with a few straightforward words unassisted by the devices which make vivid the pictures of the official masters of word painting—the accumulated detail of Balzac, the unusual images of D. H. Lawrence. But she makes us see the scene just as well as they do. The curtain rises on darkness; suddenly a brilliant light is flashed on two wild-looking children peering into a tranquil, lamp-lit drawing-room; or on a savage face backed by storm and night, gazing in at a window "with hair and coat wettened by snow" and "sharp cannibal teeth revealed by the cold and wrath, and gleaming in the darkness." Then the curtain falls. But Emily Brontë has picked out the important features of the scene with so unerring an eye that it is photographed on our memories forever.

Wuthering Heights, however, is more than vivid and real. It is also very exciting. In addition to her pictorial and dramatic gifts, Emily Brontë possessed the humbler art of the writer of thrillers. She can work /198/ up a climax as successfully as Dumas, hold the reader as breathless with suspense as Sir Arthur Conan Doyle. She can also evolve that deeper excitement which comes from a sense of the power of fate. As through *Hamlet,* there sounds through *Wuthering Heights* behind the single voices of the actors, now faint now loud, but always audible, the clash and vibration of the orchestra of destiny. Emily Brontë conveys this partly by sheer imaginative power, which enables her to invest the slightest gesture with a spiritual significance, to make the most prosaic sentence stir a cosmic echo. But she does it more especially by a mastery of the dramatic device called tragic irony. She makes her characters say something that has a prophetic significance, of which they themselves are unaware:

" 'And we must pass by Gimmerton Kirk,' cries Catherine to Heathcliff in her last interview with him, 'to go that journey! We've braved its ghosts often together, and dared each other to stand among the graves and ask them to come. But, Heathcliff, if I dare you now, will you venture? If you do, I'll keep you. I'll not lie there by myself: they may bury me twelve feet deep, and throw the church down over me, but I won't rest till you are with me.' "

She speaks only with the exaggeration of a thoughtless moment of passion, but she speaks the truth. And when four hundred pages later we watch him transfixed by the sight of her ghost, we remember her words, and with a thrilled awe recognize that behind the visible drama we are witnessing, works ever the controlling and purposeful hand of fate. /199/

But sense of form and art of narrative do not make up the tale of Emily Brontë's technical equipment. There remains her style; and it is the most powerful instrument of all. One would not think so at the first glance. Emily Brontë is not a virtuoso in the manipulation of words, like Thackeray. Her writing is marked by no artfully modulated cadences, no deliberate, adroit precision of statement. She speaks as the bird sings, instinctively, carelessly, ignorantly: and at times she is both clumsy and amateurish. Nor does her writing, like that of Charlotte, suddenly blaze up in an inspired flight of gorgeous rhetoric. She has no purple passages; no striking, unusual metaphors; she never raises her voice. Her style is a lightweight fabric, colorless, bare and direct. It understates rather than otherwise; it employs few images, and those generalized and commonplace. It is not a painted window dyeing all that passes through it to its own jeweled hues, but a clear pane, only designed to reveal her vision as completely as possible.

All the same, it transfigures that vision as only a great style can. For it is compounded of the essential precious crystal of her genius. The distinguishing qualities of Emily Brontë's imagination show themselves in her choice of words as much as in her conception of character. She may use only the humble materials of everyday speech; but out of them her intensity, her freshness and her strength enable her to forge an instrument at once extremely powerful and extremely delicate; capable of expressing with equal ease the airiest subtleties of atmosphere or the full ex- /200/ plosion of passion. It does not matter that she never raises her voice; into a fleeting whisper she can pack all the pulsing complexities of a heart at war with itself. It does not matter that she is sometimes clumsy: her freshness combines with this very clumsiness to invest her work with an untutored enchanting grace. It does not matter that she is bare; the simplicity of her melody only makes it easier for us to hear the vibrations of its thronging overtones. Nor do we mind if her words or images are commonplace. She manages to inform them with her own vitality. Drenched in the magical rejuvenating elixir of her temperament, the most faded clichés of letters gleam and shimmer with all the palpitating life that animated them on the day of their creation. Indeed, Emily Brontë achieves that rarest of literary triumphs: she writes an old language so that it seems like a new one.

As for her rhythm, it is one of the wonders of our literature. It is always a perfect echo of the sense; the movement of the sentence is modulated exactly to correspond with the movement of the emotion it conveys. It is also unfailingly beautiful; a varied, natural, haunting cadence, now buoyantly lilting, now surging like the sea, now wailing upward piercingly sweet, now dying away in a wild sadness, like the cry of the plover that circled and swooped over the Yorkshire moors which were its birthplace.

"My walk home was lengthened by a diversion in the direction of the kirk. When beneath its walls, I perceived decay had made progress, even in seven months: many a window showed black gaps deprived /201/ of glass; and slates jutted off, here and there, beyond the right line of roof, to be gradually worked off in coming autumn storms.

"I sought, and soon discovered, the three headstones on the slope next the moor: the middle one grey, and half buried in heath: Edgar Linton's only harmonized by the turf and moss creeping up its foot; Heathcliff's still bare.

"I lingered round them, under that benign sky: watched the moths fluttering among the heath and harebells, listened to the soft wind breathing through the grass, and wondered how any one could ever imagine unquiet slumbers for the sleepers in that quiet earth."

Style, structure, narrative, there is no aspect of Emily Brontë's craft which does not brilliantly exhibit her genius. The form of *Wuthering Heights* is as consummate as its subject is sublime. So far from being the incoherent outpouring of an undisciplined imagination, it is the one perfect work of art amid all the vast varied canvasses of Victorian fiction.

It seems odd that it should be so, considering the circumstances of its creation, considering that Emily Brontë's craftsmanship was self-taught, and that she evolved its principles unassisted by any common tradition. But ironically enough, her circumstances were the secret of her success. It was they that enabled her to maintain the consistent integrity of her imagination. Since she had no ready-made conventions to help her, since she always had to invent them for herself, her form is appropriate to her conception, as it could never have been if she had tried to mold her inspiration to /202/ fit the accepted Victorian formulas. Her mystical attitude to life made her approach to her subject so different from that of her contemporaries, that the forms and conventions evolved to fit a theme like that of *David Copperfield* or *Pendennis* would not have fitted it at all. But the form she evolves in *Wuthering Heights* fits it perfectly. So perfectly, indeed, that if we knew nothing about it we should never guess it to be the unique work of a lonely genius, but the culminating achievement of a whole literary civilization. Against the urbanized landscape of Victorian fiction it looms up august and alien, like the only surviving monument of a vanished race. /203/

Questions for Discussion and Writing

1. As do several other critics, Cecil points out the extent to which Emily Brontë's environment influenced the writing of *Wuthering Heights*. Assemble as much information on this subject as you can find in the essays, supporting your points with direct and original use of the novel itself.

2. Cecil presents Emily Brontë as a mystic; summarize this idea, and decide how it affects interpretation of the novel. Does it answer any objections to the novel raised by other critics?

3. What do you think of the footnote on page 155? Is Cecil hedging in his argument here? Or is he merely qualifying statements which might have been misinterpreted?

4. Cecil says that Brontë is "innocent of irony." Does he mean that there is no irony at all in *Wuthering Heights*? (See if you can find any.) Or is he speaking in some general sense that you can explain?

5. Note Cecil's two examples of improbable actions (page 159) which he says are made acceptable to us by the author's intensity. Examine these actions and determine just what it is that creates this intensity. Can you supply similar actions from other parts of the novel? What does "intense" mean as applied to action in a novel?

6. With the help of the critics, especially Cecil, define the attraction between Catherine and Heathcliff and between Cathy and Hareton.

7. What does Cecil find original in *Wuthering Heights*? To what extent is his praise of the novel based on this?

8. Cecil calls the novel "exciting." (page 177) In what sense does he find it so? Do you agree? Do you find it exciting in other ways? Or do you fail to find it exciting at all? Explain your answer, making careful use of the novel to do so.

9. Look for passages that illustrate Cecil's comments on Brontë's style as "at times . . . both clumsy and amateurish." First discuss the elements of style with your instructor.

10. What is Emily Brontë's "eagle imagination"? (page 189)

11. "*Wuthering Heights* is usually considered as artistically confused, just as it is considered intellectually confused," says Cecil on page 195. Explain this statement in detail.

12. Cecil and other critics have argued against the criticism mentioned in the question above. Explain their arguments for *Wuthering Heights* as a novel that is not confused.

Wuthering Heights

ERNEST A. BAKER

No work of literature was ever more inseparably identified with a definite spot on the earth's surface than *Wuthering Heights* (1847); and yet it is a drama of elemental conflict and suffering that might have been played out on any stage. It is the story of a passion unfettered by the limitations of the world and the flesh; time and place, though so definitely particularized,[1] are almost irrelevant; it is of any region and any age of mankind's perennial agony. At the end, the lover left on earth seeks union with the beloved even in the grave. And he attains it; for Emily has not merely grasped the modern idea of the supreme value of the individual soul, which realizes itself in its personal life and in mutual understanding, complete harmony, virtual identity with its destined mate; she sees the personality and the consummated union as eternal facts, which mortality itself cannot annul.[2]

> There is no room for Death,
> Nor atom that his might could render void.

Charlotte was much more orthodox in her heterodox ways of contriving the marriage of true minds; Emily, innocent /**70**/ libertine that she was, defied convention. Catherine, at the very moment when she is deciding to marry Linton, as a matter of worldy wisdom

From *The History of the English Novel* (London: H. F. & G. Witherby Ltd., 1937. 10 vols.), Vol. VIII.

[1] *E.g.* in Mrs Dean's conscientious effort to fix the date of Hindley's assault on the jealous Heathcliff, as the summer of 1778—*i.e.* nearly twenty-three years before (chap. vii).

[2] "Belief in the personal and positive immortality of the individual and indivisible spirit was not apparently, in her case, swallowed up or nullified or made nebulous by any doctrine or dream of simple reabsorption into some indefinite infinity of eternal life" (Swinburne, 266). /**70**/ [Algernon Charles Swinburne, *A Note on Charlotte Brontë* (London, 1877), p. 266.]

and natural expectation, declares to Nelly her unalterable sense that she and Heathcliff are fundamentally and irrevocably one.[3]

"It would degrade me to marry Heathcliff now; so he shall never know how I loved him: and that, not because he's handsome, Nelly, but because he's more myself than I am. Whatever our souls are made of, his and mine are the same; and Linton's is as different as a moonbeam from lightning, or frost from fire."

And then she relates how she wept in her dream, to find herself in heaven, away from Wuthering Heights, away from Heathcliff.[4] She knows she is doing wrong; she knows it in her heart of hearts:

"*Here!* and *here!*" replied Catherine, striking one hand on her forehead, and the other on her breast: "in whatever place the soul lives. In my soul and in my heart, I'm convinced I'm wrong."

Never will she forsake Heathcliff: "I shouldn't be Mrs Linton were such a price demanded!" With her good-natured husband's aid, she will save him from Hindley and help him to rise. Worldly connexions and worldly prejudices are of no concern to them; theirs is a bond that nothing in this existence or the one beyond can break. "Nelly, I *am* Heathcliff! If all else perished, and *he* remained, *I* should still continue to be; and if all else remained, and he were annihilated, the universe would turn to a mighty stranger: I should not seem a part of it."

The probabilities of average human nature do not apply to /71/ such a story. It has reached the dimensions of that tragedy in which the confines of mundane existence are broken down. And yet the strange thing is that a story which soars to the extreme heights of poetry is nevertheless based on the firmest and plainest realism: not alone the setting, which is as solid as the moorland rocks.[5] Cath-

---

[3] Love, not sex, is the bond of indissoluble union. The rash and innocent marriage of Catherine and Edgar Linton, when she avowedly loves Heathcliff as if he were part of her very being, is proof enough of Emily's innocence.

[4] Cp. *Aucassin et Nicolette:* "En Paradis qu-ai je à faire? je n'i quier entrer, mais que j'aie Nicolete, ma très douce amie, que j'aim tant" ("What have I to do in Paradise? I don't want to go there, but to have Nicolette, my sweetest love, whom I love so") (*Nouvelles françaises du 13e siècle,* ed. L. Moland and C. d'Héricault, 1856, 242-243). /71/

[5] As to the extent of this realism, a flood of light has been recently shed on the question where Emily Brontë found the germs of her characters, or the moulds into which she poured her conceptions of masculine strength and untamable will, by those who have studied the Methodist magazines read at Haworth parsonage, and the records of the violent revivalist movements going on in those parts in her time and earlier (see particularly *Methodist Good Companions* (1935), by Mrs. G. Elsie Harrison: *e.g.* (chap. v., "Reactions in Haworth Parsonage"). As might well

erine and Heathcliff, though /72/ they represent and express such
daring conceptions, are not merely drawn realistically, they are real-
ists themselves. Perfectly clear-sighted in their outlook on the rest
of the world, they see each other exactly as they are. Catherine
tells the lovelorn Isabella, fascinated by Heathcliff's rugged strength
and superiority to other men, what he really is: "an unreclaimed
creature, without refinement, without cultivation; an arid wilderness of furze and whinstone."

"Pray don't imagine that he conceals depths of benevolence and affection
beneath a stern exterior! He's not a rough diamond—a pearl-containing
oyster of a rustic: he's a fierce, pitiless, wolfish man. I never say to him, 'Let
this or that enemy alone, because it would be ungenerous or cruel to harm
them'; I say, 'Let them alone, because I should hate them to be wronged':
and he'd crush you like a sparrow's egg, Isabella, if he found you a troublesome charge. I know he couldn't love a Linton; and yet he'd be quite capable of marrying your fortune and expectations! avarice is growing with
him a besetting sin. There's my picture; and I'm his friend."

And, after the last wild interview, after the tempest of despair
and the caresses that bite like curses, when Nelly Dean tells Heath-

---

be supposed, Emily was not intimate with the country people of the West Riding,
even those round about her. Charlotte said: "I am bound to avow that she had
scarcely more practical knowledge of the peasantry among whom she lived, than
a nun has of the country-people that pass her convent gates" (Gaskell, xvi.). But
Mrs. Brontë was a Methodist from Cornwall, like the aunt who took her place;
and the atmosphere at the parsonage "was steeped in Methodism." The young
folk read what Charlotte called "mad Methodist magazines, full of miracles and
apparitions and preternatural warnings, ominous dreams, and frenzied fanati-
cisms." (As Mrs Harrison remarks, George Eliot also read these thrillers, and perhaps it was there that she found the story of Hetty and her murdered baby, in
Adam Bede. She too had a Methodist aunt, whom she idealized in Dinah Morris.)
Jabes Branderham, in Mr Lockwood's dream of the sermon, "divided into four
hundred and ninety parts" and of his protest which excites a riot in the chapel,
had his original in the Rev. Jabez Bunting (1779-1858), the clergyman who turned
Wesleyan and became a mighty force among the Methodists. He was the central
figure in an uproarious incident at the opening of a chapel at Woodhouse Grove,
where the Brontës' uncle John Fennel was headmaster of a school, the school, in
fact, where Patrick Brontë met his future wife and where Aunt Bramwell came from.
The "rappings and counter-rappings" which Lockwood eventually traces to the
tapping of the fir-cones on the window were a reminiscence of the row in the
chapel, and by no means the only details literally reproduced from incidents now
authenticated. A previous incumbent of the Haworth living (1742-1746) had been
William Grimshaw, Methodist preacher and friend of Wesley. His denunciations
in broad Yorkshire are echoed by old Joseph, who seemed to Lockwood "the
wearisomest self-righteous Pharisee that ever ransacked a Bible to rake the promises
to himself and fling the curses to his neighbours." The Brontë girls knew all about
the good-hearted but rugged and boisterous Grimshaw, head of the Haworth

cliff that Catherine's life has closed in a gentle dream, and prays
that she may "wake as kindly in the other world," this is his answer: /73/

"May she wake in torment!" he cried, with frightful vehemence, stamping his foot, and groaning in a sudden paroxysm of ungovernable passion.
"Why, she's a liar to the end! Where is she? Not *there*—not in heaven—not
perished—where? Oh! you said you cared nothing for my sufferings! And I
pray one prayer—I repeat it till my tongue stiffens—Catherine Earnshaw,
may you not rest as long as I am living! You said I killed you—haunt me,
then! The murdered *do* haunt their murderers, I believe. I know that
ghosts *have* wandered on earth. Be with me always—take any form—drive
me mad! only do not leave me in this abyss, where I cannot find you!
Oh, God! it is unutterable! I *cannot* live without my life! I *cannot* live
without my soul!"

It is the negation of polite romance; all this is death to sentimen-

---

Round. Sowden's Farm, on the brow of the hill, is the old parsonage to which
Wesley came, and may safely be identified with Wuthering Heights, Ponden Hill,
across the moor, being similarly recognizable as Thrushcross Grange (Harrison, 118-
119). Other corroborations abound. The Earnshaw legend is the Grimshaw legend,
and the general brutality in *Wuthering Heights* is that of the Haworth Round. It
all shows how solid Emily had laid her realistic foundations. It shows also that
her sense of humour was not defective, like Charlotte's. Only compare her Joseph
with Charlotte's timid kitcat of Barraclough, the obnoxious Methody. She gets
comic relief out of this profane representative of the apostolic Grimshaw, without
any such change of tone as would have turned tragedy into farce and have jarred
upon the feelings. It is the man's unconscious nature.

" 'Thank Hivin for all! All warks togither for gooid to them as is chozzen, and
piked out fro' the rubbidge! Yah knaw whet t' Scriptures ses.' And he began /72/
quoting several texts, referring us to chapters and verses where we might find
them."

The blending of gloom and grotesquerie, of sardonic humour with terror, is
inimitable. Had Emily wanted to be a novelist, she would have been one of the
greatest, if she had lived. Humour she kept in proper restraint; she was a poet,
writing tragedy the most austere. There is nothing incredible in the argument
that the religious passion of such as Grimshaw for the Divine Lover was translated by her "into the language of human love," or that Grimshaw's ecstasies,
during which "the communicants were sometimes held in Haworth church for
hours together," suggested the wild transports of Heathcliff. The passion of
Wuthering Heights is sexless: Heathcliff cries, "My soul's bliss kills my body."
Emily was revolted by the Methodist view of evil and the doctrine of eternal
punishment; she was a rebel, an individualist; her religion was an affair between
herself and God. "It was Emily Brontë's violent reaction to the Methodist doctrine of sin that made her best poetry" (Harrison, 133). That is true with some
grains of allowance. And, certainly, Heathcliff, with "no sort of fear of hell and
Satan or of an outraged God," is a withering retort to the plaintive, pusillani-
mous Methodist who, as Grimshaw put it, hoped "to go creeping into heaven at
last" (*Ibid.*, 135). /73/

talism. The matter-of-factness mingled with Heathcliff's heaven-defying transports appears memorably in his instructions to the sexton: his coffin to be placed close to Catherine's, and a plank removed from each so that their dust will mingle. Heathcliff is thoroughly credible; he is consistent in act and speech and emotion, from the appalling incident when he curses himself for having put out a hand and saved the life of his enemy's son,[6] to the demoniac imprecation when he tells the dying Cathy that the kisses and tears she has wrung out, "they'll blight you—they'll damn you." /74/

All the others who figure in the story, including the pair through whom, by an awkward expedient, it gets itself told, are entirely subordinate, mere accessories to the terrific duel between the protagonists; but they sustain their parts and help to establish the realistic solidity. Isabella, the commonplace, giddy young thing, who flings herself at Heathcliff's head and is devoured; her brother Ed-

---

[6] That incident (chap. ix.) inevitably calls up the scene in *Hamlet* which Dr Johnson found "so atrocious and horrible," where Hamlet will not slay his uncle while at prayer, and waits for a moment when he can catch him in some act

> That has no relish of salvation in't.

Heathcliff is like Hamlet in combining realistic vision, matter-of-factness, with the imagination that looks beyond. Coleridge said that in Hamlet Shakespeare "intended to portray a person, in whose view the external world, and all its incidents and objects, were comparatively dim, and of no interest in themselves, and which began to interest only, when they were reflected in the mirror of his mind. Hamlet," he continues, "beheld external things in the same way that a man of vivid imagination, who shuts his eyes, sees what has previously made an impression on his organs" (*Lectures on Shakspere*, ed. T. Ashe, 1893, 159—with Ashe's punctuation). Much of this applies to Emily Brontë's Heathcliff. On the other hand, Heathcliff might be taken as an example of Blake's anarchic individualism. Blake would have admitted him to his heaven. "Men are admitted into Heaven not because they have curbed & govern'd their Passions or have No Passions, but because they have cultivated their Understandings. The Treasures of Heaven are not Negations of Passion, but Realities of Intellect, from which all the Passions Emanate Uncurbed in their Eternal Glory. The Fool shall not enter into Heaven let him be ever so Holy." "This world of Imagination is Infinite & Eternal, whereas the world of Generation, /74/ or Vegetation, is Finite & Temporal" ("Vision of the Last Judgment," *Poetry and Prose of William Blake,* ed. Geoffrey Keynes, 1927, pp. 830, 842). Any coincidence of thought is, of course, probably accidental; Emily had apparently never read Blake, though she was fairly well acquainted with German fiction and perhaps German philosophy. Somehow, at any rate, she arrived at a conception parallel to Blake's of the devils as redeemers—defenders of the "freedom of the natural soul." Blake, whether she knew of him or not, throws some light on the daring course taken by her imagination.

> What immortal hand and eye
> Dare frame thy fearful symmetry? /75/

gar Linton, gentle and amiable, bewildered by his wife's infatuation; the wretched boy who is Heathcliff and Isabella's demoralized offspring; and the simple, rustic, honest-hearted Hareton, what Hindley may have been before he was brutalized by evil courses—they are distinct and lifelike, though not memorable on their own account. But Nelly Dean, old Joseph, and the younger Catherine do arrest attention; and even Lockwood, though criticism has disparaged him, is fully equal to the duty allotted him, which is not quite otiose. He has the first as well as the last word; and the temptation which he resists to fall in love with Catherine Linton is a touch that brings that sprightly creature nearer, and with its tag of irony for him, Hareton's good luck, lets the story down gently to the mundane level. But the phlegmatic Mrs Dean, whose original was Tabby Brown, an old servant at the parsonage, with her obtuseness to all the glamour, is much livelier and racier, and also a better medium for a story that may leap in a moment from the common earth to somewhere between heaven and hell. Emily Brontë has been reproached for the clumsiness of this complicated mode of narration. But much is to be said for her choice of the indirect method, though it was overdoing it perhaps to begin with the epilogue, Catherine having already departed this stormy life when the story opens, and Heathcliff /75/ being about to follow. Yet could the drama possibly have unfolded itself with such impressiveness had it kept to the straightforward order of events? Its force is concentrated in a series of tremendous climaxes; the fire and fury of one scene gives momentum enough until the next. There are, it is true, intricate complications and obscurities in between; but, when the great moment arrives, the mental and moral situation is made clear enough by the actors themselves. Lucid order may be at a discount; but the lack of it is a trifling defect; for, as Swinburne pointed out,[7] the alleged "confusion or incoherence" is only "external and accidental," not "inward and spiritual." Better, however, not to dwell too minutely on the legal points involved in Heathcliff's inheritance of the two estates. A wide ignorance of the law may be condoned in a young woman's first novel. And, after all, what are such faults of execution in the light of the almost superhuman conception realized with such power? That the would-be clever hand of Branwell Brontë is traceable in the first two chapters, with their over-literary phraseology and strained facetiousness, may perhaps be conceded to Emily's many scholiasts.[8] But a chap-

[7] *Miscellanies*—"Emily Brontë," 266.

[8] These concessions to the prevalent mode of novel-writing occur elsewhere in

ter follows at once which ushers in /76/ admirably one of the great moments. It describes Lockwood's trying night in the quaint old bedroom at Wuthering Heights, his nightmare after reading Jabes Branderham's sermon, and the worse than nightmare of the fingers clutching through the lattice and the voice sobbing "Let me in—let me in!" Catherine is there. To use her phrase about the children's plays at Haworth, Emily has "established" her tragedy. If it was clumsy to take the last events first, it was assuredly the clumsiness of genius.[9] /77/

the book; Emily was not always at the full height of poetic inspiration. But these first two chapters are particularly stilted, and do suggest that there was another hand at work as well as Emily's. Branwell put forward various rather indefinite claims to the authorship of *Wuthering Heights*. The theory that he wrote it all is, of course, as silly as the idea that Charlotte Brontë wrote it, but has not been too monstrous to find exponents. But there is good reason to believe that he was in the secret when Emily was writing the book, that they discussed it together, even if they did not collaborate further, and thus portions written wholly or in part by him, such as these two chapters, were incorporated. The tale goes that Branwell, whilst drinking with some friends, pulled some sheets of paper from his hat, and read out what proved afterwards to be a part of *Wuthering Heights*, asserting that it was his own work. The sceptic might ask whether the fact that the papers were in Branwell's hat proved anything—he was looking there for some poetry he had written. Without branding him as an out-and-out liar, no one can deny that Branwell was a *poseur*, and, what is more troublesome to those in quest of facts, a self-deceiver. He was quite capable of deluding himself into the firm belief that he had written a book in which he had had the smallest finger. The question is summarized by Benson (168-179) and argued in more detail and with an intent to rehabilitate Branwell by Leyland (*The Brontë Sisters, passim*). The theory that Heathcliff was drawn from Branwell is another of the Old Aunt Sallies erected by eccentric admirers, and hardly worth while knocking down. "No doubt," say the editors of the *Shakespeare Head Brontë*, Messrs T. J. Wyse and J. Alexander Symington, "that Branwell's experiences and behavior were the vital influences which resulted in the conception and creation of *Wuthering Heights*" (ii. 57). But that Branwell may have been the suggester, intentionally or the reverse, of such things as the dare-devil sentiments, and the violent outbursts of imprecation, is a totally different matter. One of the most grotesque of the Old Aunt Sallies was Dr William Wright's pretence, pulverized by A. M. Mackay (*The Brontës: Fact and Fiction*), that *Wuthering Heights* was a version of Brontë ancestral history in Ireland—an apocrypha originating in delusion rather than deliberate fraud, or what is almost as bad, the rage for original discovery—of mares' nests. Mr Benson's statement that "the intention to make a *motif* out of Catherine's beauty and Lockwood's complacent susceptibility" "was scrapped" is hardly true. As already noted, it gives a little touch of beauty to the close, when Lockwood realizes the chance he has missed (see above, p. 75). Lockwood does not "drop out" (Benson, 175), but utters the thoughts which make such a fine ending. /76/

[9] It is astounding to hear very superior folk talk about the "sentimental" ending of *Wuthering Heights*: they must have got the word on the brain without being

Questions for Discussion and Writing

1. Support or attack Baker's suggestion that *Wuthering Heights* is "a drama . . . that might have been played out on any stage." (page 70) Could it be played out in an executive suite? In Hamlet's Denmark? In an East-Side slum? Explain your answer.

2. Baker says that time and place are "almost irrelevant." Are they? If so, has Brontë loaded her novel with useless detail? Use later criticism to support your answer.

3. Does Baker believe *Wuthering Heights* is a modern novel? Do you find the novel modern? Do most critics? Why or why not?

4. What does Baker mean when he calls Emily Brontë an "innocent libertine"? (pages 70-71) Support your answer, of course, by use of the novel.

5. To what extent is *Wuthering Heights* a realistic novel? Does Baker find it realistic? What have other critics made of the realistic elements in the story?

6. Baker calls Heathcliff "thoroughly credible." (page 74) Explain in detail what he means and support or refute Baker's statement. What conflicting opinions of the credibility or incredibility of Heathcliff have been offered by critics?

7. Comment on Baker's statement that all characters in the story are subservient to Catherine Earnshaw and Heathcliff. If you accept this, do

---

quite clear what it means. Sentimentality is non-existent in the story of Catherine and Heathcliff; that is one of its supreme glories. Heathcliff is actuated by two passionate motives, revenge on Hindley and all belonging to him, and the furious hunger for union with Catherine. In his last hours, he feels himself on the verge of attaining this final reunion, and the lesser impulse sinks into indifference. He has ceased to love or hate anything on earth but Catherine. Hence, Hareton and Catherine the second, whom he has despised rather than actively hated, as mere accidents in the path of his vengeance, are brushed aside as no longer of the least importance, and the tale comes naturally to the symmetrical close. Heathcliff and Catherine are united in death; the Earnshaws and the Lintons reunite in the present generation. Further, vengeance is shown again defeating itself, as Emily had already shown, in the baby Hareton's escape when Heathcliff involuntarily saves his life, and also in Hareton's unconquerable affection for Heathcliff. "Poor Hareton, the most wronged, was the only one who really suffered much. He sat by the corpse all night, weeping in bitter earnest. He pressed its hand, and kissed the sarcastic savage face that every one else shrank from contemplating." Heathcliff himself had said, "It is a poor conclusion . . . an absurd termination to my violent exertions." He had slaved like Hercules to demolish the two houses, and now the will to wreak his revenge had vanished. "But where is the use? I don't care for striking; I can't take the trouble to raise my hand!" Emily wrote this, which is a sufficient reply to such fatuity. /77/

you do so with any reservations? If you reject the statement, do you in any way qualify your rejection?

8. Why does Baker call Isabella "commonplace"?

9. Compare later evaluations of Lockwood with Baker's estimate.

10. Comment on Baker's criticism of the "order of events" in *Wuthering Heights* in the light of later criticism.

11. What do other critics say of Emily Brontë's "ignorance of the law"? Cf. especially Sanger.

12. Do you find the first two chapters "particularly stilted," as if another hand had helped to write them? If so, support with references. If not, defend the chapters. Be sure you have a clear idea of what "stilted" means.

The Dramatic Novel:
Wuthering Heights

BRUCE McCULLOUGH

Although *Wuthering Heights* has been pretty generally accepted as a triumph of the imagination, there has not been the same uniformity of opinion in regard to its merits as a work of art. Some- /185/ thing of the frenzy that now and then possesses its two leading characters seems to communicate itself to those who attempt to appraise the novel and prevents them from writing in measured terms about it. One critic[1] sets loose an avalanche of adjectives, of which "stupendous" may serve as an example, and characterizes each act of Heathcliff as being "wrapt in its own infernal glamour, trailing a cloud of supernatural splendour." Another critic[2] would have it that the form of the novel is "as consummate as its subject is sublime," and calls it "the one perfect work of art" among Victorian novels. One of the recent biographers[3] of Charlotte is impatient with her for not having appreciated her sister's genius more thoroughly, and goes on to reveal his own superior appreciation by asserting that although *Wuthering Heights* is among the greatest of novels its "composition and construction are inconceivably awkward." He argues further that since "no single author could have planned a book in so topsy-turvy a manner" Branwell must have written the opening chapters. Yet another writer,[4] after a careful scrutiny of the legal aspects of the novel, says that he was inclined for a time to find the climax of the tragedy in the circumstance that the surviving young people "were to be left destitute." He ad-

From *Representative English Novelists* (New York: Harper & Brothers, 1946).

[1] May Sinclair, *The Three Brontës*, Boston, 1912, p. 245.
[2] David Cecil, *Early Victorian Novelists*, New York, 1935, p. 202.
[3] E. F. Benson, *Charlotte Brontë*, London, 1932, pp. 174, 175.
[4] C. P. S., *The Structure of Wuthering Heights*, London, 1926, p. 18.

mits, however, that such an interpretation would be going too far. It would indeed be going too far. Mrs. Dean clearly never had an inkling of such a calamitous turn of events and it was to her, after all, that Emily entrusted the telling of the story. Moreover, it is made perfectly clear by Heathcliff before his death that he is no longer consumed by the desire to destroy the two families.

It is well for us, then, in dealing with a novel that has been so variously commented upon, to avoid farfetched theories and to accept what we are plainly told. As it is, there is enough for the commentator to explain if he can. There is enough mystery in the character of Heathcliff to tax our capacity for strangeness without borrowing trouble by searching for additional hidden meanings.

The title of *Wuthering Heights* is taken from the name of the /186/ dwelling place of the Earnshaw family, in which most of the action of the story occurs. "Wuther," according to the dictionary, means to roar or bluster, and in the opening chapter "wuthering" is said to indicate the atmospheric tumult to which the house was exposed in stormy weather. We may conclude that in giving her novel such a title the author wished to suggest the warring of the elements. She wished to suggest that human passions are not unlike the ceaseless contention going on between the inanimate forces surrounding us, which follow laws of their own, hardly to be understood.

The affinity existing between Catherine Earnshaw and Heathcliff is a product of natural growth and is not amenable to reason. When frustrated, the energy which it has generated is turned into paths of destruction. By marrying Edgar Linton, Catherine thwarts Heathcliff and denies to herself the possibility of a natural outlet for her passion. Kept from union with him in life, her spirit presumably haunts him after her death. There is no peace for her because she is completely herself only in union with the man of whom she has once confessed to Nelly Dean: "He's more myself than I am." Heathcliff, the most completely frustrated character, blames Edgar Linton for robbing him of Catherine, and Hindley Earnshaw for first having made it impossible for him to win her. His frustrated passion bears fruit in hatred which can find relief only in the destruction of everything at all connected with the two men. His wrath thus falls upon their children and also upon his own child, the pitiable offspring of a hated union. It falls even upon Catherine, who in having innocently betrayed him is the cause of his torment.

The struggle suggested in the title, and made manifest in every aspect of the novel, centers in Heathcliff. His feeling for Hareton and for Catherine Linton becomes in time a blend of attraction and replusion. They are associated in his mind with what he hates and also with what he loves. He cannot dissociate them from his lost Catherine, who looks at him through the eyes of her daughter and to whom Hareton sometimes bears a striking resemblance. There are times too when Hareton, deprived as he has been of a chance for normal growth, seems to Heathcliff a personification of his own youth.

Apart from such minor complexities, Emily Brontë sees how /187/ conflicts arise within the very core of love, which is conceived not as a matter of simple attraction between two persons but as a complex of forces occupying different planes of feeling. One of the most remarkable sections in the novel is that which depicts the conflict growing in the heart of Catherine Earnshaw after she has been introduced to the quieter atmosphere of Thrushcross Grange. She acquires a different set of manners for use with the Lintons, quite without any vulgar intention to deceive. She begins also to look at Heathcliff from a different and more critical point of view. To censure her for planning to marry Linton while she loves Heathcliff is to disregard her inexperience and to fail to recognize how potent such conflicts can be in determining conduct. In any case she might not have married Linton, in spite of her plans, if Heathcliff had remained at home. Furthermore, in first planning her marriage she had hoped to use it as a means of aiding Heathcliff.

Such a way of handling love was revolutionary in English fiction in 1847. It is remarkable that the author was able to depict it so convincingly and with so little attention to the blinding conventions of the period. She was more completely honest and more convincing than Charlotte, who was much more pleasing to their own generation. In what other English novel of the period could such a scene have occurred as the one in which Catherine tries to dissuade Isabella from her fatal infatuation with Heathcliff? Catherine knows that her feeling for Heathcliff is different from her feeling for Linton—a difference which she tries to explain to Mrs. Dean in what seems to be a strange outburst coming from a Victorian heroine:

My great miseries in this world have been Heathcliff's miseries, and I watched and felt each from the beginning: my great thought in living is himself. If all else perished, and *he* remained, I should still continue to be; and if all else remained, and he were annihilated, the universe would

turn to a mighty stranger: I should not seem a part of it. My love for
Linton is like the foliage in the woods: time will change it, I'm well aware,
as winter changes the trees. My love for Heathcliff resembles the eternal
rocks beneath: a source of little visible delight, but necessary. Nelly, I *am*
Heathcliff! He's always, always in my mind: not as a pleasure, any more
than I am always a pleasure to myself, but as my own being. /188/

Those who have looked upon *Wuthering Heights* as being awkward and confused in structure have usually not bothered to consider what other method of construction the author might have
elected to follow. Neither have they devoted much attention to the
advantages of the method followed or to its suitability to the material of the novel. As matter of fact, one who reads the novel with
ordinary attentiveness to details will find not confusion but a carefully articulated plot. He will find not a surplusage of irrelevant
matters but an organically conceived story with a distinct beginning
and end, a complete cycle of change, and bearing within its narrow
confines an intensity of feeling unapproached in the more sophisticated fiction of the period. The fact that the narrative opens at a
point near the end should not occasion any difficulty to readers who
are familiar with Conrad or with the technical innovations of recent
fiction.

The subject of *Wuthering Heights* as conceived by its author was
not suited to autobiographical treatment. Charlotte's best novels
were in the nature of confessions, which could be put into the mouth
of a character more or less to be identified with the author. What
Emily had to tell may well have been intimately connected with
her feelings, but she was too reserved to open her heart in a form of
confession so little disguised as was her sister's. It is not surprising
that, being reticent by nature, she should choose a method of telling
her story that would leave her in the background. Besides, like a
true artist, she was not content to express merely what she had experienced. She possessed the type of imagination capable of representing in objective terms what she had contemplated and made
her own.

An additional reason for the choice of method can be found in
the extraordinary nature of the material. On its surface a story of
mundane revenge, the novel really has to do with a love that passes
beyond ordinary boundaries and results in behavior that seems to
be little short of madness. If one pole of the story is fixed in everyday affairs, the other pole takes us into a realm of feeling where not
everyone can venture with assurance. What better method can be
found to render such strange occurrences credible than to have them

related by a person who has witnessed them and who, more- /189/ over, is manifestly a sensible, matter-of-fact person, whose obvious disapproval of much that she has to tell is an added guarantee of its authenticity? Lockwood, as intermediary, lends further support to the story. Mrs. Dean, despite her literal-mindedness, might conceivably exaggerate the wonders of which she is, so to speak, the sole custodian. But Lockwood, being a gentleman who belongs to the world of the reader rather than to the narrow circle of the participants, is beyond such suspicion. His curiosity provides Mrs. Dean with a reason for talking. In such a simple way is the authority of the strange tale established. The author has the good sense not to make too much of her difficulties. To have done so would have been to attract more attention to them.

Great artists succeed not by avoiding difficulties but by overcoming them. There are difficulties in the method of *Wuthering Heights*. Mrs. Dean has to remember long stretches of conversation that have taken place years before. She is able to pick her way through a multitude of trivial associations and select what best suits her purpose. She has to supply gaps in her information by various devices and her presence upon some occasions seems intrusive. Catherine and Heathcliff both confide in her, although Heathcliff is by nature secretive.

There are things too in Heathcliff's manipulation of events that seem hardly plausible. Isabella's infatuation fits too neatly into the scheme of revenge. The harrowing marriage of Catherine Linton to young Heathcliff is another circumstance in which the hand of the conspirator is plainly seen. The affair is managed with such diabolical cleverness, however, and the victim of it is so eager to return to her father that, strange as it is, the action is made to seem plausible. We have the horrifying impression of being in a world in which kindness and compassion have suffered a temporary paralysis under the sway of a superior malignant power. It is remarkable, in fact, how well the author overcame her difficulties. Her story carries conviction by the sheer force of its sincerity and simplicity.

The only other character besides Mrs. Dean who might conceivably have acted as narrator was Heathcliff, who was obviously not fitted for the task. Since telling the story by letters would have been practically out of the question for such a situation, the only other /190/ obvious method was that of ordinary omniscient authorship. Self-consciousness and lack of experience were probably enough to prevent Emily from adopting the latter method, and there may have been an additional reason. As an omniscient storyteller she would

have been put into a position of having to make explanations of
things which were better left unexplained. The events of her story
needed the authority of dramatic representation, but they were not
easily to be elucidated. Mrs. Dean makes no pretense of understanding the meaning of everything that Catherine says about
Heathcliff. She is not a person to be much disturbed by what she
sees. The desire of Catherine not to be separated from Heathcliff
while she is planning to marry Linton is to Mrs. Dean so much folly
and nonsense. As a character in whose uncertain hands the fate of
the children sometimes hangs, she forms a definite part of the action, but as a narrator she becomes little more than a convention.
She and Lockwood both fade into impersonality, and the story thus
gains in objectivity. The intrusive personality of the author, so
characteristic of most Victorian novels, does not here stand between
us and the figures of the drama.

The time covered by *Wuthering Heights* is somewhere near thirty
years, of which only certain periods are presented with dramatic
continuity. Emphasis is placed upon the time when Heathcliff and
the first Catherine reach maturity and upon the corresponding
period in the lives of the succeeding generation of characters, when
Catherine Linton, Hareton Earnshaw, and Linton Heathcliff provide
the triangular situation that in the generation before has been provided by Catherine Earnshaw, Heathcliff, and Edgar Linton.

The novel opens at a point in time somewhat less than a year
before the actual close of the story, when Mr. Lockwood, a tenant
of Heathcliff, makes a call on his landlord at Wuthering Heights.
Notwithstanding his chill reception he returns the following day
and makes the acquaintance of a strange but attractive young
woman, Heathcliff's daughter-in-law, and of a boorish young man,
whom he first assumes to be his host's son but who proves to bear
the name Hareton Earnshaw. Having to remain overnight on
account of the weather, Lockwood amuses himself before going to
sleep by looking through some old books, which contain a fragmen-
tary diary, /191/ dating back about a quarter of a century and
belonging apparently to a young girl named Catherine Earnshaw.
The name is brought particularly to his attention because he has
seen the same name scratched on the paint and in some places
changed to *Catherine Heathcliff* and *Catherine Linton*. Finally he
goes to sleep and has a curious dream, in which it seems to him that
a child calling herself Catherine Linton tries to get in through the
window. She cries that she has been a waif for twenty years, thus
providing us with a time reference that does not extend back as

far as the time of the diary. So terrifying is the dream that Lockwood cries out and accidentally arouses his host, whose behavior
upon learning about what has happened is so unaccountable that
it is enough to raise some suspicion in Lockwood in regard to
Heathcliff's sanity.

Certain references in the diary, the recurrence of the name "Catherine" in the dream, the sullen and apathetic behavior of young
Mrs. Heathcliff, the viciousness of the dogs, the surliness of the old
servant Joseph—these and other circumstances have combined to
suggest something sinister about Heathcliff to his tenant, and to
link him in some mysterious way with the shadowy Catherine Earnshaw of the diary.

In the three introductory chapters the author accomplishes a
number of things. She quickly establishes the atmosphere of her
story, for one thing, subjecting us to a series of shocks that prepare
us for the cold bath of inhuman cruelty and eeriness to follow. By
the device of the dream and the old diary, the curtain is lifted
slightly upon earlier stages of the story, and the reader is catapulted
into the heart of the mystery without any essential facts being given
away. Lockwood is filled with curiosity in regard to his landlord,
and Mrs. Dean is provided with a focus for her story. What she has
to do is simply to explain the circumstances lying behind the strange
state of affairs in Heathcliff's household.

There can be little doubt that the spell cast by *Wuthering Heights*
over its reader is in some way connected with the fact that the events
come to us, for the most part, through the penumbra of distance.
We are never permitted long to forget that we are hearing of events
now dead. The narrator may refer passingly to some subsequent
period of time, or the thread of narrative may be broken /**192**/
by a colloquy between her and her listener. Eventually Mrs. Dean
brings her account up to the present and for a chapter or so the
story comes to us directly, with Lockwood making another visit to
Heathcliff, this time preparatory to going away. It is probably due
to more than mere coincidence that this portion of the novel is
comparatively dull and colorless.

How essential the element of time is to the author becomes more
evident when we consider how little use she made of the conventional stock in trade of the novel. What we call the elemental
quality of her art rests upon her unusual capacity to discard the accumulated weight of tradition—social, moral, religious, literary—
which formed the greater part of the ordinary novelist's material.
We do not find in *Wuthering Heights* the humor and sentiment of

domestic fiction or the system of rewards and punishments characteristic of the Victorian ethic. We do not find the social apparatus
of the satirical novel, or the picturesque accouterments of romance.
What *is* used is completely assimilated. Heathcliff may be a descendant of the Gothic villain or the Byronic hero, but he fits so
perfectly into his peculiar environment that the question of literary
affinity does not occur to us. Even the weather is not exploited as it
is in *Jane Eyre.* We are aware of it, as people who lived on the
moors are sure to have been. But it, like everything else, is reduced to essentials. It marks the passage of time, provides alterna-
tions between periods of calm and of storm, and reflects the recur-
rent cycles of change characteristic of all matter, both animate and
inanimate.

The setting of the novel is limited to the two dwelling places,
Wuthering Heights and Thrushcross Grange, and the fields which
lie around and between them. The nearby village of Gimmerton
is a place to which people sometimes go, but the reader is not privileged to accompany them. The characters are limited to the members of the Earnshaw and Linton families and a small number of
accessory personages. There are practically no visitors to bring in
even a slight stir from the outside world. The doctor is not a talka-
tive fellow, as he would be in a Fielding novel, but a bare func-
tionary.

With so much eliminated or reduced in scale, what remains?
Enough, it would seem, for the author's purpose. Time remains,
/193/ and the absence of distractions enables us the better to see
it in the process of functioning. The laws operating in the novel do
so on a time dimension. To see them at work to the best advantage,
we need to be placed in a position where we can witness a complete
cycle of change. Otherwise we should get only a partial view of the
resultant phenomena. We need also to be able to look back and
forth across the expanse of time. If we were limited to a strictly
chronological view we should not have the advantage which comes
from foreknowledge. We should lose ourselves in the events of the
moment, and our time sense would become less acute. It is only
when we look back across the years that the force of time as a factor
in our lives becomes fully apparent to us. The aspect of change is
kept before us in *Wuthering Heights* by the fact that we never completely forget where we are in relation to the events depicted.

It goes almost without saying that *Wuthering Heights* is one of
the most dramatic of English novels. When Mr. Earnshaw takes
home a waif from the streets of Liverpool, he unwittingly intro-

duces into his family a source of discord that comes near to destroying it and involving a neighboring family in the ruin. The arrival of Heathcliff causes division between father and son and later between brother and sister. Thence the contagion spreads to the Lintons through the agency of Catherine, whose early death is directly traceable to the conflict set up in her by her brother's degradation of the man she loves.

There is no necessity for the author to seek new and exciting turns of her plot as she proceeds. Her initial situation carries within it all the generative force required. The resentment of Heathcliff at his ill treatment accumulates until it finally breaks out with concentrated fury. Gradually thereafter it spends itself and subsides. After his death peace and tranquility return to those who are left of the two families. Hareton and the second Catherine are happy young lovers, rambling on the moors, afraid now of nothing. The novel closes on the note of tranquillity when Lockwood visits the graves where the body of Heathcliff lies besides those of his rival Linton and his beloved Catherine:

"I lingered round them, under that benign sky; watched the moths fluttering among the heath and harebells, listened to the soft wind /194/ breathing through the grass, and wondered how any one could ever imagine unquiet slumbers for the sleepers in that quiet earth."

There is no intention here to suggest that nature is indifferent to the sufferings of man, as Hardy might have done. The discord, in Emily's view, is not *between* man and nature but *within* nature. Nature is not always in a state of equilibrium. Man, being a part of nature, is subject to disturbance when the forces governing him are thrown out of balance.

Wuthering Heights is a story of terrific conflict. The fury of Heathcliff is like the ungovernable fury of a storm. The feeling aroused in the reader is akin to the sense of powerlessness that one experiences in the presence of unleashed forces of nature. One can only wait for the tumult to subside and hope that not everything in the path of destruction will succumb. As in genuine tragedy, the powers which bring the characters into conflict and collision are powers which, once having been aroused and brought into action, must run their full course before order is restored. They are the expression not simply of chance or of human caprice but of the interweaving of passions and circumstances into an insoluble complex of forces as ruthless in its working as fate.

Death . . . was frequently brought into Victorian fiction for reasons of sentiment or of sensation. The deaths in *Wuthering Heights,* of which there are several, have, however, a legitimate place in the novel. In a drama of time and of the changes wrought by time, death reminds us that we are subject to the laws of growth and decay. Moreover, the deaths of the more important characters, such as Catherine and Heathcliff, are handled dramatically, not sentimentally or melodramatically. Let us close our discussion by turning to a passage of a quieter kind. The death of Mr. Earnshaw, as related by Mrs. Dean, well illustrates the simplicity of the author and her refusal to adopt the strained, sentimental tone of the average Victorian in dealing with such occasions:

But the hour came, at last, that ended Mr. Earnshaw's troubles on earth. He died quietly in his chair one October evening, seated by the fireside. A high wind blustered round the house, and roared in the /195/ chimney: it sounded wild and stormy, yet it was not cold, and we were all together—I, a little removed from the hearth, busy at my knitting, and Joseph reading his Bible near the table (for the servants generally sat in the house then, after their work was done). Miss Cathy had been sick, and that made her still; she leant against her father's knee, and Heathcliff was lying on the floor with his head in her lap. I remember the master, before he fell into a doze, stroking her bonny hair—it pleased him rarely to see her gentle—and saying—"Why canst thou not always be a good lass, Cathy?" And she turned her face up to his, and laughed, and answered, "Why cannot you always be a good man, father?" But as soon as she saw him vexed again, she kissed his hand, and said she would sing him to sleep. She began singing very low, till his fingers dropped from hers, and his head sank on his breast. Then I told her to hush, and not stir, for fear she should wake him. We all kept as mute as mice a full half-hour, and should have done so longer, only Joseph, having finished his chapter, got up and said that he must rouse the master for prayers and bed. He stepped forward, and called him by name, and touched his shoulders; but he would not move, so he took the candle and looked at him. I thought there was something wrong as he set down the light; and seizing the children each by an arm, whispered them to "frame upstairs, and make little din—they might pray alone that evening—he had summut to do."

"I shall bid father good-night first," said Catherine, putting her arms round his neck, before we could hinder her. The poor thing discovered her loss directly—she screamed out—"Oh, he's dead, Heathcliff! he's dead!" And they both set up a heart-breaking cry.

I joined my wail to theirs, loud and bitter; but Joseph asked what we could be thinking of to roar in that way over a saint in heaven. He told me to put on my cloak and run to Gimmerton for the doctor and the parson. I could not guess the use that either would be of, then. However, I went, through wind and rain, and brought one, the doctor, back with me; the other said he would come in the morning. Leaving Joseph to explain matters; I ran to the children's room: their door was ajar, I saw they had never laid down, though it was past midnight; but they were calmer, and did not need me to console them. The little souls were comforting each other with better thoughts than I could have hit on: no parson in the world ever pictured heaven so beautifully as they did, in their innocent talk: and, while I sobbed and listened, I could not help wishing we were all there safe together./196/

Questions for Discussion and Writing

1. Bruce McCullough says that "*Wuthering Heights* has been pretty generally accepted as a triumph of the imagination, . . ." (page 185) With reference to critical evaluations of the novel, explain McCullough's statement.

2. Evidently McCullough finds some of the interpretive and critical theories connected with *Wuthering Heights* farfetched. Why? Discuss farfetched interpretations of the novel.

3. Why does McCullough say that there is enough mystery in the character of Heathcliff to tax our capacity for strangeness?

4. According to McCullough, what is the atmosphere of *Wuthering Heights*? Examine the atmosphere of the novel yourself, agreeing or disagreeing with McCullough.

5. On page 189, McCullough says that "one who reads the novel with ordinary attentiveness to details will find not confusion but a carefully articulated plot." Of course, "ordinary attentiveness" is not too precise a phrase, but do you believe the plot is as readily available as McCullough implies? What do other critics say about this? Point to aspects of structure which support the conclusion you reach.

6. Do other critics agree with McCullough that *Wuthering Heights* is, on the surface, a story of mundane revenge? What is the role of revenge in the novel?

7. Comment on the list of improbabilities on page 190; can you add to the list? Do you disagree with any items on the list?

8. Lack of experience and the desire to avoid explanations are the reasons McCullough gives for Brontë's avoiding omniscient authorship. Do the critics suggest other reasons? Can you suggest some? Discuss advantages and limitations of the omniscient point of view with your instructor.

9. Explain in detail what McCullough's phrase "penumbra of distance" means in relation to the novel.

10. Explain the problem in handling time which Emily Brontë faced in writing *Wuthering Heights*. Do you agree with McCullough that Emily Brontë's problem illustrates how essential the element of time is to a novelist? Do you think Miss Brontë handled time well in this novel?

11. Why does McCullough say *Wuthering Heights* is a dramatic novel? What do other critics make of the dramatic quality of the novel?

12. Compare McCullough's comments on the conclusion of the novel with those of other critics.

Implacable, Belligerent People
of Emily Brontë's Novel,
Wuthering Heights

V. S. PRITCHETT

I have been reading *Wuthering Heights* again, after 20 years, a novel which is often regarded as poetical, mystical and fabulous. No people like Heathcliff and Catherine, it is said, ever existed. *Wuthering Heights* is indeed a poetical novel; but when I was reading it, it seemed to me the most realistic statement about the Yorkshire people of the isolated moorland and dales that I have ever read. I am a southerner; but I spent a good deal of my childhood in those Northern cottages and I recognise the implacable, belligerent people of Emily Brontë's novel at once. The trap used to pick you up at the branch line station and in a few miles you were on the moors, the wind standing against you like an enemy, the moorland drizzle making wraiths over the endless scene, and the birds whimpering in cries of farewell, like parting ghosts. Austere, empty, ominous were the earth and sky, and the air was fiercer and more violent than in the South. The occasional small stone houses stuck up like forts, the people themselves seemed, to a southerner, as stern as soldiers, and even the common sentences they spoke were so turned that, but for a quizzical glitter in the eyes of the speaker, one might have taken their words as challenge, insult or derision. I do not mean that these remote Yorkshire people were not kindly and hospitable folk; but one had not to live among them for long, before one found that their egotism was naked, their hatred unending. They seemed to revel in an hostility which they called frankness or bluntness; but which—how can I put it?—was

From *New Statesman and Nation*, XXXI (June 22, 1946).

an attempt to plant all they were, all they could be, all they represented as people, unyieldingly before you. They expected you to
do the same. They despised you if you did not. They had the com-
bative pride of clansmen and, on their lonely farms, clans they were
and had been for hundreds of years. I can think of episodes in my
own childhood among them which are as extraordinary as some
of the things in *Wuthering Heights;* and which, at first sight, would
strike the reader as examples of pitiable hatred and harshness. Often
they were. But really their fierceness in criticism, the pride, and
the violence of their sense of sin was the expression of a view of life
which put energy and the will of man above everything else. To
survive in these parts, one had to dominate and oppose.

There is no other novel in the English language like *Wuthering
Heights.* It is unique first of all for its lack of psychological dismay.
Never, in a novel, did so many people hate each other with such
zest, such Northern zest. There is a faint, homely pretence that
Nelly, the housekeeper and narrator, is a kindly, garrulous old
body; but look at her. It is not concealed that she is a spy, a go-
between, a secret opener of letters. She is a wonderful character, as
clear and round as any old nurse in Richardson or Scott; but no
conventional sentiment encases her. She is as hard as iron and takes
up her station automatically in the battle. Everyone hates, no one
disguises evil in this book; no one is "nice." How refreshing it is
to come across a Victorian novel which does not moralise, and yet
is very far from amoral. How strange, in Victorian fiction, to see
passion treated as the natural pattern of life. How refreshing to see
the open skirmishing of egotism, and to see life crackling like a
fire through human beings; a book which *feels* human beings as
they feel to themselves.

And that brings us to the more important difference between
Wuthering Heights and the other English novels of the nineteenth
century: Emily Brontë is not concerned with man and society, but
with his unity with nature. He, too, is a natural force, not the product of a class. Her view is altogether primitive. Often wild romanticism, the fiery murk of the Gothic revival, threaten to impair her
picture; but these literary echoes are momentary. Her spirit is
naturally pagan and she appears to owe nothing at all to the general traditions of our novel which has fed upon the sociability of
men and women and the preaching of reform. (D. H. Lawrence,
who used to be compared with her in the heyday of mysticism
twenty years back, is utterly cut off from her by his preaching, by the
nonconformist ache.) This isolation of Emily Brontë is startling,

and only Conrad and Henry James, in their very different ways, were parallel to her. Here perhaps lies a clue: they were foreigners who were crossed with us. By some Mendelian accident, Emily Brontë seems to have reverted to the Irish strain in the Brontë family and to have slipped back, in the isolation and the intense life of the Yorkshire moors, to an earlier civilisation. She is pre-Christian. The vision of the union of man and nature is natural to her. Or rather, as in many writers of split racial personality, one sees two countries, two civilisations, two social histories in conflict. In an admirable essay Lord David Cecil says she is really moved by the principle of storm and the principle of rest. The gentler second generation patiently resolves the conflict of its fathers.

But storm and rest, what are they if not the Irish and the English in Emily Brontë? The actual split in the form of the novel itself, so often criticised and occasionally defended, is the split between Ireland and Yorkshire. Yorkshire has moralised her theme, brought it to earth, checked the Irish tendency to produce giants and heroes. To the Yorkshire Protestant turned pagan, the passions are not Irish demi-gods moaning tendentious poetry upon the western burial grounds; but devils incarnate, superb devils, indifferent to the denunciation of the Northern chapel. They are energies. And the authentic voice of the moorland people's realism is heard in the housekeeper's reflections on the early days of the first Catherine's marriage:

I believe I may assert that they were really in possession of deep and growing happiness.
It ended. Well, we *must* be for ourselves in the long run; the mild and generous are only more justly selfish than the domineering; and it ended when circumstances caused each to feel that the one's interest was not the chief consideration in the other's thoughts.

Or in Heathcliff's words:

I have no pity! I have no pity! The more the worms writhe, the more I yearn to crush out their entrails! It is a moral teething; and I grind with greater energy, in proportion to the increase of pain.

There is the scheme of our nature before morality has chiselled us. I remember from my childhood, what pride the Northern preachers took in the pride of the devil.

If Emily Brontë saw her leading characters as elemental spiritual types, she did not leave them simple and boring. We can see exactly the superstructure of character. We know quite well why Catherine became Catherine. An unflinching Northern shrewdness marked the duality of her character and saw that the duality gave her wilfulness, her caprice and her power to wound. Heathcliff is an understandable monster. There is a faint suggestion of the Victorian social conscience in the creation of him. He is the slum orphan. He represents, in a sense perhaps remote, the passion of the outraged poor. So utterly crushed, he will crush utterly if he arises. He has the exorbitant will to power. He would—indeed he does—run a concentration camp. In a sense the struggle between Catherine and himself is a class struggle. This is a point worth keeping at the back of one's mind because it is too easy to regard Emily Brontë as a writer who was mystical in the void. But there is another aspect of him. Compare him with Charlotte Brontë's portrait of Rochester. Charlotte's desired villain is a feminine day-dream; Emily's Heathcliff is not a day-dream at all. His ancestor in literature is Lovelace, the superb male in full possession of the power of conspiracy and seduction. Heathcliff's appalling words to the housekeeper in front of his wife, Isabella, recalls the letters of Lovelace:

> But at last, I think she begins to know me: I don't perceive the silly smiles and grimaces that provoked me at first; and the senseless incapability of discerning that I was in earnest when I gave her my opinion of her infatuation and herself. It was a marvellous effort of perspicacity to discover that I did not love her. I believed, at one time, no lessons could teach her that! And yet it is poorly learnt; for this morning she announced, as a piece of appalling intelligence, that I had actually succeeded in making her hate me! . . . Are you sure you hate me? If I let you alone for half a day, won't you come sighing and wheedling to me again? I dare say she would rather I had seemed all tenderness before you: it wounds her vanity to have the truth wholly exposed.

But Heathcliff is not so admirable a villain as Lovelace; Heathcliff lacks the force of the male intellect. He is Lucifer without the mind and with a mere appetite for property; though, here again, it is interesting to note that he, like Lovelace, is moved to act by the desire for revenge upon the woman's family. Yet, if he is inferior to Lovelace, like Lovelace he is deified by his passion. The destinies of Lovelace and Clarissa are spiritually linked for ever by Clarissa's death; the destinies of Heathcliff and Catherine are linked for ever, not spiritually, but as it were by natural law; not by the immortality of the soul only but by the immortality of the earth:

> My love for Linton is like the foliage in the woods: time will change it, I'm well aware, as winter changes the trees. My love for Heathcliff resembles the eternal rocks beneath: a source of little visible delight, but necessary. Nelly, I *am* Heathcliff. He's always, always in my mind; not as a pleasure, any more than I am always a pleasure to myself, but as my own being.

The power of *Wuthering Heights* grows and is sustained by its plain language and because, at no point, does the writer forget the detail of house or moorland. The storm is intolerable because we have to stand resisting it with our feet clinging to the earth; Emily Brontë would be lost if that storm became rhetorical. But I am one of those who are not carried on by the second part of the story. I can see its moral necessity, but I do not *feel* its logic. Grotesque elements bob up at the break between the two tales. To hear afterwards that Catherine was in advanced pregnancy during the wonderful last scene with Heathcliff, which seems to me the highest moment in the English literature of passionate love, is a physical offence. And then in the beating-up scene later, when Heathcliff breaks in and starts his Dachau act, there are descriptive excesses. One grins back at his "cannibal face" with its "sharp teeth" at the window; and when, on top of all this, Hareton comes in and announces he has been hanging puppies, one lets out the laugh one had reserved for the murder of the children in *Jude the Obscure*. This is just Gothic stuff. The second Catherine has her captivation, but you feel she is a poor creature to fall for Hareton whose long history as a problem-child will take a lot of living down. We have entered the field of psychological realism and social allegory and we are not sure that we have the proper guide. I do not mean that this part of the book is less well written. The characters, the incident, the scene are just as well done as in the earlier part, which is to say that they are beautifully done; and there is always the irresistible pleasure of seeing the wheel turn full circle. But the high power has gone, the storm has spent its force, Heathcliff has become a set character; the devil—and this is surely a decline—has become vicious instead of diabolical. Only, in the last pages, when he fancies he sees the first Catherine again and when, starving himself to death, he begins to relive that ineluctable love, does the power return. And those last pages reconcile us to the moral necessity of the second part of a novel which is not, as some have said, carelessly constructed, but unevenly felt. /453/

Questions for Discussion and Writing

1. Trace the word "fabulous" through the criticism of *Wuthering Heights*. Pritchett says that the novel is often regarded as fabulous. What does he mean by the word?

2. Is Pritchett making a case for the novel as a realistic novel? Have other critics made this assertion? Why or why not?

3. What do you understand Pritchett to mean by his phrase, "the lack of psychological dismay"?

4. Comment on Pritchett's evaluation of Nelly Dean.

5. To what extent does motivation in *Wuthering Heights* concern Pritchett in this article? Are his comments in accord with other critical appraisal of this novel?

6. Trace the idea that Emily Brontë is "pagan" and "pre-Christian" in other criticism and in the novel itself.

7. In his comment on David Cecil's study of *Wuthering Heights,* Pritchett says, "the gentler second generation patiently resolves the conflict of its fathers." How do you react to the words "gentler" and "patiently" here? Can you suggest any way in which they are or are not applicable? Does the second generation resolve the conflict of the first? If so, in what sense?

8. What is the "duality" of Catherine's character?

9. Study the idea that Heathcliff represents, in any sense, Emily Brontë's "Victorian social conscience," "the passion of the outraged poor."

10. What does Pritchett mean by the "plain language" of *Wuthering Heights?*

11. Do you think that Heathcliff is a diabolical person at any time during the novel? Do critics think this? Why?

12. Comment on Pritchett's criticism of the second half of the novel, using other critics and the novel itself to support your paper. Note especially such statements as the following: some description is "just Gothic stuff"; Catherine is a "poor creature for falling in love with Hareton, a problem child"; in the second half the "storm has spent its force."

The Brontës, or,
Myth Domesticated

RICHARD CHASE

Herbert Read cannot be right to say that Emily Brontë "is forever perplexed by the problem of evil." She does not allow herself to be perplexed; if she did she would no longer be "innocent" and she would no longer be a tragic writer, if we /500/ are to stick to Keats' stringent prescription. She has little of the grandly humane moral sense of Sophocles; she is Aeschylean. Heathcliff is a creature whose beginning and end remain, in the purely mundane moral sense, meaningless. He does not, like Oedipus, finally recognize himself as a man whose hidden deeds have bound him up with certain moral consequences. There is no such recognition of the hero's moral self anywhere in *Wuthering Heights*.

But though Emily Brontë cannot be said to be "perplexed" by evil, there is a central moral assertion in *Wuthering Heights*. This we come upon in the scene where both Heathcliff and Cathy realize the appalling consequences of Cathy's failure to fulfill her mission; which was, clearly, to marry Heathcliff. The terrible recriminations which pass between the two lovers are the anguished utterances of human beings who are finally, because of the moral failure of Cathy, being dragged down into the flux of the dehumanized universe. Cathy dissolves into pure matter and force almost before our eyes (as Heathcliff is to do later) and while she yet retains enough of sensibility to make the experience articulate. Yet though this is the single moral assertion, the whole action of the book depends upon it.

As in *Jane Eyre*, the culture heroine of *Wuthering Heights* fails. Heathcliff relentlessly charges her with her failure: "You teach me now how cruel you've been—cruel and false. *Why* did you despise

From *Kenyon Review*, IX (Autumn, 1947), 487-506.

me? *Why* did you betray your own heart, Cathy? I have not one word
of comfort. You deserve this. You have killed yourself. Yes, you
may kiss me, and cry; and wring out my kisses and tears; they'll
blight you—they'll damn you. You loved me—then what *right* had
you to leave me? What right—answer me—for the poor fancy you
felt for Linton? Because misery and degradation, and death, and
nothing that God or Satan could inflict would have parted us, *you*,
of your own free will did it." Like Jane Eyre, Cathy has refused the
act which would have set Satan at war with God in the soul of
Heathcliff. The /501/ penalty for not throwing herself into the
agony of the spiritual struggle and birth is certainly unequivocal:
she must die. This spiritual struggle Emily Brontë pictures in a
poem:

> So stood I, in Heaven's glorious sun
> And in the glare of Hell
> My spirit drank a mingled tone
> Of seraph's song and demon's moan—
> What my soul bore my soul alone
> Within itself may tell.

If, then, we are to call *Wuthering Heights* a tragedy, we must leave
room in our definition of the word for the following circumstances: a heroine comes to grasp the significance of her spiritual
mission too late; the hero degenerates into "absurdity" and dies,
since the God-Devil figure is absurd without the human protagonist
on whom he depends.

   Emily Brontë's "innocence" is partly due to her almost absolute
devotion to death. Surely no first-rate writer has ever been more of
the Other World. She was

> Weaned from life and torn away
> In the morning of [her] day.

She is also, as one would expect, devoted to her own childhood
(she seems to have taken some of her images from Wordsworth;
notice her habit of referring to infancy as a "glory," a "lost vision,"
a "light," and so forth). Cathy dies as she hopes, into a wonderful
world of light; she dies "like a child reviving." The poem beginning
"The soft unclouded blue of air" unites the theme of childhood
with the theme of the Lover-Lord. The poem concerns the thoughts
of an unnamed "I" on a day "as bright as Eden's used to be":

> Laid on the grass I lapsed away,
> Sank back again to childhood's day;
> All harsh thoughts perished, memory mild
> Subdued both grief and passion wild.

But, she asks, does the sunshine that bathes the "stern and swarthy brow" of "that iron man" elicit in his memory a sweet /502/ dream of childhood, or is

> Remembrance of his early home
> So lost that not a gleam may come?

He sits in silence.

> That stormy breast
> At length, I said, has deigned to rest;
> At length above that spirit flows
> The waveless ocean of repose . . .
> Perhaps this is the destined hour
> When hell shall lose its fatal power
> And heaven itself shall bend above
> To hail the soul redeemed by love.

But all in vain. One glance at the "iron man" reveals

> how little care
> He felt for all the beauty there

and how soon her own breast can grow as cold

> As winter wind or polar snow.

Her futile desire has been to drag the hero back into infancy— perhaps into that "Unique Society" of childish heroes and heroines who perform romantic deeds among the islands of the Pacific in Emily Brontë's juvenile writings. She has wanted to transform the universal energy of the "iron man" into the mild light of the Other World, or "home." She has thought that by detachment from this world she could deprive Hell of "its fatal power" and make Heaven "hail the soul." But detachment cannot solve the conflict between the Devil and God; that is work which must be done in This World. Cathy, too, tries to take Heathcliff into "that glorious world" which she sees "dimly through tears" and yearns for "through the walls of an aching heart." But this is only an imaginary Heathcliff, "*my* Heathcliff," she says, not the relentless inquisitor who stands before her. "*My* Heathcliff" is a child returning to what Wordsworth called the "imperial palace" and what Emily Brontë described thus: /503/

> I saw her stand in the gallery long,
> Watching the little children there,
> As they were playing the pillars among
> And bounding down the marble stair.

Virginia Woolf writes that Emily Brontë "looked out upon a world cleft into gigantic disorder and felt within her the power to unite it into a book." *Wuthering Heights* displays the schisms between the forces of the universe; we have a sense of great motions taking place without immediately recognizable relation. Things do not fit together and we are left to contemplate the estrangement of parts. The book is meaningful because it portrays human beings caught in the schisms—caught between the Other World and This World, between Childhood and Adulthood, between Savagery and Civilization, between the Devil and God, between Matter and Spirit, between Stasis and Motion.

4. WE ARE ASKED to consider three pairs of lovers in *Wuthering Heights:* Heathcliff and the elder Cathy, Linton Heathcliff and the younger Cathy, Hareton Earnshaw and the younger Cathy. Nothing could be more Victorian than the child-lovers, Linton and the younger Cathy, both aged seventeen, under the baleful influence of Heathcliff. They are sweet, innocent children; they are persecuted and forced into a morbid sex relationship. They are both spoiled—Linton is an invalid who sucks sugar candy and asks Cathy not to kiss him, because it takes his breath away; he is pettish, willful, and mortally afraid of his father. Cathy has some of the vivacity of her mother; she is pretty; but she too is pettish and spoiled. "I should never love anyone better than papa," she says.

In my family there is an illustrated Victorian autograph album, inherited from elder generations. It contains—along with many elaborately scrolled signatures, pictures of doves, and a recipe for smelling salts—an engraving of a smiling and cherubic /504/ girl sucking a stick of candy. At first glance she seems perfectly innocent; yet there is an almost wicked knowingness in her expression. Behind her is a dark, bestial face carved heavily in wood; the leg of the table on which she leans is carved in the shape of a menacing griffon or gargoyle. It is exactly the relation of Linton and Cathy to Heathcliff in those appalling love scenes on the moors. The theme of childhood, voiced by the elder Cathy on her deathbed, is thus continued in the main action of the second half of the book. We begin to see that, in one way or another, childhood is in fact the central theme of Emily Brontë's writing.

There is a childishness too about the love relationship of Hareton and the younger Cathy. They marry when Hareton is twenty-five and Cathy is nineteen, but Hareton is still a primitive waif, having been deliberately kept untaught by Heathcliff. Cathy is still a spoiled child. Their marriage promises to be a happy one, however. Hareton, though in many ways the image of Heathcliff, has little of Heathcliff's force. He can be domesticated. Cathy promises to mature into a responsible woman. As in the marriage of Jane and Rochester, the woman has a strong advantage over her lover; for Cathy is educated and intelligent and she will teach Hareton, who desperately desires to be educated. In *Jane Eyre* the principal lovers finally come together, though in a compromised relationship. *Wuthering Heights* is a more uncompromising book. Heathcliff and the elder Cathy come together only at several removes: Hareton and the younger Cathy are but pale replicas of their elders.

5. I HAVE SAID that the Brontës were essentially Victorian. The happy marriages at the end of *Jane Eyre* and *Wuthering Heights* represent the ostensible triumph of the secular, moderate-liberal, sentimental point of view over the mythical, tragic point of view. The moral texture of these novels is woven whole /505/ cloth out of the social customs of the day. To the marriage of free and godlike souls, to humane utopias of sexual society, the Brontës plainly preferred domesticity—and this despite the fact that no one knew better the readiness with which the Victorian family reverted to the primitive horde. The Brontës' tremendous displacement of the domestic values toward the tragic and mythical, though it falls short of ultimate achievement, gives their work a margin of superiority over that of other Victorian novelists. The Brontës were more fully committed to art than most of their contemporaries. They "rebelled" only in the sense that they translated the Victorian social situation into mythical forms. And this reminds us that the fault of much of our "new criticism" of the best nineteenth-century literature is to mistake art for rebellion. /506/

Questions for Discussion and Writing

1. James Hafley agrees with Herbert Read concerning Emily Brontë's attitude toward evil, but Richard Chase disagrees. Take sides.

2. Do you agree that there is "no such recognition of the hero's moral self anywhere in *Wuthering Heights*"? (page 501)

3. In his second paragraph Chase speaks of "central moral assertion," "being dragged into the flux of the dehumanized universe," and says that "Cathy dissolves into pure matter and force almost before our eyes." What is he talking about? Make a comment on this sort of criticism.

4. Is Cathy the "culture heroine" of *Wuthering Heights?* What is a culture heroine?

5. How does Chase define the word *tragedy* as he applies it to *Wuthering Heights?* Do critics think the novel is a tragedy?

6. Chase calls Heathcliff the hero; in what sense is he? In what sense is he not? Review the other critics, and decide what the concensus is.

7. Do critics generally agree that Emily Brontë's preoccupation with death governs the action and theme of *Wuthering Heights?*

8. In what sense is there a "devotion to death" (page 502) in *Wuthering Heights?*

9. What would David Cecil say to Chase's "conflict between the Devil and God"? (page 503)

10. Do you agree that the novel is meaningful because "it portrays human beings caught in the schisms"? (page 504) Is this the theme of the novel?

11. "Nothing could be more Victorian than the child-lovers, Linton and the younger Cathy. . . ." (page 504) Comment, using Chase's statements developing the above.

12. Justify Chase's statement that "Cathy promises to mature into a responsible woman." (page 505)

13. "Hareton and the younger Catherine are but pale replicas of their elders." (page 505) Does Chase here speak for the majority of critics? Who speaks for a different conclusion concerning the couple?

14. Do modern critics "mistake art for rebellion" in *Wuthering Heights?*

Tempest in the Soul: The Theme and Structure of *Wuthering Heights*

MELVIN R. WATSON

I

In the century since its publication, *Wuthering Heights,* like the plays of Shakespeare with which it has often been compared, has been the subject of many diverse criticisms and interpretations. Almost no one has been audacious enough to deny its power and its unique place in the development of English fiction, but few have made an unprejudiced attempt to understand what Emily Brontë strove for in her one full-length study of human nature—its impulses and its desires, its loves and its hates, its disasters and its triumphs, its defeats and its victories. Because of its strange elemental fierceness and barbarity, its stormy setting, divorced from the world as we know it, its seemingly crude, inartistic structure, and its superhuman emotions, *Wuthering Heights* is not an easy book to discuss. Yet if it is the masterpiece that it is admitted to be, it must present a valid interpretation of life in people who are believable, however seldom their prototypes may appear in the world as we know it; it must concern itself with a theme which we can all understand; and it must show a power of architectonics, however unconventional or imperfect from the inexperience of the architect that power might be.

Certainly *Wuthering Heights* is different, primarily, perhaps because its author was an individualist who spurned the easy road of

/87/ convention. Not for her was the typical Victorian novel with its study of normal men and women in the ordinary pursuits of life. Considered as a novel of that kind, it is a miserable failure, badly organized and badly told, with two heroes—Edgar Linton and Hareton Earnshaw—neither of whom is strong or prominent enough to carry the story, and with a villain who overrides the action and is at last triumphantly united with the heroine who has died midway through the book. The plan then becomes incontrovertibly confusing, the point of view too blatantly awkward, the presence of two generations unnecessary, and the conclusion a travesty of poetic justice.

Nor are other possibilities any more feasible as a complete explanation of what Emily Brontë was doing. Although revenge plays a large part in the story, it cannot be considered merely a revenge tragedy analogous to the dramas of Kyd, Chapman, or Marston. The dissolution of the revenge motif in the last chapters and the supreme happiness of Heathcliff as he prepares for his reunion with Catherine rule out such an explanation. To consider this merely the account of Heathcliff's and Catherine's love is equally fantastic. Love there is of a superhuman strength, and thwarted love it is which motivates much—but not all—of Heathcliff's hatred; but if this is a love story and nothing more, the importance of Hindley, Hareton, Cathy, and Linton is misplaced, the entire last half is ill-proportioned, and the ending is off key. If, on the other hand, we assume that *Wuthering Heights* is nothing more than a Gothic romance, we automatically exclude it as a serious study of any human problem.

One last possibility must be considered. In his detailed and provocative essay on Emily Brontë, Lord David Cecil contends that what we have is an allegory setting forth her conception of the universe, a universe built up from two opposing forces—storm and calm,—and that the theme is the re-establishment of the cosmic order which has been disturbed by faulty external actions, by an improper mixture of the two forces in the marriages of Catherine /88/ and Edgar, and of Isabella and Heathcliff, which produce children of love and hate respectively, and by the introduction of an extraneous element in the person of Heathcliff. Two principal weaknesses of this interpretation suggest themselves. *Wuthering Heights* is not, I believe, a metaphysical dissertation in which the Heights and Thrushcross Grange are a microcosm and their inhabitants only allegorical puppets whose wooden actions serve to envision a Brontëan universe. Doubtless, Emily Brontë had her own unconventional views of the world, which inevitably became a part of the fabric of *Wuthering Heights,* but surely she was attempting something more concrete, more closely related to human experience than this. But, more important, such an analysis relegates Heathcliff to a position of less prominence than he occupies. Heathcliff *is* the story. He not only acts and suffers, but causes others to act and suffer; his strength permeates the story; his power for good and for evil shocks and surprises the reader; his deeds and his reactions from the ghastly beginning to the pastoral close make a coherent whole out of what might have been a chaotic heap.

Wuthering Heights, then, is a psychological study of an elemental man whose soul is torn between love and hate. He is a creature about whose past nothing is known. A dark, dirty beggar, he was picked up on the Liverpool streets by Mr. Earnshaw and brought to the secluded part of the world known as the moors, where he has ample space to work out his destiny. Only the elemental passions of love and hate receive any development in the elemental environment by which he was molded. His strength of will and steadfastness of purpose he brought with him to the moors, but there they were prevented by external events from following their natural course. There he was hardened by his physical surroundings, toughened and embittered by the harsh treatment of Hindley, disillusioned by what he considered the treachery of Catherine, on whom he had poured love out of his boundless store. Then he resolves to even scores by crushing everyone who has stood in his way, everyone who has helped to thwart his happiness, the specter /89/ of which haunts him for seventeen long years during which he works out the venom which has accumulated in his soul. As soon as part of the venom is removed and the day of happiness begins to dawn, he no longer has the will to keep up his torturing.

This is a daring theme, subject to much misinterpretation, for during most of the action Heathcliff performs like a villain or like a hero who has consciously chosen evil for his companion. When completely understood, however, he is neither an Iago for whom evil is a divinity nor a Macbeth who consciously chooses evil because of his overpowering ambition, but rather a Hamlet without Hamlet's fatal irresolution. Like Hamlet, he was precipitated into a world in which he saw cruelty and unfaithfulness operating. His dilemma was not Hamlet's, for he has no father to avenge or mother to protect, but in a way he has evil thrust upon him if he is to survive among harsh surroundings. And Heathcliff was not one to hesitate when faced with an alternative, however tragic the consequences might be.

Though Heathcliff is not perhaps more sinned against than sinning, his actions are produced by the distortion of his natural personality. This distortion had already begun when Mr. Earnshaw brought him into Wuthering Heights, a "dirty, ragged, black-haired child." Already he was inured to hardship and blows; already he uncomplainingly accepted suffering, as when he had the measles, and ill treatment from Hindley if he got what he wanted. From the very first he showed great courage, steadfastness, and love. But with Mr. Earnshaw's death Hindley has the power to degrade Heathcliff to the status of a servant. A weak, vindictive character, as cruel as Heathcliff without Heathcliff's strength, Hindley prepares for his own destruction by his inhumanity to Heathcliff and the other inhabitants of the Heights. Though Heathcliff was forced down to an animal level, he took a silent delight in watching his persecutor sinking also into a life of debauchery. Nor was he alone, for he had Cathy, on whom he poured his devotion and love. They were inseparable. On the moors by day or in the chimney corner by /90/ night, they chatted and dreamed whenever Heathcliff was not busy with the chores. But the visit to Thrushcross Grange introduced Cathy to another world to which she opened her arms, and that world contained Edgar Linton. Edgar held a superficial attraction for Cathy which Heathcliff could never understand and which he feared, for, having possessed Cathy for some years, he feared losing even part of her attention. The final blow, a blow which turns Heathcliff from sullen acquiescence to tragic determination, comes when Cathy confesses to Ellen her infatuation with Edgar and her resolve to marry him so that she and Heathcliff can escape from the repressive world of Wuthering Heights. Not once did she think of giving up Heathcliff, but Heathcliff inadvertently overhears only the first part of the conversation. Cathy has deserted him for a mess of pottage, for fine clothes and refined manners; she is ashamed of his rough exterior, of his lack of polish; she would be degraded to marry him as he is. Heathcliff doesn't stay to hear Cathy confess her oneness with him:

If all else perished, and *he* remained, *I* should still continue to be; and if all else remained, and he were annihilated, the universe would turn to a mighty stranger: I should not seem a part of it. My love for Linton is like the foliage in the woods: time will change it, I'm well aware, as winter changes the trees. My love for Heathcliff resembles the eternal rocks beneath: a source of little visible delight, but necessary. Nelly, I *am* Heathcliff.

He's always, always in my mind: not as a pleasure, any more than I am always a pleasure to myself, but as my own being.

His mind is made up. If love alone is insufficient to hold Cathy, he will secure the necessary money and polish; if his only happiness is to be snatched from him, he will turn to hate; and now not only Hindley will be the object of his wrath, but Edgar also. As long as he had Cathy, his worldly condition, his suffering, was as nothing; without her, all is chaff to be trampled underfoot.

For three years, during which he vanishes from sight, he prepares himself, the poison in his system increasing all the time until love is submerged in a sea of hate which he must drain off before love can reassert itself. Union with Cathy is his one desire. Since physical /91/ union is made impossible by her death—not that it was ever important,—the union must be spiritual, but the world and the people of the world must be subjugated before such happiness can be achieved. The course is set, the wind is strong, the bark is sturdy, the journey long. For seventeen years Heathcliff wreaks his vengeance on Hindley, Edgar, and Isabella and on their children Hareton, young Cathy, and Linton. The account of the trip is not pretty. Even in the love scenes before the elder Cathy's death there is a savage passion which strikes terror to the heart of the beholder, unlike any other scenes in the course of English fiction; and before the masochistic treatment of Isabella, Hareton, young Cathy, and Linton we cringe. Here is a man haunted by a ghost of happiness for which he must exorcise his soul, a soul filled with accumulated hatred. That he ceases his reign of terror before Hareton and young Cathy have been completely broken is due not to any loss of spiritual strength but to the realization that the end of the voyage is near, that the tempest is subsiding, and that reunion with Cathy is about to be consummated. In Heathcliff one looks in vain for Christian morals or virtues; his is a primitive, pagan soul; yet love conquers even a Heathcliff in the end—after his soul has been purged of the hate in and with which he has lived for decades. The evil that he does springs not from a love of evil itself, but from the thwarting of the natural processes of love.

In the development of this theme everyone, even Catherine, is subordinated to Heathcliff, as important as many of them are in molding Heathcliff's character, in serving as contrasts to him, or in receiving the force of his hatred. Mr. Earnshaw introduces him to the Heights but exits too early to be more than a puppet, except as he favors Heathcliff over Hindley and thus encourages the waif's willful ways and prepares for the tragedy that is to follow. Hindley re-

verses his father's actions. He has inherited all the cruelty of the
moors without any of their saving strength; he vents his accumulated wrath on Heathcliff but treads himself the primrose path of
dalliance. His habits of drinking and gambling make him a clay
/92/ pigeon when Heathcliff has prepared himself for revenge.
He is a despicable character whose downfall calls forth no sympathizing tear. Edgar Linton, on the other hand, contrasts with Heathcliff in another way. In another novel he might have been a conventional Victorian hero; he is presentable and well-mannered, sincere
but somewhat smug, honest but thoroughly conventional, good-
looking but pallid, devoted to Catherine but incapable of understanding or possessing her. His moral sense the Victorian reader
could comprehend and sympathize with. In *Wuthering Heights,*
however, he is an anomaly, owning Catherine without possessing
her, resenting Heathcliff but lacking the power to thwart him.
Though he lives under the shadow of the volcano, he suffers
only as he sees those whom he loves—Isabella, Cathy, and Linton—
submerged by the lava of hate. And Edgar is as helpless as the peas-
ants who lived near Vesuvius. Isabella, as weak as Catherine is
strong, as conventional as Catherine is unconventional, as super-
ficially attracted to Heathcliff as Catherine was to Edgar, allows
Heathcliff to make his first inroads on Thrushcross Grange. An
emotional, giddy girl who had no knowledge of men or their motives, she felt only the physical attraction of a dark, handsome, well-
dressed newcomer to her small circle of acquaintances. Too late she
discovered that she was to be only a tool, used briefly and then cast
aside to be worn away by rust. Though completely convincing in
her role, she is significant only as the device which enables Heathcliff to gain control of Thrushcross Grange.

Catherine alone stands as a near equal to Heathcliff. Beautiful,
selfish, willful, she strides through the first part of *Wuthering
Heights* like the queen that she is. She understands Heathcliff because she is like him. She could control him, but she forfeits that
power by her marriage to Edgar. One of the greater ironies of the
book is this: that by her action intended primarily to help Heathcliff she partly alienates herself from him and blows to flame the fire
of hatred which produces an eruption lasting seventeen years. She
failed to think her decisions through. When she makes her fatal
/93/ confession to Ellen, not once does she consider the effect of
her choice on Heathcliff. She assumes that she can continue to
rule both Edgar and Heathcliff as she has done in the past, but she
reckons without his pride. Catherine, however, was no hypocrite;

she loved both Edgar and Heathcliff—in entirely different ways; she was faithful to her marriage vows, but they could not prevent her feeling a spiritual kinship with Heathcliff. The love scene in chapter xv, overpowering as it is, contains nothing gross, nothing merely physical. It is symbolic of a union which the two cannot resist, for it expresses a likeness of the two souls. But Catherine had deserted him and brings upon herself the curses of heaven and hell that she shall wander as a ghost until he has subjugated the world and attained spiritual union with her. During the last half of the book, Catherine is present only as a spirit, an influence which continually goads Heathcliff like the Furies of old. In the final analysis it is her *spirit,* not Catherine herself, that is important for the novel as a whole.

The presence of the second generation caused many early commentators to stumble, for they failed to recognize that Hareton, young Cathy, and Linton are essential to the theme. Time is necessary for Heathcliff to eradicate the hate from his soul in order that love can reassert itself; furthermore, in order to gain the wealth and power which, he feels, separated him from Catherine, he must possess not only Wuthering Heights but Thrushcross Grange as well. This he can accomplish only through the marriage of Cathy and Linton. His relation to Hareton is peculiar. Though he once ironically saved him from death when Hindley in a drunken fit let him fall over the banisters, he takes a savage delight in degrading him as he was once degraded by Hindley. Hareton is saved by the absence of hatred in his heart, and the fondness between him and young Cathy blossoms in time of prevent his becoming just an animal. The love which develops out of and in spite of the hate which surrounds them—but develops as that hate is subsiding—provides the calm and symbolic ending of the book. /94/

II

The structure of *Wuthering Heights* is as different and unconventional as the theme. How could it be otherwise? New wine should not be poured into old bottles. Though there are superficial awkwardnesses and old-fashioned conventions in the point of view, this seems to be the inevitable way of telling such a story. The structure provides yet another analogy with Elizabethan drama, for it is consciously organized like a five-act tragedy, with breaks always indicated at the appropriate points. The method of telling the story, "in terms of autobiography thrice involved," as William Dean Howells said, is necessary for this structure. Mr. Lockwood, the relative nonentity who records the story as told to him by Ellen Dean, lives in the community only a few months before Heathcliff dies; yet representing, as he does, normal humanity, and experiencing enough of the confusion of Wuthering Heights to make him believe anything about these creatures, and being the audience before whom their past is unfolded, a past which is broken into segments by Ellen's or Mr. Lockwood's interruptions, he lends credibility to the events and serves as a curtain marking off the divisions of the story.

The Prologue (chapters i-iii), like that of a Greek tragedy, sets the tone and character of the book. Here, through a perfectly detached spectator, an ordinary person from the outside world, we are catapulted into the story at a point just before the denouement. Lockwood observes the primitive quality of the life at Wuthering Heights, the brutality and the coldness evident on every hand, both inside and out; he witnesses the inhumanity and the hatred of Heathcliff; he experiences the ghastly night in Catherine's old bedchamber, with Cathy's spirit crying for entrance—or was it a dream? He is as confused, as shocked, and as mystified as any reader could be; naturally he is curious to discover more about these strange inhabitants of this peculiar establishment. This beginning is not accidental; it is the triumph of an artistic spirit that /95/ realized the difficulties inherent in her material. If the strange behavior of her characters was to be made believable, she must storm the citadel with the first assault; she must make Lockwood's reactions coincide with the reader's and cause both to suspend their disbelief until they have discovered the background for the present situation. Ellen Dean, fortunately, is able to satisfy all his curiosity.

Though this minor-character point of view seems the only possible one for this story, certain disadvantages loom before us. Ellen is at moments plot-ridden. The climactic last scene between Cathy and Heathcliff is arranged by Ellen, and she is the direct cause of young Cathy's and Linton's getting so friendly; yet we feel that here Ellen is merely the agent of fate; these things would have happened whether or not Ellen had intervened. Certain time-honored but slightly unnatural conventions, also, are used. Ellen gets part of the story in a letter from Isabella—hardly a person to correspond with a servant; she secures needed information about the situation at Wuthering Heights by gossiping with Zillah, the new servant there; but, more significant, she acquires mental reactions and attitudes from the confessions to her, such as Catherine's in chapter ix, Heathcliff's in chapter xxi, and Edgar's in chapter xxv. Except for the first, these are really soliloquies in the Elizabethan sense and should be accepted as such. Finally, to have Ellen Dean as narrator, we must accept the fact that a servant can be in many places where she would not ordinarily be and hear many things that she would not ordinarily hear: for example, the last scene between Cathy and Heathcliff in chapter xv, or Heathcliff's description of what he did on Catherine's burial day and of his looking at her corpse after many years, in chapter xxix. But the advantages gained by having the story told by an eyewitness are weighty enough to balance all these disadvantages. Dramatic intensity is secured by seeing the story unfold with all the freshness and vigor with which Ellen saw it. Ellen relates the story with breaks to set off the divisions as it actually happened. She has no favorites; though she may at moments betray partialities, she makes no consistent attempt to white- /96/ wash any of the characters or events. And she lends further credibility to the story by recounting only what she has seen or heard.

Act I, including chapters iv-vii, introduces the first generation, provides the initial complications in Hindley's treatment of Heathcliff, and the effect on Cathy of her visit to the Grange, and ends with Heathcliff's defiance of Hindley: "I'm trying to settle how I shall pay Hindley back. I don't care how long I wait, if I can only do it at last. I hope he will not die before I do!" Mrs. Dean interrupts herself to remind Lockwood that she should stop, but is persuaded to continue her tale.

The next section, containing only two chapters, includes the birth of the first member of the second generation, Hareton, develops Cathy's relation with Edgar Linton, and climbs to a minor climax when Heathcliff inadvertently hears Cathy declare that she has accepted Edgar's proposal of marriage. The last few pages of the act hurry over three years, at the end of which Cathy and Edgar are married. Here Ellen Dean stops because of the lateness of the hour.

After Lockwood has recovered from a four weeks' illness brought on by his first visit to Wuthering Heights, he demands more of "the history of Mr. Heathcliff." Ellen responds with Act III, leading up in its five chapters to the main climax of the novel. From the first meeting of Cathy and Heathcliff after her marriage to the arrangement for their last scene a few hours before her death, this act runs the gamut of emotional intensity. Heathcliff finishes the ruin of Hindley by catering to his taste for drink and gambling and secures mortgages on Wuthering Heights; he elopes with Isabella after she has thrown herself at his feet; he physically chastises Edgar for

daring to interfere in his talks with Catherine; he alternates between passionate love and fierce hatred in his attitude toward Catherine and helps produce in her a fever from which she dies. Instead
of ending this act with the climactic scene between Cathy and
Heathcliff from which she never recovers, Emily Brontë only prepares for it, but presents the climax itself at the beginning of the
/97/ next act. Again her technique seems right, for not only does
this break give the reader a chance to catch his breath, but it makes
of Act IV a more symmetrical structure.

The interruption at the end of chapter xiv is the last one until
Mrs. Dean has brought the story up to date at the close of chapter
xxx. In the week intervening between the close of chapter xiv
and the beginning of chapter xv, Mrs. Dean has told Mr. Lockwood the rest of the story, which he has determined to continue in
her own words. Since the structural breaks in Act IV and the beginning of Act V are not so important as the others, there is no necessity for inventing interruptions. Casual comments are enough to
mark the breaks now, of which there are three, one at the beginning
of chapter xviii ("continued Mrs. Dean") to indicate the last part
of Act IV, and another in the opening line of chapter xxv
("said Mrs. Dean") to indicate the start of Act V. The other break,
slightly more prominent than these, sets off the climactic scene, the
birth of young Cathy, and the death of Catherine from the rest of
this section and occurs in the middle of chapter xvi. These events,
though a bridge between the rising and the falling actions, were to
be clearly marked off from the less dramatic events of this act: the
birth of Linton after Isabella's escape from Wuthering Heights, the
mention of her death some years later, the death of Hindley—these
occupy the middle of the act,—and the development of the second
generation, which fills up the last "scene" of the act.

By the close of the first "scene" of Act V, Nelly Dean has brought
Lockwood up to date. The machinations of Heathcliff have
accomplished the marriage of young Cathy and Linton, and with
the death of Edgar, and then of Linton, Heathcliff has come into
possession of Thrushcross Grange. Lockwood's visit to Wuthering
Heights after his recovery, described in chapter xxxi and forming
the second part of this last act, prepares the reader for the final resolution of the drama. Several crucial months have elapsed since the
memorable night spent in Catherine's former bedchamber, months
during which the inhabitants of the Heights have changed. /98/
Heathcliff now wonders about the wisdom of his treatment of
Hareton, for when he looks for Hindley in his face, he sees only

Catherine. Hareton is making gigantic efforts to pull himself up by his bootstraps by learning to read in order to impress Cathy. Cathy, though still bitter and morose from her harsh treatment, and changed less than the other two, totters on the verge of a readjustment. Wisely, this scene has been inserted to make the reformation in the last chapters easier to accept.

When Lockwood saw Wuthering Heights for the first time, he was impressed in this manner:

Pure, bracing ventilation they must have up there at all times, indeed; one may guess the power of the north wind blowing over the edge, by the excessive slant of a few stunted firs at the end of the house; and by a range of gaunt thorns all stretching their limbs one way, as if craving alms of the sun. Happily, the architect had foresight to build it strong: the narrow windows are deeply set in the wall, and the corners defended with large jutting stones.

The locked gate, the padlocked door, and the fierce dogs added to his sense of awe. On his last visit, after a nine months' absence from the moors, he was struck by a different atmosphere:

Before I arrived in sight of it, all that remained of day was a beamless amber light along the west: but I could see every pebble on the path, and every blade of grass, by that splendid moon. I had neither to climb the gate nor to knock—it yielded to my hand. That is an improvement, I thought. And I noticed another, by the aid of my nostrils; a fragrance of stocks and wallflowers wafted on the air from amongst the homely fruit-trees.

The explanation for the difference both in external and internal atmosphere is supplied by Nelly Dean as she once again brings Lockwood up to date, detailing the increasing friendship and then love between Cathy and Hareton and the dissolution and final death of Heathcliff as the possibility of permanent reunion with his Cathy makes his face glow with a ghastly happiness. To escape the lovers, Lockwood vanishes through the kitchen door; and as he later meditates on the quietness of the kirk where Edgar, Cathy, and Heathcliff lie buried side by side, the story whispers itself out. /99/

As careful as she was in constructing the story, so meticulous was Emily Brontë in maintaining unity of place and tone. The reader never leaves the moors, once he has arrived there with Mr. Lockwood. He travels between Wuthering Heights and Thrushcross Grange; he sees the graves on the hillside and catches an occasional glimpse of Peniston Crag; he knows where the road to Gimmerton branches off from the road with which he is well acquainted, but

never does he follow that road to the outer world. When Mr. Earnshaw travels to Liverpool, when Heathcliff disappears, when Isabella escapes, when Edgar goes to get Isabella's son, the reader remains on the moors, awaiting their return or news of their death.
Wuthering Heights, Thrushcross Grange, and the rippling moors
between—these are the physical bounds of the story. And so with the
tone. No comic scenes or characters lighten the dramatic intensity
of the action. Even Joseph is more ironic than comic, and Mr. Lockwood's occasional facetious comments are outside the action and
have no influence upon it. Though incapable of understanding the
book, Charlotte Brontë sensed the power attained through this
unity: "Its power fills me with renewed admiration; but yet I am
oppressed; the reader is scarcely ever permitted a taste of unalloyed
pleasure; every beam of sunshine is poured down through black
bars of threatening cloud; every page is surcharged with a sort of
moral electricity."

Wuthering Heights is not the "work of immature genius,"
"awkwardly and illogically constructed," a study of "unnatural passion"; nor is it, I believe, the "one perfect work of art amid all
the vast varied canvases of Victorian fiction." In theme and structure, however, it is the product of a mature artist who knew what
effects she wished to achieve and possessed the ability to carry her
scheme through to a logical and satisfying conclusion. Her theme
of the relationship between love and hate is universal in its significance; her structure, if not unique in English fiction, is the ideal one
for this story which could not be confined within the relatively
narrow bounds of the drama. /100/

Questions for Discussion and Writing

1. By what other critics and in what ways has *Wuthering Heights* been
compared to the plays of Shakespeare?

2. From your reading of criticism of *Wuthering Heights,* explain what
Watson means by "unprejudiced" in his statement that "few have made
an unprejudiced attempt to understand what Emily Brontë strove for. . . ."
(page 87)

3. State precisely the ways in which *Wuthering Heights* is "divorced from
the world as we know it." (page 87) In what way(s) *does* the novel represent the world as we know it? What have the critics said about this?

4. What does Watson mean by the "dissolution of the revenge motif in
the last chapters" (page 88) of *Wuthering Heights?*

5. With use of Watson's article and others, discuss *Wuthering Heights* as primarily a love story.

6. Watson dismisses the possibility of *Wuthering Heights* as a Victorian novel, a novel of revenge, or a Gothic romance. What critics do you find who make a claim for one of these? If you find one or more, test the claim against Watson's assertions. If you do not find any, why do you suppose Watson has taken the time to argue against them?

7. Contrast Cecil's and Watson's readings of the novel and explain which one you believe to be more convincing.

8. Discuss Heathcliff as an "elemental man" with "elemental passions" in an "elemental environment." (page 89)

9. Explain what Watson means by saying that Edgar Linton is "incapable of understanding or possessing" Catherine. (page 92)

10. " . . . in order to gain the wealth and power which . . . separated [Heathcliff] from Catherine, he must possess not only Wuthering Heights but Thrushcross Grange as well." (page 94) Since Catherine is already dead, why must Heathcliff possess the wealth and power? And why isn't there enough wealth and power in owning Wuthering Heights? How much more does he get from Thrushcross Grange?

11. Why does Watson find the ending of the book symbolic? Do other critics deny this or support it?

12. Identify the "superficial awkwardness and old-fashioned conventions in the point of view. . . ." (page 95)

13. Why does Watson call Lockwood a "relative nonentity" (page 95) rather than just a "nonentity"?

14. Does Lockwood represent "normal humanity"? (page 95) Consult the critics.

15. Do other critics find a disadvantage in Ellen's being "at moments plot-ridden"? (page 96) If so, how do they account for this disadvantage? If not, how do they explain what Watson objects to in Ellen's role?

16. Contrast Watson's discussion of the structure of *Wuthering Heights* with other discussions of it.

17. What does Watson mean by "external and internal atmosphere"? (page 99)

18. Is *Wuthering Heights* unified in place and tone?

19. This study takes issue with Cecil's interpretation of *Wuthering Heights;* read Cecil again, and decide whether Watson is in any way indebted to David Cecil. Note what kinds of material you find, and how Watson fits them into his atricle.

Introduction to
Wuthering Heights

MARK SCHORER

From her early girlhood, Emily Brontë was a solitary being whose important life was never in the world around her but in the interior world of her fancy, a life of reverie, a secret life, and a fantastic one. She lived for only thirty years, and for those thirty years she chose solitude. Her three or four timid ventures into the world beyond Haworth Parsonage all proved unsatisfactory, and served only to heighten for her the value of the isolate, unobstructed venture of the dreaming mind. Unobstructed and, therefore, uninstructed, until, in her single novel, she wandered into a school. *Wuthering Heights,* a novel born of her loneliness and published just a year before her death, was also her education, her initiation into life. One of the most curious imaginative experiences in literature is recorded in the substrata of this novel, where we can watch the drama of a creative mind being thrust, by the quality and the logic of its own material, into full reality.

The history of the Brontë family, that dismal drama of a Yorkshire parsonage, is well known. The fantasy life that ran parallel with it can never be known so well. It began for the four Brontë children in 1826 and 1827, when Charlotte was ten, Emily was eight, Branwell, the brother, was seven, and Anne was six. "Our plays," Charlotte Brontë fortunately recorded, "were established: *Young Men,* June 1826; *Our Fellows,* July 1827; *Islanders,* December 1827 . . . The *Young Men's* play took its rise from some wooden soldiers Branwell had; *Our Fellows* from Aesop's Fables; and the *Islanders* from several events /v/ which happened. I will sketch out the origin of our plays more explicity if I can. First: *Young*

Men. Papa bought Branwell some wooden soldiers at Leeds; when Papa came home it was night, and we were in bed, so next morning Branwell came to our door with a box of soldiers. Emily and I jumped out of bed, and I snatched up one and exclaimed, 'This is the Duke of Wellington! This shall be the Duke!' When I had said this Emily likewise took one up and said it should be hers; when Anne came down she said one should be hers." There is an ingenuousness in this account that suggests neither the scope and system nor the grip upon the mind that "our plays" were to gain. Some years later, Charlotte wrote,

> We wove a web of childhood,
> A web of sunny air . . .

and again, there is no suggestion that what had started as a game with wooden soldiers was to become a private mythology of lonely, upland wishes.

That four children should share a fantasy game of soldiers is not remarkable, but the importance of their game to these four is remarkable. That importance is shown by the fact that the game was turned into a literary project, and that, when the whole thing had been written down, it was equal in wordage to their combined publications. The elaborate exfoliations of this subjective world of reverie grew into a reality substantial enough to exist for years beside the emptier world of externals, and the one world imposed itself upon the other.

They imagined a kingdom called Angria, and with it, an invented geography, a fabulous history, and a saga of military and political, academic and, finally, sentimental adventure. When Charlotte was sent off to school at Roe Head in 1831, Emily and the milder Anne broke off from the saga of Angria and began afresh with their own legends of Gondal and its associated kingdom, Gaaldine. In 1835, when Charlotte took Emily with her to Roe Head as a pupil, Emily endured the dislocation for only /vi/ three months and nearly died of it. It was not that she was sick for home, but that she was sick for those conditions at home which enabled her to live in her preferred world. "My sister Emily loved the moors," Charlotte wrote. "Flowers brighter than the rose bloomed in the blackest of the heath for her; out of a sullen hollow in a livid hillside her mind could make an Eden. She found in the bleak solitude many and dear delights; and not the least and best-loved was—liberty. Liberty was the breath of Emily's nostrils; without it she perished." Liberty, this must mean, to move unimpeded in the world of her choice, and among the circumstances that made that choice possible. Twice more she tried to survive outside. In 1836 she succeeded for six months in acting as governess at Halifax. Six years later, she managed nine months at Brussels as a student of French, returned, and never left home again. Within the narrow bounds of Haworth Parsonage, she was perfectly free; in the large and unfamiliar world outside, she lost the only liberty that mattered.

Except for her single novel and her poems, we have almost nothing from her pen. The prose portions of the Gondal legend have not been recovered, if they exist; she kept, except for a few scraps, no diaries; unlike garrulous Charlotte, she was no letter writer, and the few letters that are extant are stiff with reserve; unlike Charlotte, she had no friends at all. Yet she was not timid; she was simply and completely isolate—isolate in Gondal, where, among imagined people irresponsibly aggressive and lavishly febrile, she had as the single unimagined companion her pale sister, Anne.

From Charlotte—who in 1839 wrote a compunctious farewell to her Angria, a land that had jarred her conscience increasingly as she grew older—Emily had now, there is reason to think, shut off her secret life. Since she was seventeen she had been writing poems, and writing them in such a small and crabbed hand that it can in itself be regarded as nearly a protective cryptography. How, in 1845, Charlotte came upon them, and how, in 1846, through her efforts, a volume called *Poems by Currer, Ellis,* /vii/ *and Acton Bell* obtained its unspectacular publication, Charlotte recounts in her "Biographical Notice." What she does not say there, and has only recently been discovered, is that the bulk of Emily's poems are Gondal poems—lyrical reflections spoken by Gondal people on occasions of emotional intensity. Emily resisted the publication of these poems, and when they appeared under those three names (intended to confess to neither sex, and both), they had been taken completely out of their Gondal framework. They seemed to be lyrics, simply.

They cannot be taken as personal, argues Miss Fannie Ratchford, the chief investigator of Angria and Gondal, since they are dramatic; to which one can only reply that then they are subpersonal; certainly no other poetry has ever expressed so boldly and so badly—not an autobiography, of course, but, precisely, a personality. The Brontës, Charlotte and Emily both, differ from most other novelists in the extremity to which they drive their art as a means of extending the self, the will. Their dramas, in poems or novels, are dramas enacted by *personae;* and under these masks are their aspiring selves. Emily's poems are better than Charlotte's by the degree to which social convention has not smothered candor of imagination; *Wuthering Heights* is greater than *Jane Eyre* by the same measure. Charlotte, eschewing her dreaming youth in Angria, wrote more and more out of that censorious half of her mind that clung to duty; Emily submitted to her Gondal, submerged herself in it, wrote out of it into her fullest maturity, and made it mean—well, revelation.

The prose or narrative portions of the Gondal legend are not known to us; the poems are lyrical punctuations of that legend. The poems suggest that Gondal varies significantly from Angria, which we know in Charlotte's early prose and in Branwell's. Angria was a magnificent kingdom of marble palaces, luxurious accouterments, velvet and furs, whereas Gondal was a nothern kingdom, more like the Yorkshire moors than any other country—somber, foggy, sullen, capricious, without *décor*. Emily's par- /viii/ tisans also argue that her drama is different, that hers is a world of consequence, even of moral consequence, that evil begets evil, and good, good, and that the whole is controlled by a certain ethical logic. One can, it is true, infer a more responsible *narrative* sense from Emily's Gondal poems that one can from the Charlotte-Branwell material, most of which was produced at an earlier age. The Gondal poems have been linked together into different Gondal narratives by different Gondal interpreters; yet in each interpretation the narrative, while sequential in a superficial way, remains puerile—from the point of view of serious fiction, simply frivolous. What signifies in the Gondal world is not the story, let alone the moral sense, but the emotional quality, and that is always dark, Byronic, and excessive.

The experiences of Emily's violently passionate Gondal heroine, Augusta Geraldine Almeda (described by Louise Bogan as "a kind of female Don Juan"), have a certain historic interest in that they show the extent to which, by 1835, the notion of *la femme fatale* had sunk into the popular consciousness, even of juveniles, but their chief interest is in the kind of world they imply, in the kind of imagination that selects that world, and in the kind of literary problem that Emily would pose to her imagination once we can think of it seriously as mature.

Gondal is a world of sensibility unleashed from responsibility, a world in which the extremes rather than the causes of feeling are important. From the point of view of humanity as it is generally known or as Emily Brontë knew it, Gondal is a world of declaiming ghosts, where passions and sufferings always overshadow their motives. Certain familiar situations from late eighteenth- and early nineteenth-century fiction and poetry emerge: characters of an intractable and tyrannical pride; violent crimes and sexual sins resulting in lamentable exile and imprisonment; children doomed to incomprehensible conditions of terror. Yet the Gondal legend gives us not so much themes or plots or even clear persons as it does an emotional quality, an atmosphere of secret value in which sexual and political power /ix/ are major and one. This is the world that, for twenty years, Emily Brontë chose to live in.

2

After the unhappy publication of their poems, Currer, Ellis, and Acton Bell agreed that each should write a novel. It was still in a way a family game, and Charlotte again tells us how these three novels came into public being. Emily's novel begins where Gondal broke off. *Wuthering Heights* reveals again the same secret world of value, but this time, through what may in part be an accident of technique, the revelation is meaningfully accomplished.

From the tone of somnambulistic excess that her prose generates, we can assume that this world of monstrous passion, of dark and gigantic emotional and nervous energy, was in the first place a realm of ideal value, like Gondal, and that the book sets out to persuade us and its skeptical characters, especially Lockwood, of the moral magnificence of such unmoral passion. We are expected in the first place to take at their own valuation these demonic beings, Heathcliff and Cathy: as special creatures, set apart from the cloddish world about them by their heightened capacity for feeling, set apart even from the ordinary objects of human passion as, in their transcendent, supersexual relationship, they present themselves in the stature of beings larger than life, as mythical powers, nearly, in their identification with an uncompromising landscape and cosmic force. This is an absurd demand for a novelist to place upon himself, and the novelist Emily Brontë had to discover the absurdity to the girl Emily. Her novelistic art had to evaluate her world, so that we are persuaded that it is not Emily who is mistaken in her estimate of her characters, but they who are mistaken in their estimate of themselves. The theme of the moral magnificence of unmoral passion is an impossible theme to sustain, and, the needs of her temperament to the contrary, all personal longing and reverie /x/ to the contrary, Emily Brontë teaches herself that this was indeed not at all what her material must mean as art.

In any realm except one like Gondal, at any rate, the theme of the moral magnificence of unmoral passion is impossible, and Emily Brontë had first of all taken her passions out of that dreamy world and put them in Yorkshire. The landscape remained essentially the same, perhaps, but, fatally, she gave it names—Gimmerton and Thrushcross Grange, Penistone Crags and Wuthering Heights. She named it with the rough names of the real world, and doing that, she invited the real world in, that other world from the one whose values so far in her life she had wished to prove.

Then, to lay before us the full character of this passion, to show us how it first comes into being and then comes to dominate the world about it and the life that follows upon it, Emily Brontë gives her material a broad scope in time, lets it, in fact, cut across three generations. The relationships of these three generations seem to a new reader impossibly confusing; yet actually they are as neat and tidy as the cupboard of a spinster. They are shown on page xii.

To manage material which is so extensive, the novelist must find a means of narration, points of view, to encompass that material and justify its being told at all. So she chooses two persons who are really outside the story. The first is a foppish traveler who stumbles into this world of passionate violence, a traveler representing the thin and conventional emotional life of the far world of fashion, who wishes to hear the tale told, and himself tells us as much of it as occurs in the present. For her second, who tells everything that has occurred in the past, Emily Brontë chooses, almost inevitably, the old family retainer who knows everything, a character as conventional as the other, but this one representing not the conventions of fashion, but the conventions of the humblest moralism. To these she adds a third, as a kind of chorus—Joseph. His dourly evangelical observations on the central actors are comic in their contrast, and they light /xi/ up the consuming passions abovestairs in a way to suggest that when someone who is not feeling those passions looks at them, they look different.

What has happened is, first, that Emily Brontë has chosen as her narrative perspective those very elements, conventional emotion and conventional morality and conventional piety, which her hero and heroine are meant to transcend with such spectacular magnificence; and second, that she has permitted this perspective to operate throughout a long period of time. And these two elements compel the novelist to see what her unmoral passions come to. Moral magnificance? Not at all; rather, a devastating spectacle of human

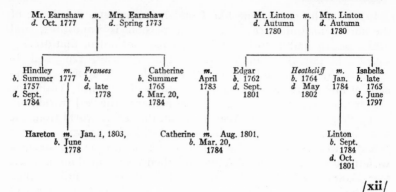

/xii/

waste: ashes. For the time of the novel is carried on long enough
to show Heathcliff at last an emptied man, burned out by his fever
ragings, exhausted and will-less, his passion meaningless at last. And
it goes even a little further, to Lockwood, the fop, in the grave-
yard, sententiously contemplating headstones. Thus in the end the
triumph is on the side of the cloddish world, which survives.

Not entirely there, to be sure—and in that partiality lies the great
power of the book. For the moment, however, it is enough to see
that the character of Gondal has been altered, and that the alteration has come about through structural means. This novel, which
seemed to Charlotte Brontë so irregular, so Gothic, and impelled
her to attempt in her editor's preface to the second edition, which
she had "corrected," a kind of defense of her sister's rude genius,
is, actually, one of the most carefully constructed novels in the language. C. P. Sanger pointed out not only the nearly mathematical
regularity of the character relationships within their apparent confusion, but the niceness and care with which the novelist handled
problems of time, so that the day, month, and year of every important event can be calculated. A very scrupulous order, in short,
contains this disorderly material; highly regulative intelligence
is working in cooperation with exceedingly flamboyant emotions.
There are tensions here that make both for strangeness and for
greatness. /xiii/

We can trace out this same general movement through an element
of style no less than through the larger patterns of structure. Let us
assume again that *Wuthering Heights* means to be a work of edification, that Emily Brontë begins by wishing to instruct her narrator
the sentimental dandy Lockwood, in the nature of a grand passion,

and that somehow she ends by instructing herself in the vanity of human wishes. She means to dramatize with something like approval what George Eliot, in another connection in *Middlemarch*, called "the sense of a stupendous self and an insignificant world." But Emily Brontë's style, her rhetoric, specifically her metaphors, signify rather the impermanence of self and the permanence of something larger.

To exalt the power of human feeling, she roots her analogies with extraordinary consistency in the fierce life of animals and in the relentless life of the elements—fire, wind, water. "Wuthering," we are told at once, is "a significant provincial adjective, descriptive of the atmospheric tumult to which its station is exposed in stormy weather," and, immediately after, that "one may guess the power of the north wind, blowing over the edge, by the excessive slant of a few stunted firs at the end of the house; and by a range of gaunt thorns all stretching their limbs one way, as if craving alms of the sun." The application of this landscape to the characters becomes explicit in the second half of the novel, when Heathcliff says, "Now, my bonny lad, you are *mine*! And we'll see if one tree won't grow as crooked as another, with the same wind to twist it!" The natural elements provide at least half of the metaphorical base of the novel.

Human conditions are like the activities of the landscape, where rains *flood*, blasts *wail*, and the snow and wind *whirl wildly*. Faces, too, are like landscapes, always *darkening* or *brightening*, *beclouded*, *overcast*, *shaded*, and so on. People are weather vanes, registering tumultuous moral conditions. When the imagery is not of wind and cloud and water, it is of fire; and from the outset, the fire on the hearth is the center of pictorial interest in every interior. Somewhat suprisingly, perhaps, meta- /xiv/ phors of earth are much rarer in this novel than those of wind and water and fire; and earth, we may remind ourselves, takes more solid and durable forms than these other elements, which, while permanent in themselves, are fickle and transient in their forms.

The second large area of metaphorical interest is animal life, yet animals here are almost never drawn upon in a domestic or a pastoral vein, but almost always to make analogies with violence and savagery, or for purposes of scorn and abuse. Most of the animals are wild, and strength is equal to brutishness. The domestic and the gentler animals generally are used for purposes of harsh satire or vilification. In this thick context of brute qualities, either fierce or contemptible, there is eloquent suggestiveness in the second

Cathy's carving, near the end of the novel, "figures of birds and beasts out of the turnip parings in her lap," and something deeper than pathos and nearer horror when suddenly she cries out, "Oh! I'm tired—I'm *stalled*, Hareton!"

Emily Brontë's metaphors color all her diction. As her epithets are charged with passion—"jealous guardianship," "vexatious phlegm," "importunate branch"—so her verbs are verbs of violent movement and conflict: *writhe, drag, crush, grind, struggle, yield, sink, recoil, outstrip, tear, drive asunder,* and so on, page after page. Here is a rhetorical texture in which everything is at a pitch from which it can only subside. And, interestingly, there is an antithetical chorus in this rhetoric, or a contrapuntal warning, which, usually in the voice of Nelly Dean but not alone in her voice, says, "Hush! Hush!" all through the novel, at the beginning of paragraph after paragraph. At the end, everything is hushed. And the moths that *flutter* over Heathcliff's grave and "the soft wind *breathing* through the grass" that grows on it have at last more power than he, for all his passion. These soft and fragile things paradoxically endure.

If Heathcliff's life, which is exhausted at the end, has not been, as he once said of it, "a moral teething," and the novel, therefore, not quite a tragedy, the story of his life has been a moral teething /xv/ for the author. Lockwood is instructed in the nature of a grand passion, but he and Emily Brontë together are instructed in its final fruits: even roaring fires end in a bed of ashes. In Emily Brontë's metaphors and verbs, one may find what Gerard Manley Hopkins said one can often find in the stylistic texture of a great work—an "underthought," worked in counterpoint to the "overthought." Thus, while the human and the nonhuman are equated, the work itself yet somehow develops a stronger and stronger contrast between the obligations of the human and the nonhuman creation.

These rhetorical and structural functions should suggest some of the imaginative stresses with which this work is imbued and which give it the strange charm it has always had for its readers. At the end, the voice that drones on is the perdurable voice of the country, Nelly Dean's. No more than Heathcliff did Emily Brontë quite intend that homespun finality. Like the older Catherine, she could have said of her book, "I've dreamt in my life dreams that have stayed with me ever after, and changed my ideas; they've gone through and through me, like wine through water, and altered the colour of my mind."

3

Yet the triumph is not all on the side of convention and the cloddish world. It has sometimes been argued that Branwell had a part in the writing of this book, and, because of the relative weakness of the opening scenes, these have been atttributed to his unsteady hand. There is enough evidence of other kinds to demonstrate the implausibility of the claim. The best evidence is simply that, when Emily began her novel, she was still writing out of Gondal, that unanchored world of fitful movement and inchoate feeling which was her secret and her sole pleasure. Only after she was well into her book was the movement steadied and the feeling, as it were, "framed" by that other world which, in what was the only serious infraction of her privacy, she had /xvi/ joined with hers. In *Wuthering Heights,* one world explodes within another—the world of unconscious yearning and of those primary passions from which we construct our myths, within the world of conscious propriety, literary no less than social, and of those secondary sentiments on which we base our manners. The fires of this eruption must be put down—that is the habit of civilization; but the outer world has been enriched and cleansed as well as seared by them, and that is the function of art.

"There is an art of the flood," wrote William Butler Yeats, "of Shakespeare when he shows us Hamlet broken away from life by the passionate hesitations of his reverie. And we call this art poetical, because we must bring more to it than our daily mood if we would take our pleasure; and because it delights in picturing the moment of exaltation, of excitement, of dreaming. . . . And there is an art that we call real, because character can only express itself perfectly in a real world, being that world's creature, and because we understand it best through a delicate discrimination of the senses which is but entire wakefulness, the daily mood grown cold and crystalline."

In *Wuthering Heights* these two arts become one, and the enigmatic power of the novel lies in our response to the tensions between the two kinds, the tensions that strain deep in the very texture of the style and at the solid girders of its dramatic structure—tensions between romance and convention, mythical force and rural manners, the amoral values of nature and the inadequately moral values of men, desire and the destiny of things as they really are. From these tensions, this conjuncture, arises the paradox that is the characteristic of all great art—a strange spaciousness freer than life, our release and elevation into liberty.

Nothing more happened in the life of Emily Brontë. She lived on in solitude. She was angry with her sister when, one day, Charlotte stepped into her publisher's office in London and exposed the mysterious secret of the Bell's with the announcement, "We are three sisters." When Emily fell ill, she died much like Heathcliff, with stubborn reserve, as if emptied of wishes: she /xvii/ would not go to bed; she would not see a doctor. That was in December, 1848, less than a year after *Wuthering Heights* had been given to the world outside. /xviii/

Questions for Discussion and Writing

1. In terms of the novel, try to explain Schorer's phrase, "the moral magnificence of unmoral passion." Does it help you to understand the novel?

2. Mark Schorer describes Lockwood as a "foppish traveler." (page xi) What does he mean? Do you agree with the application of this word to Lockwood? Do other critics see Lockwood as a fop?

3. Discuss Nelly Dean as a character representing "the conventions of the humblest moralism." (page xi)

4. Elaborate on Schorer's statement that Joseph is a "kind of chorus" (page xi), explaining in full the function of Joseph in the novel.

5. Do you agree with Schorer that the unmoral passion of *Wuthering Heights* ends in "a devastating spectacle of human waste"? (page xiii) Do you think Heathcliff or Catherine would agree? Consult the other critics.

6. Comment on Schorer's statement that at the end of the novel Heathcliff is "an emptied man, burned out by his fever ragings, exhausted and will-less, his passion meaningless at last." (page xiii)

7. Is it "the childish world" (page xiii) which triumphs in the novel? What implications does this conclusion have for the novel? How does it conflict with the comments of other critics?

8. Discuss further Emily Brontë's use of metaphors.

9. On pages xiv-xv, Schorer provides an impressive list of quotations from *Wuthering Heights* to support his idea that "The natural elements provide at least half of the metaphorical base of the novel." Consider Schorer's problem as critic here. Is his list long enough to convince you? Would it be possible to find an equal number of similar expressions in another novel used merely for description and not for the purpose to which Schorer ascribes Emily Brontë's use of them? If you think so, do you consider this to invalidate Schorer's argument? Would a longer list convince you? What is a critic's responsibility in supplying evidence to support his ideas?

Emily Brontë:
Wuthering Heights (1847)

ARNOLD KETTLE

Wuthering Heights, like all the greatest works of art, is at once concrete and yet general, local and yet universal. Because so much nonsense has been written and spoken about the Brontës and because Emily in particular has been so often presented to us as a ghost-like figure surrounded entirely by endless moorland, cut off from anything so banal as human society, not of her time but of eternity, it is necessary to emphasize at the outset the local quality of the book.

Wuthering Heights is about England in 1847. The people it reveals live not in a never-never land but in Yorkshire. Heathcliff was born not in the pages of Byron, but in a Liverpool slum. The language of Nelly, Joseph and Hareton is the language of Yorkshire people. The story of *Wuthering Heights* is concerned not with love in the abstract but with the passions of living people, with property-ownership, the attraction of social comforts, the arrangement of marriages, the importance of education, the validity of religion, the relations of rich and poor.

There is nothing vague about this novel; the mists in it are the mists of the Yorkshire moors; if we speak of it as having an elemental quality it is because the very elements, the great forces of nature are evoked, which change so slowly that in the span of a human life they seem unchanging. But in this evocation there is nothing sloppy or uncontrolled. On the contrary the realization is intensely concrete: we seem to smell the kitchen of Wuthering Heights, to feel the force of the wind across the moors, to sense the

From *An Introduction to the English Novel,* 2 vols. (London: Hillary House Ltd., 1951) , Vol. 1, Chap. V.

very changes of the seasons. Such concreteness is achieved not by mistiness but by precision.

It is necessary to stress this point but not, of course, to /139/ force it to a false conclusion. The power and wonder of Emily Brontë's novel does not lie in naturalistic description, nor in a detailed analysis of the hour-by-hour issues of social living. Her approach is, quite obviously, not the approach of Jane Austen; it is much nearer to the approach of Dickens. Indeed, *Wuthering Heights* is essentially the same kind of novel as *Oliver Twist*. It is not a romance, not (despite the film bearing the same title) an escape from life to the wild moors and romantic lovers. It is certainly not a picaresque novel and it cannot adequately be described as a moral fable, though it has a strong, insistent pattern. But the pattern, like that of Dicken's novel, cannot be abstracted as a neat sentence: its germ is not an intellectualized idea or concept.

Emily Brontë works not in ideas but in symbols, that is to say concepts which have a significance and validity on a level different from that of logical thought. Just as the significance of the workhouse in *Oliver Twist* cannot adequately be conceived in merely logical terms but depends on a host of associations—including its physical shape and colour—which logical analysis may penetrate but is unlikely adequately to convey, so the significance of the moors in *Wuthering Heights* cannot be suggested in the cold words of logic (which does not mean that it is illogical). The symbolic novel is an advance on the moral fable just in the sense that a symbol can be richer—can touch on more of life—than an abstract moral concept.

The opening sentence of the *Social Contract* gives a simple example: "Man was born free, but everywhere he is in chains." Of the two statements in this sentence the first is abstract, the second symbolic. And the impact of the second on our imagination is greater than that of the first for this very reason. (If one were concerned to go deeper into the matter one might suggest that Rousseau *knew* that man was in chains but merely speculated that he had been born free.) Now, whereas the symbolism of the moral fable (and the fable is itself a kind of extended symbol) is inherently limited by the abstract concept behind it, the symbolism of *Wuthering Heights* or the good part of *Oliver Twist* is the expression of the very terms in which the /140/ novel has been conceived.* In

---

* A simple, though not infallible, indication of the kind of novel one is dealing with is given by the naming of characters. In allegory and the novel of 'humours' names always denote character—e.g., Faithful and Squire Allworthy. In totally non-symbolic novelists like Jane Austen the names are quite without signifi-

fact, it *is* the novel and the novel stands or falls by its validity, its total adequacy to life.

Wuthering Heights is a vision of what life in 1847 was like. Whether it can be described as a vision of what life as such—all life—is like is a question we will consider later. It is, for all its appearance of casualness and the complexity of its family relationships, a very well-constructed book, in which the technical problems of presentation have been most carefully thought out. The roles of the two narrators, Lockwood and Nelly Dean, are not casual. Their function (they the two most 'normal' people in the book) is partly to keep the story close to the earth, to make it believable, partly to comment on it from a common-sense point of view and thereby to reveal in part the inadequacy of such common sense. They act as a kind of sieve to the story, sometimes a double sieve, which has the purpose not simply of separating off the chaff, but of making us aware of the difficulty of passing easy judgments. One is left always with the sense that the last word has not been said.

The narrators do not as a rule talk realistically, though sometimes Nelly's part is to slip into a Yorkshire dialect that 'places' what she is describing and counteracts any tendency (inherent in symbolic art) to the pretentious. At critical points in the narrative we are not conscious of their existence at all; there is no attempt at a limiting verisimilitude of speech. They do not impose themselves between us and the scene. But at other times their attitudes are important.

One of the subtleties of the book is the way these attitudes change and develop; Lockwood and Nelly, like us, learn from what they experience, though at first their limitations are made use of, as in the very first scene when the expectations of the conventional Lockwood are so completely shocked by what he finds at Wuthering Heights. He goes there, he the normal /141/ Victorian gentleman, expecting to find the normal Victorian middle-class family. And what he finds—a house seething with hatred, conflict, horror— is a shock to us, too. The attack on our complacency, moral, social and spiritual, has already begun.

The centre and core of the book is the story of Catherine and Heathcliff. It is a story which has four stages. The first part, ending

---

cance: Emma Woodhouse might equally well be called Anne Elliot. In novels which have a certain symbolic quality the names of characters generally have a peculiar rightness of their own: Heathcliff, Noah Claypole, Henry James's characters.

in the visit to Thrushcross Grange, tells of the establishing of a special relationship between Catherine and Heathcliff and of their common rebellion against Hindley and his régime in Wuthering Heights. In the second part is revealed Catherine's betrayal of Heathcliff, culminating in her death. The third part deals with Heathcliff's revenge, and the final section, shorter than the others, tells of the change that comes over Heathcliff and of his death. Even in the last two sections, after her death, the relationship with Catherine remains the dominant theme, underlying all else that occurs.

It is not easy to suggest with any precision the quality of feeling that binds Catherine and Heathcliff. It is not primarily a sexual relationship. Emily Brontë is not, as is sometimes suggested, afraid of sexual love; the scene at Catherine's death is proof enough that this is no platonic passion, yet to describe the attraction as sexual is surely quite inadequate. Catherine tries to express her feelings to Nelly (she is about to marry Linton).

"My great miseries in this world have been Heathcliff's miseries, and I watched and felt each from the beginning: my great thought in living is himself. If all else perished, and *he* remained, *I* should still continue to be; and if all else remained, and he were annihilated, the universe would turn to a mighty stranger: I should not seem a part of it. My love for Linton is like the foliage in the woods: time will change it, I'm well aware, as winter changes the trees. My love for Heathcliff resembles the eternal rocks beneath: a source of little visible delight, but necessary. Nelly, I *am* Heathcliff! He's always, always in my mind: not as a pleasure, any more than I am always a pleasure to myself, but as my own being."[1]

and Heathcliff cries, when Catherine is dying: "I *cannot* live without my life, I *cannot* live without my soul."[2] What is conveyed to us here is the sense of an affinity deeper than sexual attraction, something which it is not enough to describe /142/ as romantic love.

This affinity is forged in rebellion and, in order to grasp the concrete and unromantic nature of this book, it is necessary to recall the nature of that rebellion. Heathcliff, the waif from the Liverpool slums, is treated kindly by old Mr. Earnshaw but insulted and degraded by Hindley. After his father's death Hindley reduces the boy to the status of a serf. "He drove him from their company to the servants, deprived him of the instructions of the curate, and insisted that he should labour out of doors instead; compelling him to do so as hard as any other hand on the farm."[3] The situation at Wuth-

---

[1] *Wuthering Heights*, Chap. IX.
[2] *Ibid.*, Chap. XVI.
[3] *Ibid.*, Chap. VI.

ering Heights is wonderfully evoked in the passage from Catherine's journal, which Lockwood finds in his bedroom:

" 'An awful Sunday!' commenced the paragraph beneath. 'I wish my father were back again. Hindley is a detestable substitute—his conduct to Heathcliff is atrocious—H. and I are going to rebel—we took our initiatory step this evening.

'All day had been flooding with rain; we could not go to church, so Joseph must needs get up a congregation in the garret, and, while Hindley and his wife basked downstairs before a comfortable fire—doing anything but reading the Bibles, I'll answer for it—Heathcliff, myself, and the unhappy plough-boy, were commanded to take our Prayer-books, and mount: were ranged in a row, on a sack of corn, groaning and shivering, and hoping that Joseph would shiver too, so that he might give us a short homily for his own sake. A vain idea! The service lasted precisely three hours: and yet my brother had the face to exclaim, when he saw us descending, "What, done already?" On Sunday evenings we used to be permitted to play, if we did not make much noise; now a mere titter is sufficient to send us into corners!

' "You forget you have a master here," says the tyrant. "I'll demolish the first who puts me out of temper! I insist on perfect sobriety and silence. Oh, boy! was that you? Frances darling, pull his hair as you go by: I heard him snap his fingers." Frances pulled his hair heartily, and then went and seated herself on her husband's knee: and there they were, like two babies, kissing and talking nonsense by the hour—foolish palaver that we should be ashamed of. We made ourselves as snug as our means allowed in the arch of the dresser. I had just fastened our pinafores together, and hung them up for a curtain, when in comes Joseph on an errand from the stables. He tears down my handiwork boxes my ears and croaks—

' "T' maister nobbut just buried, and Sabbath no o'ered, and /143/ t'sound o' t' gospel still i' yer lugs, and ye darr be laiking! Shame on ye! Sit ye down, ill childer! There's good books enough if ye'll read em! sit ye down, and think of yer sowls!' "

'Saying this, he compelled us so to square our positions that we might receive from the far-off fire a dull ray to show us the text of the lumber he thrust upon us. I could not bear the employment. I took my dingy volume by the scroop, and hurled it into the dog-kennel, vowing I hated a good book. Heathcliff kicked his to the same place. Then there was a hubbub!

' "Maister Hindley!" shouted our chaplain. "Maister, coom hither! Miss Cathy's riven th' back of 'Th' Helmet O' Salvation,' un Heathcliff's pawsed his fit into t' first part o' 'T' Brooad Way to Destruction.' It's fair flaysome, that ye yet 'em go on this gait. Ech! th' owd man wad ha' laced 'em properly—but he's goan!"

'Hindley hurried up from his paradise on the hearth, and seizing one of us by the collar, and the other by the arm, hurled both into the back

kitchen, where, Joseph asseverated, "owd Nick" would fetch us as sure as
we were living, and so, comforted, we each sought a separate nook to await
his advent.' "[4]

This passage reveals, in itself, a great deal of the extraordinary
quality of *Wuthering Heights*. It is a passage which, in the typical
manner of the novel, evokes, in language which involves the kind
of attention we give to poetry, a world far larger than the scene it
describes, and evokes it through the very force and concreteness of
the particular scene. The rebellion of Catherine and Heathcliff is
made completely concrete. They are not vague romantic dreamers.
Their rebellion is against the régime in which Hindley and his
wife sit in fatuous comfort by the fire whilst they are relegated to
the arch of the dresser and compelled for the good of their souls
to read the *Broad Way to Destruction* under the tutelage of the
canting hypocrite Joseph. It is a situation not confined, in the
year 1847, to the more distant homesteads of the Yorkshire moors.

Against this degradation Catherine and Heathcliff rebel, hurling
their pious books into the dog-kennel. And in their revolt they discover their deep and passionate need of each other. He, the outcast
slummy, turns to the lively, spirited, fearless girl who alone offers
him human understanding and comradeship. And she, born into
the world of Wuthering Heights, senses that to achieve a full humanity, to be true to /144/ herself as a human being, she must associate herself totally with him in his rebellion against the tyranny
of the Earnshaws and all that tyranny involves.

It is this rebellion that immediately, in this early section of the
book, wins over our sympathy to Heathcliff. We know he is on
the side of humanity and we are with him just as we are with Oliver
Twist, and for much the same reasons. But whereas Oliver is presented with a sentimental passivity, which limits our concern,
Heathcliff is active and intelligent and able to carry the positive
values of human aspiration on his shoulders. He is a conscious
rebel. And it is from his associaton in rebellion with Catherine that
the particular quality of their relationship arises. It is the reason
why each feels that a betrayal of what binds them together is in
some obscure and mysterious way a betrayal of everything, of all
that is most valuable in life and death.

Yet Catherine betrays Heathcliff and marries Edgar Linton, kid-
ding herself that she can keep them both, and then discovering that
in denying Heathcliff she has chosen death. The conflict here is,

[4] *Ibid.*, Chap. III.

quite explicitly, a social one. Thrushcross Grange embodying as it does the prettier, more comfortable side of bourgeois life, seduces Catherine. She begins to despise Heathcliff's lack of 'culture.' He has no conversation, he does not brush his hair, he is dirty, whereas Edgar, besides being handsome, "will be rich and I shall like to be the greatest woman of the neighbourhood, and I shall be proud of having such a husband."[5] And so Heathcliff runs away and Catherine becomes mistress of Thrushcross Grange.

Heathcliff returns, adult and prosperous, and at once the social conflict is re-emphasized. Edgar, understandably, does not want to receive Heathcliff, but Catherine is insistent:

" 'I know you didn't like him,' she answered, repressing a little the intensity of her delight. 'Yet, for my sake, you must be friends now. Shall I tell him to come up?'

'Here,' he said, 'into the parlour?'

'Where else?' she asked.

He looked vexed, and suggested the kitchen as a more suitable place for him. Mrs. Linton eyed him with a droll expression—half angry, half laughing at his fastidiousness. / 145 /

'No,' she added after a while; 'I cannot sit in the kitchen. Set two tables here, Ellen: one for your master and Miss Isabella, being gentry, the other for Heathcliff and myself, being the lower orders. Will that please you, dear? . . . ' "[6]

And from the moment of Heathcliff's reappearance Catherine's attempts to reconcile herself to Thrushcross Grange are doomed. In their relationship now there is no tenderness, they trample on each other's nerves, madly try to destroy each other; but, once Heathcliff is near, Catherine can maintain no illusions about the Lintons. The two are united only in their contempt for the values of Thrushcross Grange. "There it is," Catherine taunts Edgar, speaking of her grave, "not among the Lintons, mind, under the chapel roof, but in the open air, with a headstone."[7] The open air, nature, the moors are contrasted with the world of Thrushcross Grange. And the contempt for the Lintons is a *moral* contempt, not a jealous one. When Nelly tells Heathcliff that Catherine is going mad, his comment is:

" 'You talk of her mind being unsettled. How the devil could it be otherwise in her frightful isolation? And that insipid paltry creature attending her from *duty* and *humanity!* From *pity* and *charity!* He might as well plant an oak in a flower pot, and expect it to thrive, as imagine he can restore her to vigour in the soil of his shallow cares!' "[8]

[5] *Ibid.,* Chap. IX.   [7] *Ibid.,* Chap. XII.
[6] *Ibid.,* Chap. X.   [8] *Ibid.,* Chap. XIV.

The moral passion here is so intense, so deeply imbedded in the rhythm and imagery of the prose, that it is easy to be swept along without grasping its full and extraordinary significance. Heathcliff at this point has just perpetrated the first of his callous and ghastly acts of revenge, his marriage to Isabella. It is an act so morally repulsive that it is almost inconceivable that we should be able now to take seriously his attack on Edgar Linton, who has, after all, by conventional, respectable standards, done nobody any harm. And yet we do take the attack seriously because Emily Brontë makes us. The passion of the passage just quoted has the quality of great poetry. Why?

We continue to sympathize with Heathcliff, even after his marriage with Isabella, because Emily Brontë convinces us that what Heathcliff stands for is morally superior to what /146/ the Lintons stand for. This is, it must be insisted, not a case of some mysterious 'emotional' power with which Heathcliff is charged. The emotion behind his denunciation of Edgar is *moral* emotion. The words "duty" and "humanity," "pity" and "charity" have precisely the kind of force Blake gives such words in his poetry.*

They are used not so much paradoxically as in a sense inverted but more profound than the conventional usage. Heathcliff speaks, apparently paradoxically, of Catherine's "frightful isolation," when to all appearances she is in Thrushcross Grange less isolated, more subject to care and society, than she could possibly be with him. But in truth Heathcliff's assertion is a paradox only to those who do not understand his meaning. What he is asserting with such intense emotional conviction that we, too, are convinced, is that what he stands for, the alternative life *he* has offered Catherine is more natural (the image of the oak enforces this), more social and more moral than the world of Thrushcross Grange. Most of those who criticize Heathcliff adversely (on the grounds that he is unbelievable, or that he is a neurotic creation, or that he is merely the Byronic satan-hero revived) fail to appreciate his significance because they fail to recognize this moral force. And as a rule they fail to recognize the moral force because they are themselves, consciously or not, of the Linton party.

---

* E.g. Pity would be no more
          If we did not make somebody Poor;
          And Mercy no more could be
          If all were as happy as we

or

          Was Jesus humble? or did he
          Give any proofs of Humility.

The climax of this inversion by Heathcliff and Catherine of the common standards of bourgeois morality comes at the death of Catherine. To recognize the revolutionary force of this scene one has only to imagine what a different novelist might have made of it.

The stage is all set for a moment of conventional drama. Catherine is dying, Heathcliff appears out of the night. Two possibilities present themselves: either Catherine will at the last reject Heathcliff, the marriage vow will be vindicated and /147/ wickedness meet its reward; or true love will triumph and reconciliation proclaim the world well lost. It is hard to imagine that either possibility ever crossed Emily Brontë's mind, for either would destroy the pattern of her book, but her rejection of them is a measure of her moral and artistic power. For instead of its conventional potentialities the scene acquires an astonishing moral power. Heathcliff confronted with the dying Catherine, is ruthless, morally ruthless: instead of easy comfort he offers her a brutal analysis of what she has done.

" 'You teach me now how cruel you've been—cruel and false. *Why* did you despise me? *Why* did you betray your own heart Cathy? I have not one word of comfort. You deserve this. You have killed yourself. Yes, you may kiss me, and cry: and wring out my kisses and tears: they'll blight you—they'll damn you. You loved me—then what *right* had you to leave me? What right—answer me—for the poor fancy you felt for Linton? Because misery and degradation, and death, and nothing that God or Satan could inflict would have parted us, *you*, of your own will, did it. I have not broken your heart—*you* have broken it; and in breaking it you have broken mine. So much the worse that I am strong. Do I want to live? What kind of living will it be when you—oh, God! would *you* like to live with your soul in the grave?' "[9]

It is one of the harshest passages in all literature, but it is also one of the most moving. For the brutality is not neurotic, nor sadistic, nor romantic. The Catherine-Heathcliff relationship, standing as it does for a humanity finer and more morally profound than the standards of the Lintons and Earnshaws has to undergo the kind of examination Heathcliff here brings to it. Anything less, anything which smudged or sweetened the issues involved, would be inadequate, unworthy. Heathcliff knows that nothing can save Catherine from death but that one thing alone can give her peace, a full and utterly honest understanding and acceptance of their relationship and what it implies. There is no hope in comfort or compromise. Any such weakness would debase them both and make a futile waste

⁹ *Ibid.*, Chap. XV.

of their lives and death. For Heathcliff and Catherine, who reject
the Lintons' chapel roof and the consolations of Christianity, know,
too, that their relationship is more important than death. /148/

In the section of the book that follows Catherine's death Heathcliff continues the revenge he has begun with his marriage to Isabella. It is the most peculiar section of the novel and the most
difficult because the quality of Heathcliff's feeling is of a kind most
of us find hard to comprehend. All normal and healthy human
feeling is rejected. He cries:

> " 'I have no pity! I have no pity! The more the worms writhe, the more
> I yearn to crush out their entrails! It is a moral teething; and I grind with
> greater energy, in proportion to the increase of pain.' "[10]

"It is a moral teething"—the phrase is both odd and significant,
giving as it does the answer to our temptation to treat this whole
section as a delineation of pathological neurosis. Heathcliff becomes a monster: what he does to Isabella, to Hareton, to Cathy, to
his son, even to the wretched Hindley, is cruel and inhuman beyond normal thought. He seems concerned to achieve new refinements of horror, new depths of degradation. And we tend to feel,
perhaps, unless we read with full care and responsiveness, that
Emily Brontë has gone too far, that the revenge (especially the
marriage of Cathy and Linton Heathcliff) has o'erflown the measure.

And yet it is only one side of our minds, the conscious, limited
side that refers what we are reading to our everyday measures of experience that makes this objection. Another side, which is more
completely responding to Emily Brontë's art, is carried on. And the
astonishing achievement of this part of the book is that, despite our
protests about probability (protests which, incidentally, a good
deal of twentieth-century history makes a little complacent), despite
everything he does and is, we continue to sympathize with Heathcliff—not, obviously, to admire him or defend him, but to give him
our inmost sympathy, to continue in an obscure way to identify
ourselves with him *against* the other characters.

The secret of this achievement lies in such a phrase as "it is a
moral teething" and in the gradually clarifying pattern of the book.
Heathcliff's revenge may involve a pathological condition of hatred,
but it is not at bottom merely neurotic. It has a moral force. For
what Heathcliff does is to use against /149/ his enemies with
complete ruthlessness their own weapons, to turn on them

[10] *Ibid.*, Chap. XIV.

(stripped of their romantic veils) their own standards, to beat them at their own game. The weapons he uses against the Earnshaws and Lintons are their own weapons of money and arranged marriages. He gets power over them by the classic methods of the ruling class, expropriation and property deals. He buys out Hindley and reduces him to drunken impotency, he marries Isabella and then organizes the marriage of his son to Catherine Linton, so that the entire property of the two families shall be controlled by himself. He systematically degrades Hareton Earnshaw to servility and illiteracy. "I want the triumph of seeing *my* descendant fairly lord of *their* estates! My child hiring their children to till their father's lands for wages."[11] (This is a novel which, some critics will tell you, has nothing to do with anything as humdrum as society or life as it is actually lived.) And what particularly tickles Heathcliff's fancy is his achievement of the supreme ruling-class triumph of making Hareton, the boy he degrades, feel a deep and even passionate attachment towards himself.

Heathcliff retains our sympathy throughout this dreadful section of the book because instinctively we recognize a rough moral justice in what he has done to his oppressors and because, though he is inhuman, we understand *why* he is inhuman. Obviously we do not approve of what he does, but we understand it; the deep and complex issues behind his actions are revealed to us. We recognize that the very forces which drove him to rebellion for a higher freedom have themselves entrapped him in their own values and determined the nature of his revenge.

If *Wuthering Heights* were to stop at this point it would still be a great book, but a wholly sombre and depressing one. Man would be revealed as inevitably caught up in the meshes of his own creating; against the tragic horror of Heathcliff's appalling rebellion the limited but complacent world of Thrushcross Grange would seem a tempting haven and the novel would resolve itself into the false antithesis of Thrushcross Grange/Wuthering Heights, just as in *Oliver Twist* the real antithesis becomes sidetracked into the false one of Brownlow/Fagin. But *Wuthering Heights,* a work of supreme /150/ and astonishing genius, does not stop here. We have not done with Heathcliff yet.

For at the moment of this horrible triumph a change begins to come over Heathcliff.

" 'It is a poor conclusion, is it not?' he observed, having brooded a

[11] *Ibid.,* Chap. XX.

while on the scene he had just witnessed: 'an absurd termination to my
violent exertions? I get levers and mattocks to demolish the two houses, and
train myself to be capable of working like Hercules, and when everything
is ready and in my power, I find the will to lift a slate off either roof has
vanished! My old enemies have not beaten me; now would be the precise
time to revenge myself on their representatives: I could do it, and none
could hinder me. But where is the use? I don't care for striking; I can't
take the trouble to raise my hand! That sounds as if I had been labouring
the whole time only to exhibit a fine trait of magnanimity. It is far from
being the case: I have lost the faculty of enjoying their destruction, and
I am too idle to destroy for nothing.

'Nelly, there is a strange change approaching: I'm in its shadow at
present.' "[12]

And he goes on to speak of Cathy and Hareton, who "seemed a
personfication of my youth, not a human being." "Hareton's aspect was the ghost of my immortal love; of my wild endeavour to
hold my right; my degradation, my pride, my happiness and my
anguish." When Nelly asks "But what do you mean by a *change*
Mr. Heathcliff?" he can only answer "I shall not know that till it
comes," he said "I'm only half conscious of it now." Once more the
stage is set for a familiar scene, the conversion of the wicked who
will in the final chapter turn from his wickedness. And once more
the conventional must look again.

The change that comes over Heathcliff and the novel and leads
us on to the wonderful, quiet, gentle, tentative evocation of nature in
the final sentence, is a very subtle one. It has something of the quality of the last two acts of *The Winter's Tale* but is much less complete, less confident. Mr. Klingopulos in his interesting essay on
Wuthering Heights[13] has commented on the ambiguous nature of
this final tranquillity. I do not agree with his analysis but he has
caught the tone most convincingly. Heathcliff, watching the love
of Cathy and Hareton grow, comes to understand something of the
failure of his own /151/ revenge. As Cathy teaches Hareton to write
and stops laughing at his ignorance we too are taken back to the
first Catherine.

Cathy and Hareton are not in the novel as easy re-creation of
Catherine and Heathcliff; they are, as Mr. Klingopulos remarks,
different people, even lesser people, certainly people conceived on
a less intense and passionate scale than the older lovers. But they do
symbolize the continuity of life and human aspirations, and it is

[12] *Ibid.*, Chap. XXXIII.
[13] *Scrutiny*, Vol. XIV, No. 4.

through them that Heathcliff comes to understand the hollowness of his triumph. It is when Hareton, who loves him, comes to Cathy's aid when he strikes her that the full meaning of his own relationship with Catherine comes back to him and he becomes aware that in the feeling between Cathy and Hareton there is something of the same quality. From the moment that Cathy and Hareton are drawn together as rebels the change begins. For now for the first time Heathcliff is confronted not with those who accept the values of Wuthering Heights and Thrushcross Grange but with those who share, however remotely, his own wild endeavours to hold his right.

Heathcliff does not repent. Nelly tries to make him turn to the consolations of religion.

" 'You are aware, Mr. Heathcliff,' I said, 'that from the time you were thirteen years old, you have lived a selfish, unchristian life; and probably hardly had a Bible in your hands during all that period. You must have forgotten the contents of the Book, and you may not have space to search it now. Could it be hurtful to send for some one—some minister of any denomination, it does not matter which—to explain it, and show you how very far you have erred from its precepts; and how unfit you will be for its heaven, unless a change takes place before you die?'

'I'm rather obliged than angry, Nelly,' he said, 'for you remind me of the manner in which I desire to be buried. It is to be carried to the churchyard in the evening. You and Hareton may, if you please, accompany me: and mind, particularly, to notice that the sexton obeys my directions concerning the two coffins! No minister need come; nor need anything be said over me.—I tell you I have nearly attained my heaven, and that of others is altogether unvalued and uncoveted by me.' "[14]

One sentence here, in its limpid simplicity, especially evokes the state of mind Heathcliff has come to. He speaks of the manner /152/ in which he wishes to be buried. "It is to be carried to the churchyard in the evening." The great rage has died in him. He has come to see the pointlessness of his fight to revenge himself on the world of power and property through its own values. Just as Catherine had to face the full moral horror of her betrayal of their love, he must face the full horror of his betrayal too. And once he has faced it he can die, not nobly or triumphantly, but at least as a man, leaving with Cathy and Hareton the possibility of carrying on the struggle he has begun, and in his death he will achieve again human dignity, "to be carried to the churchyard in the evening."

It is this re-achievement of manhood by Heathcliff, an under-

[14] *Wuthering Heights,* Chap. XXXIV.

standing reached with no help from the world he despises, which, together with the developing relationship of Cathy and Hareton and the sense of the continuity of life in nature, gives to the last pages of *Wuthering Heights* a sense of positive and unsentimental hope. The Catherine-Heathcliff relationship has been vindicated. Life will go on and others will rebel against the oppressors. Nothing has been solved but much has been experienced. Lies, complacencies and errors, appalling errors, have been revealed. A veil has been drawn from the conventional face of bourgeois man; he has been revealed, through Heathcliff, without his mask.

Above all, the quality of the feeling that binds Catherine and Heathcliff has been conveyed to us. Their love, which Heathcliff can without idealism call immortal, is something beyond the individualist dream of two soul-mates finding full realization in one another; it is an expression of the necessity of man, if he is to choose life rather than death, to revolt against all that would destroy his inmost needs and aspirations, of the necessity of all human beings to become, through acting together, more fully human. Catherine, responding to this deep human necessity, rebels with Heathcliff but in marrying Edgar (a 'good' marriage if ever there was one) betrays her own humanity; Heathcliff, by revenging himself on the tyrants through the adoption of their own standards makes more clear those standards but betrays too his humanity and destroys his relationship with the dead Catherine whose spirit must haunt the moors in terror and dismay. /153/

Only when the new change has come over Heathcliff and he again recognizes through Hareton (and remotely, therefore, through Catherine herself) the full claims of humanity can Catherine be released from torment and their relationship re-established. Death is a matter of little importance in *Wuthering Heights* because the issues the novel is concerned with are greater than the individual life and death. The deaths of Catherine and Heathcliff are indeed a kind of triumph because ultimately each faces death honestly, keeping faith. But there is no suggestion that death itself is a triumph: on the contrary it is life that asserts itself, continues, blossoms again.

Mr. David Wilson in his excellent essay on Emily Brontë[15] to which I am deeply indebted (though I do not agree with all of his interpretation) suggests an identification, not necessarily conscious in Emily Brontë's mind, of Heathcliff with the rebellious working

[15] *Modern Quarterly*, Miscellany No. 1 (1947).

men of the hungry 'forties' and of Catherine with that part of the
educated class which felt compelled to identify itself with their
cause. Such a formulation, suggestive as it is, seems to me to be too
far removed from the actual impact of *Wuthering Heights* as a
novel, to be satisfactory. But Mr. Wilson has done a valuable service in rescuing *Wuthering Heights* from the transcendentalists and
in insisting on the place of Haworth (generally assumed to be a
remote country village) in the industrial revolution and its attendant social unrest.* The value of his suggestion with regard to Heathcliff and Catherine seems to me in the emphasis it gives to the
concrete, local particularity of the book.

It is very necessary to be reminded that just as the values of
Wuthering Heights and Thrushcross Grange are not simply the
values of *any* tyranny but specifically those of Victorian society, so
is the rebellion of Heathcliff a particular rebellion, that of the
worker physically and spiritually degraded by the conditions and
relationships of this same society. That Heathcliff ceases to be one
of the exploited is true, but it is also true that just in so far as he
adopts (with a ruthlessness that frightens even the ruling class
itself) the standards of the ruling class, /154/ so do the human
values implicit in his early rebellion and in his love for Catherine
vanish. All that is involved in the Catherine-Heathcliff relationship,
all that it stands for in human needs and hopes, can be realized
only through the active rebellion of the oppressed.

Wuthering Heights then is an expression in the imaginative
terms of art of the stresses and tensions and conflicts, personal and
spiritual, of nineteenth- century capitalist society. It is a novel without idealism, without false comforts, without any implication that
power over their destinies rests outside the struggles and actions of
human beings themselves. Its powerful evocation of nature, of
moorland and storm, of the stars and the seasons is an essential
part of its revelation of the very movement of life itself. The men
and women of *Wuthering Heights* are not the prisoners of nature;
they live in the world and strive to change it, sometimes successfully, always painfully, with almost infinite difficulty and error.

This unending struggle, of which the struggle to advance from
class society to the higher humanity of a classless world is but an
episode, is conveyed to us in *Wuthering Heights* precisely because
the novel is conceived in actual, concrete, particular terms, because

* One of the most interesting exhibits in the Haworth museum today is a
proclamation of the Queen ordering the reading of the Riot Act against the
rebellious workers of the West Riding.

the quality of oppression revealed in the novel is not abstract but concrete, not vague but particular. And that is why Emily Brontë's novel is at the same time a statement about the life she knew, the life of Victorian England, and a statement about life as such. Virginia Woolf, writing about it, said:

"That gigantic ambition is to be felt throughout the novel, a struggle half thwarted but of superb conviction, to say something through the mouths of characters which is not merely 'I love' or 'I hate' but 'we, the whole human race' and 'You; the eternal powers . . .' the sentence remains unfinished."[16]

I do not think it remains unfinished. /155/

Questions for Discussion and Writing

1. Why is *Wuthering Heights* not a romance? What, precisely, is a romance?

2. Does Kettle believe *Wuthering Heights* is a realistic novel? How would he define the word "realistic" as it applies to this novel? Do other critics find the novel realistic or romantic?

3. On page 141 Kettle says that one of the functions of the two narrators is to make the reader aware "of the difficulty of passing easy judgments." If you agree, present a situation from the novel that so affects the reader.

4. Do you agree with Kettle that "The narrators do not as a rule talk realistically . . ."? (page 141) How do you suppose Kettle decided what realistic speech is for such people as Lockwood and Nelly?

5. Compare what Kettle has to say about Lockwood's change of attitude with what is said by those who argue that he in no way changes in the novel.

6. Kettle divides the novel into four stages; other critics have suggested different divisions. Which of these best helps you to understand the novel? Do you think accepting one kind of division necessarily invalidates the others?

7. How does Kettle define the nature of the love between Catherine and Heathcliff? Does his definiton satisfy you? Contrast critical opinions on the nature of this love. Why do critics feel this definition to be central to an understanding and appreciation of the novel?

8. Would Kettle label *Wuthering Heights* a social-purpose novel (another term might be "novel of manners")? If so, why? If not, what would he label it? What labels do other critics put on *Wuthering Heights*? How would you label it?

[16] *The Common Reader* (Pelican ed.), p. 158.

9. What is the exact nature of the "betrayal" of which Kettle speaks on page 145? Is it the sort of betrayal in which a woman jilts her lover for another man? Is it something more than this—or something completely different from this? Had Heathcliff and Catherine been lovers before her betrothal to Edgar Linton? Had she promised to marry Heathcliff? What are her reasons for marrying Edgar?

10. Catherine's attitude toward her husband is not treated at length by many critics, yet it is of obvious importance. Beginning with the brief remarks of Kettle on this subject (page 146), gather material for a comprehensive report on it; note especially whether Catherine's attitude is stable or changing.

11. Kettle offers two alternatives (pages 147-148) for the deathbed scene of Catherine, claiming that either would destroy the pattern of the novel. Suggest ways in which each alternate scene would injure *Wuthering Heights*.

12. Kettle says that Heathcliff's revenge has a "moral force." (page 149) In what sense is this possible?

13. The role of Cathy and Hareton has been much debated by critics. How do Kettle's comments fit into the general critical commentary? What does he add to the debate?

14. On page 154 Kettle says, "Death is a matter of little importance in *Wuthering Heights*." But death is a prime mover in the book. How does Kettle get around or face that fact? Note other critical commentary on this problem.

15. In what ways and for what reasons do Kettle's statements about the role of nature in *Wuthering Heights* conflict with statements by other critics?

On *Wuthering Heights*

DOROTHY VAN GHENT

Emily Brontë's single novel is, of all English novels, the most treacherous for the analytical understanding to approach. It is treacherous not because of failure in its own formal controls on its meaning—for the book is highly wrought in form—but because it works at a level of experience that is unsympathetic to, or rather, simply irrelevant to the social and moral reason. One critic has spoken of the quality of feeling in this book as "a quality of suffering":

> It has anonymity. It is not complete. Perhaps some ballads represent it in English, but it seldom appears in the main stream, and few writers are in touch with it. It is a quality of experience the expression of which is at once an act of despair and an act of recognition or of worship. It is the recognition of an absolute hierarchy. This is also the feeling in Aeschylus. It is found amongst genuine peasants and is a great strength. Developing in places which yield only the permanent essentials of existence, it is undistracted and universal.[1]

We feel the lack of "completeness," which this critic refers to, in the nature of the dramatic figures that Emily Brontë uses: they are figures that arise on and enact their drama on some ground of the psychic life where ethical ideas are not at home, at least such ethical ideas as those that inform our ordinary experience of the manners of men. They have the "anonymity" of figures in dreams or in religious ritual. The attitude toward life that they suggest is rather one of awed contemplation of an unregenerate universe than a feeling for values or disvalues in types of human intercourse. It is an attitude that is expressed in some of the great

Reprinted from Dorothy Van Ghent's *The English Novel: Form and Function,* copyright 1953. By permission of Holt, Rinehart and Winston, Inc., publishers.

[1] G. D. Klingopulos, "The Novel as Dramatic Poem (II): 'Wuthering Heights,'" in *Scrutiny* XIV:4 (1946-1947).

Chinese paintings of the Middle Ages, where the fall of a torrent from an enormous /153/ height, or a single huge wave breaking under the moon, or a barely indicated chain of distant mountains lost among mists, seems to be animated by some mysterious, universal, half-divine life which can only be "recognized," not understood.

The strangeness that sets *Wuthering Heights* apart from other English novels does not lie alone in the attitude that it expresses and the level of experience that it defines, for something of the same quality of feeling exists, for instance, in Conrad's work. Its strangeness is the perfect simplicity with which it presents its elemental figures almost naked of the web of civilized habits, ways of thinking, forms of intercourse, that provides the familiar background of other fiction. Even Conrad's adventurers, no matter how far they may go into the "heart of darkness," carry with them enough threads of this web to orient them socially and morally. We can illustrate what we mean by this simplicity, this almost nakedness, if we compare Emily Brontë's handling of her materials with Richardson's handling of materials that, in some respects, are similar in kind. For example, the daemonic character of Heathcliff, associated as it is with the wildness of heath and moors, has a recognizable kinship with that of Lovelace, daemonic also, though associated with town life and sophisticated manners. Both are, essentially, an anthropomorphized primitive energy, concentrated in activity, terrible in effect. But Emily Brontë insists on Heathcliff's gypsy lack of origins, his lack of orientation and determination in the social world, his equivocal status on the edge of the human. When Mr. Earnshaw first brings the child home, the child is an "it," not a "he," and "dark almost as if it came from the devil"; and one of Nelly Dean's last reflections is, "Is he a ghoul or a vampire?" But Richardson's Lovelace has all sorts of social relationships and determinations, an ample family, economic orientation, college acquaintances, a position in a clique of young rakes; and Richardson is careful, through Lovelace's own pen, to offer various rationalizations of his behavior, each in some degree cogent. So with the whole multifold *Clarissa*-myth: on all sides it is supported for the understanding by historically familiar morality and manners. But *Wuthering Heights* is almost bare of such supports in social rationalization. Heathcliff might *really* be a demon. The passion of Catherine and Heathcliff is too simple and undeviating in its intensity, too uncomplex, for us to find in it any echo of practical social reality. To say that the motivation of this passion is "simple" is not to say that it is easy to de-

fine: much easier to define are the motivations that are some-
/154/ what complex and devious, for this is the familiar nature of
human motivations. We might associate perfectly "simple" motivations with animal nature or extrahuman nature, but by the same
token the quality of feeling involved would resist analysis.

But this nakedness from the web of familiar morality and manners is not quite complete. There is the framework formed by the
convention of narration (the "point of view"): we see the drama
through the eyes of Lockwood and Nelly Dean, who belong firmly
to the world of practical reality. Sifted through the idiom of their
commonplace vision, the drama taking place among the major characters finds contact with the temporal and the secular. Because
Lockwood and Nelly Dean have witnessed the incredible violence
of the life at the Heights, or rather, because Nelly Dean has witnessed the full span and capacity of that violence and because Lockwood credits her witness, the drama is oriented in the context of
the psychologically familiar. There is also another technical bulwark that supports this uneasy tale in the social and moral imagination, and that is its extension over the lives of two generations and
into a time of ameliorated and respectable manners. At the end, we
see young Cathy teaching Hareton his letters and correcting his
boorishness (which, after all, is only the natural boorishness consequent on neglect, and has none of the cannibal unregeneracy of
Heathcliff in it); the prospect is one of decent, socially responsible
domesticity. For this part of the tale, Lockwood alone is sufficient
witness; and the fact that now Nelly Dean's experienced old eyes
and memory can be dispensed with assures us of the present reason-
ableness and objectivity of events, and even infects retrospection on
what has happened earlier—making it possible for the dream-reject-
ing reason to settle complacently for the "naturalness" of the entire
story. If ghosts have been mentioned, if the country people swear
that Heathcliff "walks," we can, with Lockwood at the end, affirm
our skepticism as to "how anyone could ever imagine unquiet slumbers for the sleepers in that quiet earth."

Let us try to diagram these technical aspects of the work, for the
compositional soundness of *Wuthering Heights* is owing to them.
We may divide the action of the book into two parts, following each
other chronologically, the one associated with the earlier generation (Hindley and Catherine and Heathcliff, Edgar and Isabella Linton), the other with the later generation (young Cathy and Linton
and Hareton). The first of these actions is centered in what we
shall call a "mythological romance" /155/ —for the astonishingly

ravenous and possessive, perfectly amoral love of Catherine and
Heathcliff belongs to that realm of the imagination where myths
are created. The second action, centered in the protracted effects of
Heathcliff's revenge, involves two sets of young lives and two small
"romances": the childish romance of Cathy and Linton, which
Heathcliff manages to pervert utterly; and the successful assertion
of a healthy, culturally viable kind of love between Cathy and Hareton, asserted as Heathcliff's cruel energies flag and decay. Binding
the two "actions" is the perduring figure of Heathcliff himself,
demon-lover in the first, paternal ogre in the second. Binding them
also is the framing narrational convention or "point of view": the
voices of Nelly Dean and Lockwood are always in our ears; one or
the other of them is always present at a scene, or is the confidant
of someone who was present; through Lockwood we encounter
Heathcliff at the beginning of the book, and through his eyes we
look on Heathcliff's grave at the end. Still another pattern that
binds the two actions is the repetition of what we shall call the "two
children" figure—two children raised virtually as brother and
sister, in a vibrant relationship of charity and passion and real or
possible metamorphosis. The figure is repeated, with variation,
three times, in the relationships of the main characters. Of this we
shall speak again later. The technical continuities or patterning of
the book could, then, be simplified in this way:

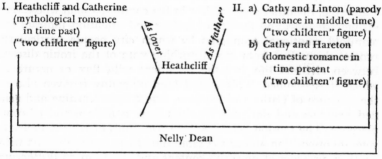

What, concretely, is the effect of this strict patterning and binding? What does it "mean"? The design of the book is drawn in the
spirit of intense compositional rigor, of *limitation;* the characters
act in the spirit of passionate immoderacy, of *excess.* Let us consider this contrast a little /156/ more closely. Essentially, *Wuthering
Heights* exists for the mind as a tension between two kinds of reality:

the raw, inhuman reality of anonymous natural energies, and the restrictive reality is given to the imagination in the violent figures of Catherine and Heathcliffe, portions of the flux of nature, children of rock and heath and tempest, striving to identify themselves as human, but disrupting all around them with their monstrous appetite for an inhuman kind of intercourse, and finally disintegrated from within by the very energies out of which they are made. It is this vision of a reality radically alien from the human that the ancient Chinese landscape paintings offer also. But in those ancient paintings there is often a tiny human figure, a figure that is obviously that of a philosopher, for instance, or that of a peasant—in other words, a human figure decisively belonging to and representing a culture—who is placed in diminutive perspective beside the enormously cascading torrent, or who is seen driving his water buffalo through the overwhelming mists or faceless snows; and this figure is outlined sharply, so that, though it is extremely tiny, it is very definite in the giant surrounding indefiniteness. The effect is one of contrast between finite and infinite, between the limitation of the known and human, and the unlimitedness of the unknown and the nonhuman. So also in *Wuthering Heights:* set over against the wilderness of inhuman reality is the quietly secular, voluntarily limited, safely human reality that we find in the gossipy concourse of Nelly Dean and Lockwood, the one an old family servant with a strong grip on the necessary emotional economies that make life endurable, the other a city visitor in the country, a man whose very disinterestedness and facility of feeling and attention indicate the manifold emotional economies by which city people particularly protect themselves from any disturbing note of the ironic discord between civilized life and the insentient wild flux of nature in which it is islanded. This second kind of reality is given also in the romance of Cathy and Hareton, where book learning and gentled manners and domestic charities form a little island of complacence. The tension between these two kinds of reality, their inveterate opposition and at the same time their *continuity* one with another, provides at once the content and the form of *Wuthering Heights.* We see the tension graphically in the diagram given above. The inhuman excess of Heathcliff's and Catherine's passion, an excess that is carried over into the sec- /157/ ond half of the book by Heathcliff's revenge, an excess everywhere present in language[2]—

[2] Mark Schorer examines this aspect of *Wuthering Heights* in his essay, "Fiction and the 'Analogical Matrix,'" in *Critiques and Essays on Modern Fiction* (New York: The Ronald Press Company, 1952).

in verbs and modifiers and metaphors that seethe with a brute fury—this excess is held within a most rigorous pattern of repeated motifs and of what someone has called the "Chinese box" of Nelly Dean's and Lockwood's interlocution. The form of the book, then—a form that may be expressed as a tension between the impulse to excess and the impulse to limitation or economy—*is* the content. The form, in short, is the book itself. Only in the fully wrought, fully realized, work of art does form so exhaust the possibilities of the material that it identifies itself with these possibilities.

If there has been any cogency in what we have said above, we should ask now how it is that the book is able to represent dramatically, in terms of human "character," its vision of the inhuman. After all, Catherine and Heathcliff *are* "characters," and not merely molecular vibrations in the primordial surge of things; indeed, they are so credibly characterized that Hollywood has been able to costume and cosmeticize them. As "characters," what are they? As lovers, what kind of love is theirs? They gnash and foam at each other. One could borrow for them a line from a poem by John Crowe Ransom describing lovers in hell: "Stuprate, they rend each other when they kiss." This is not "romantic love," as that term has popular meaning; and it is not even sexual love, naturalistically considered—the impulse to destruction is too pure in it, too simple and direct. Catherine says she *is* Heathcliff, and the implication is not of the possiblity of a "mating," for one does not "mate" with oneself. Similarly, after her death, when Heathcliff howls that he cannot live without his *life,* he cannot live without his *soul* (and Nellie says that he "howled, not like a man, but like a savage beast"), the relationship and the density suggested are not those of adult human lovers, because the complex attendant motivations of adult life are lacking. But the emotional implications of Catherine's and Heathcliff's passion are never "adult," in the sense of there being in that passion any recognition of the domestic and social responsibilities, and the spiritual complexities, of adult life. Whatever could happen to these two, if they could be happily together, would be something altogether asocial, amoral, savagely irresponsible, wildly impulsive: it would be the enthusiastic, experimental, quite random activity of child- /158/ hood, occult to the socialized adult. But since no conceivable *human* male and female, not brutish, not anthropologically rudimentary, could be together in this way as adults, all that we can really imagine for the grown-up Catherine and Heathcliff, as "characters" on the human plane, is what the book gives of them—their mutual destruction by tooth and nail in an effort, through death, to get back to the lost state of gypsy freedom in childhood.

Caught in the economical forms of adult life—concepts of social and intellectual "betterment" (such as lead Catherine to marry Edgar Linton), the frames of wealth and property ownership (which Heathcliff at first exploits in order to "raise" himself to Catherine's standard, and then as an engine of revenge against both the Earnshaws and the Lintons), marital relationships, and parenthood—they are, for the imagination, "humanized," endowed with "character," at least to the extent that we see their explosive confusions, resistances, and misery convulsing the forms usual to human adulthood. Their obsession, their prime passion, is also "human" although it is utterly destructive of the values signified by that word: the passion to lose the self in some "otherness," whether in complete identification with another person (an identification for which "mating" is a surrogate only of a temporary and lapsing kind), or by absorption into "nature"—but it is a passion that is tabooed for the socialized adult, disguised, held in check by the complex cultural economies, safely stabled in the unconscious, at best put to work in that darkness to turn the mill of other objectives. This regressive passion is seen in uncompromised purity in Catherine and Heathcliff, and it opens the prospect of disintegration—disintegration into the unconsciousness of childhood and the molecular fluidity of death—in a word, into anonymous natural energy.

If the story of Catherine and Heathcliff had not been a story told by an old woman as something that had had its inception many years ago, if the old woman who tells the story had not been limited in imagination and provincial in her sympathies, if the story had been dramatized immediately in the here-and-now and not at a temporal remove and through a dispassioned intermediator, it is doubtful that it would resonate emotionally for us or carry any conviction—even any "meaning." Because of the very fact that the impulses it represents are taboo, they can conveniently be observed only at a remove, as someone else's, as of the past, and from the judicial point of view of conventional manners. The /159/ "someone else's" and the "long ago" are the mind's saving convention for making a distance with itself such as will allow it perspective. Thus the technical *displacement* of Heathcliff's and Catherine's story into past time and into the memory of an old woman functions in the same way as dream displacements: it both censors and indulges, protects and liberates.

Significantly, our first real contact with the Catherine-Heathcliff drama is established through a dream—Lockwood's dream of the ghost-child at the window. Lockwood is motivated to dream the dream by the most easily convincing circumstances; he has fallen asleep while reading Catherine's diary, and during his sleep a tempest-blown branch is scratching on the windowpane. But why should Lockwood, the well-mannered urbanite, dream *this?*

I pulled its wrist on to the broken pane, and rubbed it to and fro till the blood ran down and soaked the bedclothes . . .

The image is probably the most cruel one in the book. Hareton's hanging puppies, Heathcliff's hanging the springer spaniel, Hindley's forcing a knife between Nelly's teeth or throwing his baby over the staircase, Catherine's leaving the blue print of her nails on Isabella's arm, Heathcliff stamping on Hindley's face—these images and others like them imply savagery or revengefulness or drunkenness or hysteria, but always a motivating set of emotional circumstances. But this is the punctilious Lockwood—whose antecedents and psychology are so insipid that we care little about them—who scrapes the dream-waif's wrist back and forth on broken glass till the blood runs down and soaks the bedclothes. The cruelty of the dream is the gratuitousness of the violence wrought on a child by an emotionally unmotivated vacationer from the city, dreaming in a strange bed. The bed is an old-fashioned closet bed ("a large oak case . . . it formed a little closet" with a window set in it): its paneled sides Lockwood has "pulled together" before going to sleep. The bed is like a coffin (at the end of the book, Heathcliff dies in it, behind its closed panels); it had been Catherine's bed, and the movable panels themselves suggest the coffin in which she is laid, whose "panels" Heathcliff bribes the sexton to remove at one side. Psychologically, Lockwood's dream has only the most perfunctory determinations, and nothing at all of result for the dreamer himself, except to put him uncomfortably out of bed. /160/ But poetically the dream has its reasons, compacted into the image of the daemonic child scratching at the pane, trying to get from the "outside" "in," and of the dreamer in a bed like a coffin, released by that deathly privacy to indiscriminate violence. The coffin-like bed shuts off any interference with the wild deterioration of the psyche. Had the dream used any other agent than the effete, almost epicene Lockwood, it would have lost this symbolic force; for Lockwood, more successfully than anyone else in the book, has shut out the powers of darkness (the pun in his name is obvious in this context); and his lack of any dramatically thorough motivation for dreaming the cruel dream suggests those powers as existing autonomously, not only in the "outsideness" of external nature, beyond the physical windowpane, but also within, even in the soul least prone to passionate excursion.

The windowpane is the medium, treacherously transparent, separating the "inside" from the "outside," the "human" from the alien and terrible "other." Immediately after the incident of the dream, the time of the narrative is displaced into the childhood of Heathcliff and Catherine, and we see the two children looking through the window of the Lintons' drawing room.

"Both of us were able to look in by standing on the basement, and clinging to the ledge, and we saw—ah! it was beautiful—a splendid place carpeted with crimson, and crimson-covered chairs and tables, and a pure white ceiling bordered by gold, a shower of glass-drops hanging in silver chains from the centre, and shimmering with little soft tapers. Old Mr. and Mrs. Linton were not there; Edgar and his sister had it entirely to themselves. Shouldn't they have been happy? We should have thought ourselves in heaven!"

Here the two unregenerate waifs look *in* from the night on the heavenly vision of the refinements and securities of the most privileged human estate. But Heathcliff rejects the vision: seeing the Linton children blubbering and bored there (*they* cannot get *out!*), he senses the menace of its limitations; while Catherine is fatally tempted. She is taken in by the Lintons, and now it is Heathcliff alone outside looking through the window.

"The curtains were still looped up at one corner, and I resumed my station as a spy; because, if Catherine had wished to return, I intended / 161 / shattering their great glass panes to a million of fragments, unless they let her out. She sat on the sofa quietly . . . the woman-servant brought a basin of warm water, and washed her feet; and Mr. Linton mixed a tumbler of negus, and Isabella emptied a plateful of cakes into her lap . . . Afterwards, they dried and combed her beautiful hair . . ."

Thus the first snare is laid by which Catherine will be held for a human destiny—her feet washed, cakes and wine for her delectation, her beautiful hair combed (the motifs here are limpid as those of fairy tale, where the changeling in the "otherworld" is held there mysteriously by bathing and by the strange new food he has been given to eat). By her marriage to Edgar Linton, Catherine yields to that destiny; later she resists it tormentedly and finds her way out of it by death. Literally she "catches her death" by throwing open the window.

> "Open the window again wide: fasten it open! Quick, why don't you move?" [she says to Nelly].
> "Because I won't give you your death of cold," I answered.
> "You won't give me a chance of life, you mean," she said . . .

In her delirium, she opens the window, leans out into the winter wind, and calls across the moors to Heathcliff,

> "Heathcliff, if I dare you now, will you venture? . . . Find a way, then!
> . . . You are slow! . . . you always followed me!"

On the night after her burial, unable to follow her (though he digs up her grave in order to lie beside her in the coffin from which the side panels have been removed), he returns to the Heights *through the window*—for Hindley has barred the door—to wreak on the living the fury of his frustration. It is years later that Lockwood arrives at the Heights and spends his uncomfortable night there. Lockwood's outcry in his dream brings Heathcliff *to the window,* Heathcliff who has been caught ineluctably in the human to grapple with its interdictions long after Catherine has broken through them. The treachery of the window is that Catherine, lost now in the "other," can look through the transparent membrane that separates her from humanity, can scratch on the pane, but cannot get "in," while Heathcliff, though he forces the window open and howls into the night, cannot get "out." When he dies, Nelly Dean discovers the window swinging open, the window of that old fashioned coffin-like /162/ bed where Lockwood had had the dream. Rain has been pouring in during the night, drenching the dead man. Nelly says,

I hasped the window; I combed his black long hair from his forehead; I tried to close his eyes: to extinguish, if possible, that frightful, life-like gaze of exultation before any one else beheld it. They would not shut; they seemed to sneer at my attempts . . .

Earlier, Heathcliff's eyes have been spoken of as "the clouded windows of hell" from which a "fiend" looks out. All the other uses of the "window" that we have spoken of here are not figurative but perfectly naturalistic uses, though their symbolic value is inescapable. But the fact that Heathcliff's eyes refuse to close in death suggests the symbol in a metaphorical form (the "fiend" has now got "out," leaving the window open), elucidating with simplicity the meaning of the "window" as a separation between the daemonic

depths of the soul and the limited and limiting lucidities of consciousness, a separation between the soul's "otherness" and its hu-
manness.

There is still the difficulty of defining, with any precision, the
quality of the daemonic that is realized most vividly in the conception of Heathcliff, a difficulty that is mainly due to our tendency
always to give the "daemonic" some ethical status—that is, to relate
it to an ethical hierarchy. Heathcliff's is an archetypal figure, un-
traceably ancient in mythological thought—an imaged recognition
of that part of nature which is "other" than the human soul (the
world of the elements and the animals) and of that part of the soul
itself which is "other" than the conscious part. But since Martin Luther's revival of this archetype for modern mythology, it
has tended to forget its relationship with the elemental "otherness"
of the outer world and to identify itself solely with the dark functions of the soul. As an image of soul work, it is ethically relevant,
since everything that the soul does—even unconsciously, even
"ignorantly" (as in the case of Oedipus)—offers itself for ethical
judgment, whereas the elements and the animals do not. Puritanism
perpetuated the figure for the imagination; Milton gave it its greatest aesthetic splendor, in the fallen angel through whom the divine
beauty still shone; Richardson introduced it, in the person of
Lovelace, to an infatuated middle class; and always the figure was
ethically relevant through the conception of "sin" and "guilt." (Let
us note here, however, the ambivalence of the figure, an ambivalence that the medieval devil does not have. The medieval devil is
/163/ a really ugly customer, so ugly that he can even become a
comedy figure—as in the medieval moralities. The daemonic archetype of which we are speaking here is deeply serious in quality because of his ambivalence: he is a fertilizing energy and profoundly
attractive, and at the same time horribly destructive to civilized
institutionalism. It is because of his ambivalence that, though he
is the "enemy," ethically speaking, he so easily takes on the stature and beauty of a hero, as he does in the Satan of *Paradise Lost*.)
In Byron's *Manfred*, the archetype underwent a rather confusing
sea-change, for Manfred's crime is, presumably, so frightful that it
cannot be mentioned, and the indefinable nature of the crime
blurs the edges of the figure and cuts down its resonance in the
imagination (when we guess that the crime might be incest, we are
disposed to find this a rather paltry equation for the Byronic incan-
tation of guilt); nevertheless, the ethical relevancy of the figure
remains. Let us follow it a little further, before returning to Emily

Brontë's Heathcliff. In the later nineteenth century, in the novels of Dostoevski, it reappears with an enormous development of psychological subtlety, and also with a great strengthening and clarification of its ethical significance. In the work of André Gide, it undergoes another sea-change: the archetypal daemonic figure now becomes the principle of progress, the spirit of free investigation and creative experience; with this reorientation, it becomes positively ethical rather than negatively so. In Thomas Mann's *Doctor Faustus*, it reverts to its earlier and more constant significance, as the type of the instinctive part of the soul, a great and fertilizing power, but ethically unregenerate and therefore a great danger to ethical man.

Our interest in sketching some phases of the history of this archetype has been to show that it has had, in modern mythology, constantly a status in relation to ethical thought. The exception is Heathcliff. Heathcliff is no more ethically relevant than is flood or earthquake or whirlwind. It is as impossible to speak of him in terms of "sin" and "guilt" as it is to speak in this way of the natural elements or the creatures of the animal world. In him, the type reverts to a more ancient mythology and to an earlier symbolism. *Wuthering Heights* so baffles and confounds the ethical sense because it is not informed with that sense at all: it is profoundly informed with the attitudes of "animism," by which the natural world—that world which is "other" than and "outside of" the consciously individualized human—*appears* to act with an energy similar to the energies of the soul; to be permeated with soul energy but of a mysterious /164/ and alien kind that the conscious human soul, bent on securing itself through civilization, cannot identify itself with as to purpose; an energy that can be propitiated, that can at times be canalized into humanly purposeful channels, that *must* be given religious recognition both for its enormous fertility and its enormous potential destructiveness. But Heathcliff does have human shape and human relationships; he is, so to speak, "caught in" the human; two kinds of reality intersect in him—as they do, with a somewhat different balance, in Catherine; as they do, indeed, in the other characters. Each entertains, in some degree, the powers of darkness—from Hindley, with his passion for self-destruction (he, too, wants to get "out"), to Nelly Dean, who in a sense "propitiates" those powers with the casuistry of her actions, and even to Lockwood, with his sadistic dream. Even in the weakest of these souls there is an intimation of the dark Otherness, by which the soul is related psychologically to the inhuman world of pure energy, for it carries within itself an "other-ness" of its own, that inhabits below consciousness.

The imagery of the windowpane is metamorphic, suggesting a total change of mode of being by the breaking-through of a separating medium that exists between consciousness and the "other." The strangest and boldest and most radiant figuration that Emily Brontë has given to her subject is the "two children" figure, also a metamorphic figure of break-through and transformation. The *type* or classic form of this figure is a girl with golden hair and a boy with dark hair and shadowed brow, bound in kinship and in a relationship of charity and passion, and with a metamorphosis of some kind potential in the relationship. The beautiful dark boy will be brightened, made angelic and happy, by the beautiful golden girl: this, apparently, is what *should* happen. But the dynamics of the change are not perfectly trustworthy. In one of Emily Brontë's poems, describing a child who might be the child Heath-cliff, the ambivalent dark boy will evidently sink further into his darkness.

> *I love thee, boy; for all divine,*
> *All full of God thy features shine.*
> *Darling enthusiast, holy child,*
> *Too good for this world's warring wild,*
> *Too heavenly now but doomed to be*
> *Hell-like in heart and misery.*[3] /165/

In the 1850 printing of the Brontë poems (the printing supervised by the Brontë sisters) two companion pieces appear under the title "The Two Children," in the first of which the dark boy is still un-changed.

> *Frowning on the infant,*
> *Shadowing childhood's joy,*
> *Guardian angel knows not*
> *That melancholy boy . . .*[4]

In the second of these companion pieces, the golden child is evoked, and now the change in the dark one is promised.

> *Child of Delight! with sunbright hair,*
> *And seablue, seadeep eyes;*
> *Spirit of Bliss, what brings thee here,*
> *Beneath these sullen skies?*

[3] *The Complete Poems of Emily Jane Brontë,* edited by C. W. Hatfield (New York: Columbia University Press, 1941), p. 121.

[4] *Ibid.,* p. 229.

> *Thou shouldest live in eternal spring,*
> *Where endless day is never dim;*
> *Why, Seraph, has thy erring wing*
> *Borne thee down to weep with him?*

She answers that she is "not from heaven descended," but that she has seen and pitied "that mournful boy."

> *And I swore to take his gloomy sadness,*
> *And give to him my beamy joy . . .*[5]

Here, with the change of the dark child, the golden child will be changed also, for she will take his "gloomy sadness." In another set of verses, the light-dark contrast is turned around bewilderingly.

> *And only he had locks of light,*
> *And she had raven hair;*
> *While now, his curls are dark as night,*
> *And hers as morning fair.*[6]

What really seems to be implied by all these shifts is not a mere exchange of characteristics but a radical identification of the two children, so that each can appear in the mode of the other, the bright one in the mode of darkness and the dark one in the mode of light. /166/

In still another of those poems that dramatize affairs in the kingdom of Gondal that occupied Emily Brontë's youthful fantasy, a brooding phantom figure haunts the moonlit grounds of a castle. Its face is "divinely fair," but on its "angel brow"

> *Rests such a shade of deep despair*
> *As nought divine could ever know.*

Apparently the cause of his death was adoration of another man's wife ("Lord Alfred's idol queen"), and it is for this reason that his spirit is "shut from heaven—an outcast for eternity." The woman for whom he died is represented as an "infant fair," looking from a golden frame in a portrait gallery.

> *And just like his its ringlets bright,*
> *Its large dark eye of shadowy light,*
> *Its cheeks' pure hue, its forehead white,*
> *And like its noble name.*

A deliberate confusion of the planes of reality—a shifting into the life inside the picture frame (like the shifts "through the window"

[5] *Ibid.,* p. 230.
[6] *Ibid.,* p. 174.

in *Wuthering Heights*), and with it a shifting from despairing adulthood into childhood—is suggested with the following questions:

> And did he never smile to see
> Himself restored to infancy?
>
> Never part back that golden flow
> Of curls, and kiss that pearly brow,
> And feel no other earthly bliss
> Was equal to that parent's kiss?[7]

The suggestions are those of metamorphic changes, but all under the aspect of frustration: the despairing lover cannot get through the picture frame where the child is. Other motifs here are reminiscent of those of *Wuthering Heights*. The spectral lover is an ambivalent figure, of divine beauty, but an outcast from heaven. Kinship is suggested between him and the child in the picture ("And just like his its ringlets bright . . . And like its noble name"), and one is left to imagine that "Lord Alfred's idol queen" was his sister, wherefore the frustration of their love. The last stanza quoted above remarks ambiguously on the parental feeling /167/ involved in the relationship: is it not the infant who is the "parent" here? Parental charity is the feeling of the golden "guardian angel" for her dark charge in "The Two Children" poems, as it is, in a degree, of Catherine for Heathcliff during their childhood, and of young Cathy first for Linton and then for Hareton. The fact that, in the poem, both the infant and the spectral lover have golden hair seems, in this elusive fantasy, to be a mark of perversion of the metamorphic sequence, at least of its having gone awry (as in the case, too, of young Cathy and Linton, who is not dark but fair).

In the relationship of Catherine and Heathcliff, the fantasy has its typical form. She is golden, he is dark. His daemonic origin is always kept open, by reiterations of the likelihood that he is really a ghoul, a fiend, an offspring of hell, and not merely so in behavior. And Catherine also, like the guardian child in "The Two Children" poems, is "not from heaven descended": she has furious tantrums, she lies, she bites, her chosen toy is a whip. They are raised as brother and sister; there are three references to their sleeping in the same bed as infants. She scolds and orders and mothers and cherishes him ("much too fond of him" as a child, Nelly says). The

[7] *Ibid.*, pp. 177-178.

notions of somatic change and discovery of noble birth, as in fairy tale, are deliberately played with; as, when Catherine returns from her first sojourn at the Lintons' and Heathcliff asks Nelly to "make him decent," he says, comparing himself with Edgar,

"I wish I had light hair and a fair skin, and was dressed and behaved as well, and had a chance of being as rich as he will be!"

and Nelly answers,

"You're fit for a prince in disguise . . . Were I in your place, I would frame high notions of my birth . . ."

(If Heathcliff is really of daemonic origin, he is, in a sense, indeed of "high birth," a "prince in disguise," and might be expected, like the princess of fairy tale, to drop his "disguise" at the crisis of the tale and be revealed in original splendor: the dynamics of the "two children" figure also points to that potential transformation.) Some alluring and astonishing destiny seems possible for the two. *What* that phenomenon might be or mean, we cannot know, for it is frustrated by Catherine's marriage to Edgar, which dooms Heathcliff to be "hell-like in heart and misery." /168/ Catherine's decision dooms her also, for she is of the same daemonic substance as Heathcliff, and a civilized marriage and domesticity are not sympathetic to the daemonic quality.

With the second generation, the "two children" figure is distorted and parodied in the relationship of Catherine's daughter and Heathcliff's son. Young Cathy, another "child of delight, with sun-bright hair," has still some of the original daemonic energy, but her "erring wing" has brought her down to "weep with" a *pale-haired* and pallid little boy whose only talents are for sucking sugar candy and torturing cats. She does her best, as infant mother, to metamorphose him, but he is an ungrateful and impossible subject. Her passionate charity finally finds her "married" to his corpse in a locked bedroom. With Cathy and Hareton Earnshaw, her cousin on her mother's side, the "two children" are again in their right relationship of golden and dark, and now the pathos of the dark child cures the daemon out of the golden one, and the maternal care of the golden child raises the dark one to civilized humanity and makes of him a proper husband.

In these several pairs, the relation of kinship has various resonances. Between Catherine and Heathcliff, identity of "kind" is greatest, although they are foster brother and sister only. The foster kinship provides an imaginative implicit reason for the unnaturalness and impossibility of their mating. Impassioned by their brother-and-sisterlike identity of kind, they can only destroy each other, for it is impossible for two persons to *be* each other (as Catherine says she "is" Heathcliff) without destruction of the physical limitations that individualize and separate. In Emily Brontë's use of the symbolism of the incest motive, the incestual impulse appears as an attempt to make what is "outside" oneself identical with what is "inside" oneself—a performance that can be construed in physical and human terms only by violent destruction of personality bounds, by rending of flesh and at last by death.

With Catherine's daughter and young Linton, who are cousins, the implicit incestuousness of the "two children" figure is suggested morbidly by Linton's disease and by his finally becoming a husband only as a corpse. With Cathy and Hareton Earnshaw, also cousins, Victorian "ameliorism" finds a way to sanction the relationship by symbolic emasculation; Cathy literally teaches the devil out of Hareton, and "esteem" between the two takes the place of the old passion for identification. With this successful metamorphosis and mating, the daemonic quality /169/ has been completely suppressed, and, though humanity and civilization have been secured for the "two children," one feels that some magnificent bounty is now irrecoverable. The great magic, the wild power, of the original two has been lost.

We are led to speculate on what the bounty might have been,* had the windowpane not stood between the original pair, had the golden child and the dark child not been secularized by a spelling book. Perhaps, had the ideal and impossible eventuality taken place, had the "inside" and the "outside," the bright child and the dark one, become identified in such a way that they could freely assume each other's modes, then perhaps the world of the animals and the elements—the world of wild moor and barren rock, of fierce wind and attacking beast, that is the strongest palpability in *Wuthering Heights*—would have offered itself completely to human understanding and creative intercourse. Perhaps the dark powers that exist within the soul, as well as in the outer elemental world, would have assumed the language of consciousness, or consciousness would have bravely entered into companionship with those dark powers and transliterated their language into its own. Emily

* A stimulating and enlightening interpretation of the book is to be found in Richard Chase's "The Brontës, or, Myth Domesticated," in *Forms of Modern Fiction*, edited by William Van O'Connor (Minneapolis: University of Minnesota Press, 1948). [First published in the *Kenyon Review*, IX (Autumn, 1947), 487-506.]

Brontë's book has been said to be nonphilosophical— as it is certainly nonethical; but all philosophy is not ethics, and the book seizes, at the point where the soul feels itself cleft within and in cleavage from the universe, the first germs of philosophic thought, the thought of the duality of human and nonhuman existence, and the thought of the cognate duality of the psyche. /170/

Questions for Discussion and Writing

1. Explain what Mrs. Van Ghent means when she says ". . . the book is highly wrought in form . . ." (page 153) Do you agree? Do other critics?

2. Ethical ideas are "not at home" in *Wuthering Heights,* says Mrs. Van Ghent. (page 153) What does this mean? What other critical comments can you find to support or refute this statement?

3. Define more fully the "web of civilized habits" (page 154) which Mrs. Van Ghent says are missing from the novel. Taking a scene from *Wuthering Heights,* indicate some of the "ways of thinking, forms of intercourse," and social habits that might have been included; then decide whether adding such material would help or hurt the scene.

4. "Heathcliff might *really* be a demon." (page 154) Evaluate this comment on the character.

5. With added examples from the novel, explain in detail what Mrs. Van Ghent means by the "inhuman excess of Heathcliff's and Catherine's passion." (page 157) Develop this explanation into a full discussion of "inhuman excess" in *Wuthering Heights* by examining other criticism of the novel.

6. Disagree with Mrs. Van Ghent's statement that "The form [of *Wuthering Heights*] . . . is the book itself" (page 158), or write a paper which gives added support to her statement.

7. Evidently Mrs. Van Ghent considers *Wuthering Heights* dramatic. Make a case for *Wuthering Heights* as a dramatic novel.

8. With the use of Mrs. Van Ghent's essay and other criticism of *Wuthering Heights* discuss the theme of destruction in the novel.

9. Mrs. Van Ghent joins several other critics in speaking of the child-like quality of the relationship between Heathcliff and Catherine. Explicate this idea as completely as you can, and demonstrate it by reference to the novel.

10. Commentators on the novel make a great deal of Lockwood's dream of the ghost-child at the window. How important does Mrs. Van Ghent think this scene is? Why? Compare and contrast her interpretation of it to those of other critics.

11. Put into your own words the idea that Mrs. Van Ghent has about the use of windows (pages 161-163). See if you can find any further instances of this use, and discuss its validity as a comment on the method of the novel.

12. Explain as thoroughly as you can what the irrecoverable "magnificent bounty" (page 170) is that Mrs. Van Ghent feels has been lost by the end of *Wuthering Heights*. You may wish to compare, in some detail, the characters of Heathcliff and Catherine, and Hareton and the younger Catherine, in your explication. Use comments of other critics if you wish, but try to work predominantly within the novel.

13. If Mrs. Van Ghent were to write an essay called *"Wuthering Heights: a Novel of Contrasts,"* what points do you suppose she would make? Write a documented essay with this title yourself.

Nelly Dean and the Power of *Wuthering Heights*

JOHN K. MATHISON

The memorable quality of *Wuthering Heights,* its power, has often been mentioned; numerous elements of the work have been considered the source of this power. No one element can be expected to account completely for it, and no combination of causes is likely to produce an answer that is fully satisfying. But examinations of the various elements in the structure of the novel have suggested clear connections between method and results, between technique and meaning.

In this essay I am attempting a partial explanation of the power of the book through a detailed examination not of the general question of the use of a narrator but specifically of the fully developed character of Nelly Dean. Nelly Dean is not a mere technical device: we cannot forget as the story progresses that we are /106/ hearing it from her rather than from the author. She is a minute interpreter. She tells us what events mean, what is right or wrong, what is praiseworthy or despicable or unforgivable behavior. Her morality is a result of her training, experiences, and reading, combined with her native temperament. The reader's degree of acceptance of her explanations and moral judgments determines his understanding of the meaning of the story and its power over him.

Nelly is an admirable woman whose point of view, I believe, the reader must reject. She is good-natured, warmhearted, wholesome, practical, and physically healthy. Her interpretation of her reading and her experiences, her feelings on various occasions, are, to a large extent, the consequence of her physical health. When the reader refuses to accept her view of things, which he continually does and must do, he is forced to feel the inadequacy of the normal, healthy, hearty, good-natured person's understanding of life and human nature. He is consquently forced into an active participation in the book. He cannot sit back and accept what is given him as the explanation of the actions of the characters. He must continually provide his own version.

For the reader to disagree with Nelly would be easy, if Nelly were not admirable. But to prevent the reader's turning Nelly into a cliché of simple and narrow piety, Emily Brontë has provided /107/ Joseph. He makes clear through his actions and his explicit statements to Nelly that she is not conventionally or rigidly pious. Her condemnations and approvals do not result from an unintelligent or fanatical acceptance of rigid rules of conduct. Joseph is sure she is destined for hell because of her warmth and human kindness, and because of her enjoyment of such pleasures as folk song and dancing. Joseph's strictures intensify the reader's favorable impressions of Nelly, the favorable impressions that make his rejection of her views more intense and significant.

And enough other servants are introduced to increase still further our realization of Nelly's superiority, intellectual and moral. Her pipe-smoking successor at the Grange[1] is apparently what might be expected of a servant. One need not more than mention Zillah, who has some mental alertness, to be made strongly aware of Nelly's superiority.

But more strongly than her superiority is shown by contrast with Joseph, with Zillah, or with the servant Lockwood finds at the Grange on his return, it is shown by the affection of the major characters, including Heathcliff, for her, as seen not in their words but in their behavior to her. And of course there is her narrative, full as it is of her ideas. In spite of all her fine qualities, nevertheless, she fails to understand the other characters and, more important, fails in her behavior in important crises of the action. From the emphasis on her admirable qualities, and from her final inadequacy, the reader is led to see that the insight of the normal, wholesome person cannot penetrate into all feelings justly: the reader becomes the active advocate of the extremes of passion of Cathy and Heathcliff, troublesome as they are to a peaceful, domestic routine.

Emily Brontë could not have succeeded in a direct attempt to de-

---

[1] *Wuthering Heights*, p. 324. This page reference and all subsequent ones are to the Rinehart Edition with an Introduction by Mark Schorer.

mand our sympathy for or understanding of two such characters as Heathcliff and Cathy. Approached directly, the reader would not have to exercise his own perceptions; he would remain /108/ passive. Some readers might say that such violent behavior is exciting enough to read about in romantic novels, but that in real life it would not do to encourage such people as Cathy and Heathcliff. To other readers, the novel might have appeared merely as a tremendous protest against conventional standards, but the interest in it would be merely biographical, sociological, or psychological.

By indirection, Emily Brontë has produced not a personal protest but a work of art. The reader's reaction is not, of course, the precise opposite of any of those mentioned above, not a simple stamp of approval bestowed on Heathcliff and Cathy, but a realization that the "normal" person is often incapable of feeling for the tortured, emotionally distraught person, and that the latter's tortured failure to understand himself and the sources of his misery partly results from the failure of imagination of the majority. The question is not whether Heathcliff and Cathy are good or bad. They are the result of psychological isolation and misunderstanding working on a particular native temperament, and the "good" are as much the doers of the damage as the "bad," either Hindley or Joseph.

The better we come to know Nelly, the more we recognize her lack of understanding of the principals. To know her we need to watch her character as it is revealed through her opinions, and, even more, through her reports of her own actions. It is this person, whom we come to know well, whose judgments we finally interpret. Not abstract judgments of a merely nominal narrator, they are the particular limited judgments of a person of a distinct emotional and intellectual viewpoint. Knowing the judge, or interpreter, knowing the giver of advice as well as the advice given, we realize the inadequacy of the interpretation, the advice, and the judgments; we become as we read active interpreters, protesters, explicators, and possibly judges.

II

Nelly's physical vigor is emphatically part of her character. Impressing us generally from her account of her actions throughout the novel, her abundant good health is specifically alluded to as /109/ well. Her one illness, a bad cold after she had been obliged to sit for a long while in "soaked shoes and stockings," was a great surprise to her; up to the time of the narrative it is the only indisposition in her life that she can recall. By this accident, which most would accept as in the course of things, her spirits were depressed: "it is wearisome, to a stirring active body—but few have slighter reasons for complaint than I had" (p. 257). Elsewhere, responding to the terrors of Cathy, who fears that everyone she knows may die and leave her alone, Nelly confidently boasts: ". . . I am strong, and hardly forty-five. My mother lived till eighty, a canty dame to the last" (p. 244). Numerous examples of illness, decline, wasting away, and death in her experience make little impression on her, who feels herself so strong. Although she once remarks "I am stout, and soon put out of breath" (p. 286), this reference confirms rather than contradicts her feeling of "ruddy" health; the picture is that of the Shepherd's wife in *The Winter's Tale:*

> when my old wife liv'd, upon
> This day she was both pantler, butler, cook;
> Both dame and servant; welcom'd all, serv'd all,
> Would sing her song and dance her turn; now here,
> At upper end o' the table, now i' the middle;
> On his shoulder, and his; her face o' fire
> With labour and the thing she took to quench it . . .
>
> (IV, iii, 55-61)

Her own health makes her a poor sympathizer with the illnesses of others; she tends to view even those illnesses in the novel which end in death as partly willful, partly acting. The physique and the temperament which goes with it of the weak or sick she cannot really believe in. An early example is her view of Hindley's consumptive wife; throughout the book further examples abound, to the last case of the frail son of Isabella whom she finds revolting largely because he will not exert himself and be vigorous. But to resume, of Hindley's wife, who had expressed fear of dying, she says: /110/

I imagined her as little likely to die as myself. She was rather thin, but young, and fresh complexioned, and her eyes sparkled as bright as diamonds. I did remark, to be sure, that mounting the stairs made her breathe very quick, that the least sudden noise set her all in a quiver, and that she coughed troublesomely sometimes: but, I knew nothing of what these symptoms portended, and had no impulse to sympathize with her. We don't in general take to foreigners here, Mr. Lockwood, unless they take to us first (pp. 46-47).

Since Nelly regards the idea of her own death as absurd, she sees no reason that Hindley's wife should be entitled to a fear of death. Such nonsense is just what one expects of foreigners (from a

different county of England). This passage, very early in the
novel, makes the reader aware of Nelly's fallibility of judgment
combined with her satisfaction wtih her own attitudes. It conditions our expectations regarding her probable actions in later
episodes, and helps us know her and hence discount her judgments
and substitute our own. These early suspicions are confirmed when
Cathy becomes ill:

> . . . Mr. Kenneth, as soon as he saw her, pronounced her dangerously ill;
> she had a fever.
> He bled her, and he told me to let her live on whey, and water gruel;
> and take care she did not throw herself down stairs, or out of the window;
> and then he left. . . .
> Though I cannot say I made a gentle nurse, and Joseph and the master
> were no better; and though our patient was as wearisome and headstrong
> as a patient could be, she weathered it through (p. 92).

Why should Cathy have chosen to come down with a fever, become
dangerously delirious, and consequently be "wearisome" to healthy,
reasonable people?

If we knew less of Nelly we might be able to sympathize with
her jogging of Lockwood during his illness: " 'You shouldn't lie till
ten. There's the very prime of the morning gone long before that
time. A person who has not done one half his day's work by ten
o'clock, runs a chance of leaving the other half undone' " (p. 64).
As it is, however, we know her advice is little more than justification of her own natural urges to be "busy and stirring" /111/ always; it is her failure to grasp the possibility of people's being
less vigorous than herself.

Most serious is her deficiency in Cathy's later illness and delirium, foreshadowed by the illness already mentioned. Inevitably,
she views it as an act:

> "Catherine ill?" he [Edgar Linton] said, hastening to us. "Shut the
> window, Ellen! Catherine, why . . ."
> He was silent; the haggardness of Mrs. Linton's appearance smote him
> speechless, and he could only glance from her to me in horrified astonish-
> ment.
> "She's been fretting here," I continued, "and eating scarcely anything,
> and never complaining, she would admit none of us till this evening, and
> so we couldn't inform you of her state, as we were not aware of it our-
> shelves, *but it is nothing*" [italics mine] (pp. 134-135).

One might suppose Ellen's "it is nothing" were a well-meant if
unsuccessful effort to cheer Edgar, if the scene ended at this point,

and if we had not begun to know Nelly rather well, but as it continues, it becomes clear that she really considers the illness both willful and minor:

"Her mind wanders, sir," I interposed. "She has been talking nonsense the whole evening; but let her have quiet and proper attendance, and she'll rally. Hereafter, we must be cautious how we vex her."

"I desire no further advice from you," answered Mr. Linton. "You knew your mistress's nature, and you encouraged me to harass her. And not to give me one hint of how she has been these three days! It was heartless! Months of sickness could not cause such a change!"

I began to defend myself, thinking it too bad to be blamed for another's wicked waywardness! (pp. 135-136).

As Edgar Linton says, Nelly had had a lifetime of experience with Cathy, but the last quoted sentence alone makes clear the triumph of constitution and temperament over experience. Nelly never will grasp the less wholesome, physically or emotionally.

It may need to be said that objectively it would be possible for the reader to find Cathy a difficult person. But the healthy Nelly's complacent self-justification and lack of surmise of stronger passions and more highly strung temperaments, make the reader Cathy's advocate in the context, and while he reads they lower /112/ his enthusiasm for the vigorously normal and, it appears, consequently obtuse.

Nelly's health is only one, though a significant, feature of the total character. Her "philosophy" on all sorts of matters is presented in detail. It is primarily a matter of avoiding any really strong passions, but continually encouraging a good deal of "natural affection." Children must "take to her." On a visit to the Heights she encounters the five-year-old Hareton near the building, and he begins to throw stones at her, and curses, distorting "his baby features into a shocking expression of malignity" (p. 115). Her reaction is unperceptively conventional.

You may be certain this grieved, more than angered me. Fit to cry, I took an orange from my pocket, and offered it to propitiate him.

He hesitated, and then snatched it from my hold, as if he fancied I only intended to tempt and disappoint him (p. 115).

Here, too, she is clearly more concerned with her picture of herself as affectionately motherly, than with understanding.

She believes in forgiving one's enemies, but she herself, not having to struggle hard in this respect, does not realize that for others placid domestic normality may not be the strongest drive. After a serious crisis in which Hindley had confined Heathcliff (during childhood) fasting in the garret for more than twenty-four hours, she broke Hindley's commands by letting him into the kitchen to feed him: "he was sick and could eat little . . ."; he remained "wrapt in dumb meditation."

On my inquiring the subject of his thoughts, he answered gravely—
"I'm trying to settle how I shall pay Hindley back. I don't care how long I wait, if I can only do it, at last. I hope he will not die before I do!"
"For shame, Heathcliff!" said I. "It is for God to punish wicked people; we should learn to forgive."
"No, God won't have the satisfaction that I shall," he returned. "I only wish I knew the best way! Let me alone, and I'll plan it out: while I'm thinking of that, I don't feel pain."
But, Mr. Lockwood, I forget these tales cannot divert you. I'm annoyed how I should dream of chattering on at such a rate . . . I could have told Heathcliff's history, all that you need hear, in half a dozen words (p. 63).

Nelly is sorry for Heathcliff and sneaks him some supper. As /113/ usual she compromises, helping Heathcliff a little and disobeying Hindley a little. Perhaps that is what was possible. But in her role as narrator she looks back upon the event, having seen the whole history of the subsequent years, and takes it in stride, still blaming Heathcliff conventionally for his lapses, still blaming others moderately, and still keeping her picture of herself as normally affectionate and good. Heathcliff should have listened to her and forgiven his enemies.

She allows, of course, for normal selfishness. Since the marriage of Cathy to Edgar Linton does take place, she hopefully finds signs that there is a "deep and growing happiness" in their union. At least she is able to be a bustling housekeeper; there are no domestic storms. But this happy period ended. "Well, we *must* be for ourselves in the long run; the mild and generous are only more justly selfish than the domineering—and it ended when circumstances caused each to feel that the one's interest was not the chief consideration in the other's thoughts" (p. 97). To her this situation is normal. No allowance is made for the enduring passion of Cathy and Heathcliff. No doubt Cathy's marriage would have appeared more successful had she forgotten Heathcliff, but it is too easy for Nelly to take this stand for the reader to go along with her. He begins to sympathize with the course that Cathy and Heathcliff did take.

Later when the reader might have been exasperated with a tantrum of Cathy's, Nelly's stolidity makes him take Cathy's part against the printed interpretation:

The stolidity with which I received these instructions was, no doubt, rather exasperating; for they were delivered in perfect sincerity; but I believed a person who could plan the turning of her fits of passion to account, beforehand, might, by exerting her will, manage to control herself tolerably even while under their influence; and I did not wish to "frighten" her husband, as she said, and multiply his annoyances for the purpose of serving her selfishness (p. 124).

For Nelly to control "fits of passion" and "manage to control herself while under their influence" have never required a struggle. /114/ She is too ruddy, healthy, physically busy and emotionally placid to know what such a struggle would be. When a few pages later she confidently announces that "the Grange had but one sensible soul in its walls, and that lodged in my body" (p. 127), we agree, but the value we place on being "sensible" is far lower than hers. Nelly is as much opposed to cold lack of visible affection as to violent passion. Normally approving of Edgar Linton, she fails to understand the feeling behind his apparent coldness and is quite ready to condemn him in his treatment of Isabella:

"And you won't write her a little note, sir?" I asked imploringly.
"No," he answered. "It is needless. My communication with Heathcliff's family shall be as sparing as his with mine. It shall not exist!"
Mr. Edgar's coldness depressed me exceedingly; and all the way from the Grange, I puzzled my brains how to put more heart into what he said, when I repeated it; and how to soften his refusal of even a few lines to console Isabella (p. 155).

She is "depressed" by "coldness," although all she wants from Edgar is a few futilely affectionate, meaningless, brotherly words not calculated to achieve any helpful result. That there is more "heart" in his coldness than in her superficiality does not occur to her. To make things well, and it really seems so to those like her, she will soften his refusal, in some compromising way, and thus receive the congratulations of her own conscience. On arriving at the Heights a few minutes later, she is actually able to say, "There never was such a dreary, dismal scene as the *formerly cheerful* house presented" [italics mine] (pp. 155-156).

The reader's first view of the house had been Lockwood's on his first visit, the history Nelly has told started with the discord resulting from the introduction into the house of the orphan Heathcliff (and the reactions to this say little enough in favor of the Earnshaws), and he has subsequently been concerned with Heathcliff, Cathy, and their agonized growing up in the house, not to mention Hindley, Joseph and Hindley's consumptive wife. The reader, consequently, cannot help placing a low value on the judgment of the wholesome Nelly, and he reassesses her narrative with quite a different emphasis. /115/

Edgar, except for his coldness to Isabella, is admired by Nelly. No unleashed and distressing passions are usually his, but a sensible and quiet affection, comforting to the housekeeper. Referring to Edgar's mourning for his deceased wife, Nelly approvingly says: "But he was too good to be thoroughly unhappy long. *He* didn't pray for Catherine's soul to haunt him: Time brought resignation, and a melancholy sweeter than common joy. He recalled her memory with ardent, tender love, and hopeful aspiring to the better world, where, he doubted not, she was gone" (p. 194). How much of this is Nelly's attribution, and how much was Edgar's real state remain doubtful; surely the part about "melancholy sweeter than common joy" is something she picked up from her boasted reading in the Linton library, but much is her natural wholesomely sentimental feeling about the decorous way for a bereaved husband to act. Possibly, too, Emily Brontë is indicating a tendency in Nelly to show off her elegance to impress Lockwood, a gentleman.

Of those aspects of experience which threaten to upset her outlook she forbids discussion, admitting her uneasiness, but willing to push aside the difficulty. Cathy, wishing to reveal a seriously troubling dream to Nelly is abruptly halted: " 'Oh! don't, Miss Catherine!' I cried. 'We're dismal enough without conjuring up ghosts and visions to perplex us. Come, come, be merry, and like yourself! Look at little Hareton—*he's* dreaming nothing dreary. How sweetly he smiles in his sleep!" (p. 84). Apart from the unwillingness to hear the dream, for Nelly to characterize Cathy as "merry and like yourself" is a stretch in making the desired the actual at any time during Cathy's adolescence, and her preference for babies is again apparent. Cathy replies: " 'Yes; and how sweetly his father curses in his solitude! You remember him, I dare say, when he was just such another as that chubby thing—nearly as young and innocent' " (p. 84). Nelly interrupted her story to explain the situation to Lockwood:

I was superstitious about dreams then, and am still; and Catherine had /116/ an unusual gloom in her aspect, that made me dread something from which I might shape a prophecy, and foresee a dreadful catastrophe.

She was vexed, but she did not proceed. Apparently taking up another subject, she recommenced in a short time.

"If I were in heaven, Nelly, I should be extremely miserable."

"Because you are not fit to go there," I answered. "All sinners would be miserable in heaven."

"But it is not for that. I dreamt, once, that I was there."

"I tell you I won't hearken to your dreams, Miss Catherine! I'll go to bed," I interrupted again (p. 84).

Little help can the distracted girl get from the only one from whom she can even try to get it. Nothing must interfere with Nelly's determination to impose her own meaning on events, and that meaning must be ordinary and cheerful. But Cathy and Heathcliff persist in a fatal tendency to try to confide in Nelly. Even at the end of his life Heathcliff confesses to her, although, dreading to hear anything unsettlingly appalling, she half refuses to listen.

The customary always triumphs with Nelly. Admirable feelings in Heathcliff, if strange or uncustomary, are shut out of her mind. Far from admirable attitudes in Edgar are approved without question, if they would be shared by most normal people in his station. When Isabella is attracted to Heathcliff, Nelly observes it merely as a new trouble to Edgar: "Leaving aside the degradation of an alliance with a nameless man, and the possible fact that his property, in default of heirs male, might pass into such a one's power, he had sense to comprehend Heathcliff's disposition . . ." (p. 106). No reader can approve such merely conventional objections, introduced without a qualm. Such attitudes had been responsible for much of the maiming of Heathcliff already. And Heathcliff is here blamed, as often, merely for not knowing his place.

Nelly is similarly imperceptive when Isabella, who has really suffered from Heathcliff, reviles him. Nelly's attempt is simply to "hush" her railings. To Isabella's "would that he could be blotted out of creation, and out of my memory!" Nelly replies, /117/ "Hush, hush! He's a human being . . . Be more charitable; there are worse men than he is yet!" (p. 183). What appears is her hatred of extremes; she does not want even Heathcliff to be unique, but merely a normally bad man, one of the well-known class of sinners. What she advocates is some conventional verbal charity and to forget, to proceed as if nothing had happened.

Nelly is a woman whom everyone in her circle, employers, the children of employers, the other servants in the neighborhood, the people of Gimmerton, and Lockwood have recognized as superior, and admirable. How superior to Joseph, Zillah, and to various other characters the reader readily perceives. To insist that she should have shown a fuller understanding of Cathy and Heathcliff would be to show a lack of understanding of what is possible or probable. From day to day she did her best, with regard to her own welfare and peace of comfort; few would have done better.

Nonetheless, her character, a representation of the normal at its best, is inadequate to the situation. As will be shown, failing to understand them, she advises them poorly, and her actions in relation to them are also harmful. Emily Brontë does not plead for them. She lets us see them as they were seen and dealt with by a good woman. The reader must progressively lower his estimate of the value of the normal and healthy, develop a comprehension of and sympathy for genuine emotions however extreme and destructive, and in so doing become an active interpreter of the meaning of the novel. The reader's active involvement and sympathy with the conventionally despicable makes the power of the book.

III

Resulting from qualities in themselves admirable, Nelly's judgments based on her understanding of events and other people result in advice and action which are parts of the total harm done to Cathy and Heathcliff. Describing the first days of Heathcliff in the Earnshaw household, she makes it apparent to the reader /118/ that her presence there will do nothing to better the little Heathcliff's situation. Speaking of the child's silent endurance of Hindley's torments, she says:

This endurance made old Earnshaw furious when he discovered his son persecuting the poor, fatherless child, as he called him. He took to Heathcliff strangely, believing all he said (for that matter, he said precious little, and generally the truth), and petting him up far above Cathy, who was too mischievous and wayward for a favourite.

So, from the very beginning, he bred bad feeling in the house ... (p. 38).

Heathcliff is, at this early point in the story, obviously blameless, yet Nelly sides with the persecutors, concerned with the trouble caused by an unusual, and hence somehow wrong situation. Looking back through the years, she can only suppose that all would have been well had Mr. Earnshaw never had so freakish a notion as to introduce a waif into the neighborhood, not that the waif become warped through continued mistreatment and helpless suffering. The parenthetical words, whose significance she disregards, reveal the almost inevitable obtuseness of interpretation by a person of her type.

One page further on, another anecdote makes a point opposite from what Nelly intends it to. Heathcliff's colt (a gift from old Earnshaw) becoming lame, the boy tries to exchange it for Hindley's sound one. " 'You must exchange horses with me; I don't like mine,

and if you won't I shall tell your father of the three thrashings
you've given me this week, and show him my arm, which is black to
the shoulder' " (p. 39). The result is that Hindley "cuffs his
ears," then threatens him with an iron weight, which he finally
hurls at him, hitting him in the chest. Nelly prevents Heathcliff
from revealing this blow to old Earnshaw, and Hindley suddenly
says: " 'Take my colt, gipsy, then! . . . And I pray that he may break
your neck; take him, and be damned, you beggarly interloper!
and wheedle my father out of all he has, only afterwards show him
what you are, imp of Satan—and take that, I hope he'll kick out
your brains!' " (p. 40). Of the words or blows, which were more
damaging to young Heathcliff may be debated, /119/ but Nelly's
actively taking the part of Hindley certainly contributes to the
harm. And beyond that, she teaches Heathcliff to lie about the
episode: "I persuaded him easily to let me lay the blame of his
bruises on the horse; he minded little what tale was told since
he had what he wanted. He complained so seldom, indeed of
such stirs as these, that I really thought him not vindictive—I was
deceived, completely, as you will hear" (p. 40). From the beginning, Nelly deals with Heathcliff through a policy of expediency,
preserving outward tranquillity, preventing "stirs" in the family.
Later when events demand even more or her, we recollect her
habitual patterns of behavior, and know she will continue to fail,
with increasingly serious results.

After old Earnshaw's death when Hindley becomes "Master,"
Nelly is not much troubled by the resulting deliberate degradation
of Heathcliff. "He bore his degradation pretty well at first, because
Cathy taught him what she learnt, and worked or played with him
in the fields. They both promised fair to grow up as rude as savages
. . ." (p. 47). More surprising is her assumption that the fanatical
Joseph's discipline would have been successful unless there was something basically wrong with Heathcliff and Cathy: "The curate
might set as many chapters as he pleased for Catherine to get by
heart, and Joseph might thrash Heathcliff till his arm ached; they
forgot everything the minute they were together again, at least
the minute they had contrived some naughty plan of revenge . . ."
(pp. 47-48). Another of her methods of helping Heathcliff is seen
slightly later in a reproof: " 'You are incurable, Heathcliff, and
Mr. Hindley will have to proceed to extremities, see if he won't' "
(p. 53).

Dramatically, with no recourse to the essay technique of Fielding as he restores the wayward Tom Jones to the favor of the

reader, the reader's sympathies are being directed powerfully toward Heathcliff, and Cathy. More powerfully, perhaps, because unless he is making a deliberate analysis of the book he does not feel his sympathies being directed by a device of the author. Field- /120/ ing's reader, directly exhorted, may argue back; Emily Brontë's reader reacts spontaneously in favor of Heathcliff.

The most Nelly can admit is that Hindley was a bad "example" for Heathcliff. This way of going to ruin—evil companions showing the way to vice—is familiar, and she makes allowance for Heath-cliff in this way. It is a qualified allowance, for Heathcliff, she says, seemed "possessed of something diabolical at that period" (p. 68). Her evidence is that Heathcliff rejoiced to see Hindley degrade himself. But the portrait of Heathcliff is far from the depravity suggested in miscellaneous remarks:

In the first place, he had, by that time, lost the benefit of his early education: continual hard work, begun soon and concluded late, had extinguished any curiosity he once possessed in pursuit of knowledge, and any love for books or learning. His childhood's sense of superiority, instilled into him by the favours of old Mr. Earnshaw, was faded away. He struggled long to keep up an equality with Catherine in her studies, and yielded with poignant though silent regret: but he yielded completely; and there was no prevailing on him to take a step in the way of moving upward, when he found he must, necessarily, sink beneath his former level (pp. 70-71).

It is hard to see how Nelly could account for Heathcliff's behavior at the same time both by diabolical possession and as she does here, but her ability to describe accurately, and yet disregard the facts in favor of explanation by a conventional formula, is a major feature of her character and her inadequacy as a counselor.

Usually, of course, Cathy and Heathcliff are being simultaneously influenced. When Cathy returns from her stay at Thrushcross Grange, Nelly is deceived by the surface improvement in her manners (p. 54). But Heathcliff's consequent desire for reform and self-improvement gets discouragingly brisk treatment:

"Nelly, make me decent, I'm going to be good."
"High time, Heathcliff," I said; "you have grieved Catherine; she's sorry she ever came home, I dare say! It looks as if you envied her, because she is more thought of than you" (p. 58).

Nelly, complacently quoting herself in such passages, still realizes no shortcomings in herself (her questions to Lockwood on moral problems from time to time never touch such failings). Had /121/ Heathcliff told his story, excusing all his actions through harsh portraits of these adults, the effect would be reversed: the reader would excuse the adults and blame Heathcliff, saying that they were no worse than most normal conventional people, and that others have survived better in worse circumstances.

Nelly's major failure (though few could have done better) is in the decisive episode during which Cathy reveals her intention of marrying Linton, despite her lack of love for him, and her intense love for, her identity with, Heathcliff. Nelly dissembles her knowledge of Heathcliff's presence, but worse, her knowledge of his departure at the worst possible moment: "Having noticed a slight movement, I turned my head, and saw him rise from the bench, and steal out, noiselessly. He had listened till he heard Catherine say it would degrade her to marry him, and then he stayed to hear no farther" (p. 85). And when Catherine wants to be assured that Heathcliff, unlike herself, does not know what deep love is, Nelly answers equivocally, " 'I see no reason that he should not know, as well as you . . . and if *you* are his choice, he'll be the most unfortunate creature that ever was born!" (*ibid.*), automatically putting Cathy in the wrong, getting herself over a difficult moment. What this moment has done is let Heathcliff overhear and leave, and the plans for marriage to Edgar go forward; Nelly has not let Cathy know that Heathcliff has heard her say that it would degrade her to marry him, but has not heard her say the words describing her real feelings, leading up to "I am Heathcliff." Nelly's view of the scene, in which her own inconvenience is more important than either Heathcliff's or Cathy's sufferings, is summarized by herself at the conclusion of Cathy's tremendous confession: "She paused, and hid her face in the folds of my gown; but I jerked it forcibly away. I was out of patience with her folly!" (p. 86).

The reader, prepared by earlier passages in which Nelly has shown, on lesser occasions, her inevitable adherence to expediency or her own comfort, is not surprised by the major failure here: moral habits are not likely to be overcome in a crisis where there /122/ is little time for struggle and deliberation. Heathcliff enters and leaves while Cathy is talking and Nelly cannot but act from habit, on the spur of the moment, but the defects revealed in this scene are her customary ones. Here, perhaps more than anywhere, the reader is sharply aware not only of her future as an interpreter of the past, but more important, of her failure as a counselor at the time of the action. Both failures co-operate to affect the reader and produce the power of the scene.

The following page, on which Nelly admits that Heathcliff had

heard much, confirms the disaster: Cathy searches for Heathcliff
during the storm, and stays up all night in wet clothes while Nelly,
at one here with Joseph, is chiefly concerned about the interruption in the household routine, even after Heathcliff is clearly gone
and Cathy has come down with a serious illness. This whole passage,
too well remembered to need detailed citation, is the turning point.
We see it as Nelly tells it. Our necessity of disagreeing completely
with the narrator's version, made very easy owing to the great detail, gives our total sympathy to Cathy and Heathcliff. We give,
perhaps, more than they deserve; we become unduly severe towards
Nelly, but to make us feel powerfully the inadequacy of the "steady
reasonable kind of body," Emily Brontë's technique could not be im-
proved. Neither a direct plea nor a narrator who was a moralizing,
narrow-minded, hypocritically pious guardian could have placed
us so completely with Heathcliff and Cathy. It needs above all
Nelly's admirable qualities including particularly the affection she
arouses in both Cathy and Heathcliff, and the awareness that her
failure is the result of them. Heathcliff and Cathy would have
fared better with worse parental guidance. The failure of the ordinarily good being made apparent, the reader, attempting to supply the fuller comprehension, becomes fully involved in the novel.[2]
/123/

To emphasize the significance of the whole scene, Emily Brontë
has Nelly sum up her attitude:

One day, I had the misfortune, when she provoked me exceedingly, to lay
the blame of his disappearance on her (where indeed it belonged, as she
well knew). From that period for several months, she ceased to hold any
communication with me, save in the relation of a mere servant. Joseph fell
under a ban also; he *would* speak his mind, and lecture her all the same
as if she were a little girl . . . (p. 93).

Later on, a dialogue between Heathcliff and Nelly emphasizes
this superficiality of hers by contrasting her explanation with his.

---

[2] A very different case of the same fundamental problem is shown with Lady
Russell in *Persuasion*. Lady Russell is admirable but has certain qualities (dislike
of wit and cleverness, and veneration of position) which cause her to fail as an
adviser to Anne. Unless an admirable character in Anne's original social group
had been shown wanting, it would not be clear that Anne was correct in emotionally and intellectually abandoning her family and their values. (Her one regret on marriage is that she has no friends or relations to introduce to Went-
worth who will add to his social pleasures.) If she were only abandoning the
stand of her absurd father and sister, she could still have accepted the group as
Emma did in marrying Knightley. But with the inclusion of Lady Russell, the
best type that the group can offer, Anne's revolt from the group itself is complete.

To his inquiry, after Cathy's marriage and illness, concerning her
condition, Nelly first replies, "I blamed her, as she deserved, for
bringing it all on herself," and continues, "the person [Edgar]
who is compelled, of necessity, to be her companion, will only sustain his affection hereafter, by the rememberance of what she once
was, by common humanity, and a sense of duty!" She is speaking
not out of any true knowledge of Edgar, but out of her determination
to edify Heathcliff. His refusal to be edified produces his reply
and reveals once more Nelly's inadequacy: " 'That is quite possible,' remarked Heathcliff, forcing himself to seem calm, 'quite
possible that your master should have nothing but common humanity and a sense of duty to fall back upon. But do you imagine
that I shall leave Catherine to his *duty* and *humanity?* and can
you compare my feelings respecting Catherine, to his?' " (p. 157).

Heathcliff finally forces her to agree to arrange an interview between him and Cathy; her motives are not a genuine feeling for the
two, but the desire to avoid an "explosion":

Was it right or wrong? I fear it was wrong, though expedient. I thought I
prevented another explosion by my compliance; and I thought, too, it
might create a favourable crisis in Catherine's mental illness: and then I
remembered Mr. Edgar's stern rebuke of my carrying tales; and I tried to
smooth away all disquietude on the subject, by affirming, with frequent
iteration, /124/ that that betrayal of trust, if it merited so harsh an appel-
lation, should be the last (p. 163).

Worse is the smugness in reporting the actual meeting when she
sarcastically remarks "it seemed Heathcliff *could* weep on a great
occasion like this" (p. 171). And conventionally, she weeps herself
for Heathcliff after Cathy's death:

"She's dead!" he said; "I've not waited for you to learn that. Put your
handkerchief away—don't snivel before me. Damn you all! she wants none
of *your* tears!"
    I was weeping as much for him as her: we do sometimes pity creatures
that have none of the feeling either for themselves or others; and when I
first looked into his face, I perceived that he had got intelligence of the
catastrophe; and a foolish notion struck me that his heart was quelled, and
he prayed, because his lips moved, and his gaze was bent on the ground.
    "Yes, she's dead!" I answered, checking my sobs, and drying my cheeks.
"Gone to heaven, I hope, where we may, every one, join her, if we take
due warning, and leave our evil ways to follow good!"
    "Did *she* take due warning, then?" asked Heathcliff, attempting a sneer.
"Did she die like a saint? Come, give me a true history of the event. How
did . . ." (p. 176).

The death of Cathy and its repercussions, however, do not end Nelly's failures that result from the great good fortune, for her own survival, of her native endowments. There remain young Cathy and the sickly son of Isabella for her to fail to comprehend. Dealing with them, she reveals her unimpaired self-confidence. Suspecting that young Cathy is corresponding with Linton, rather than question Cathy as might seem her duty as a guardian, she automatically uses the method of trying all her household keys on Cathy's locked drawer:

> . . . I emptied the whole contents into my apron, and took them with me to examine at leisure in my own chamber. . . .
> Some of them struck me as singularly odd compounds of ardour and flatness; commencing in strong feeling and concluding in the affected, wordy way that a schoolboy might use to a fancied, incorporeal sweetheart.
> Whether they satisfied Cathy, I don't know, but they appeared very worthless trash to me.
> After turning over as many as I thought proper, I tied them in a handkerchief and set them aside, re-locking the vacant drawer (p. 238). /125/

Catherine's agony on realizing that the letters have been discovered is great, but Nelly sympathizes with her not at all, since to her both the letters and their author are contemptible.

Still harsher is her treatment of Cathy after the revelation of the visits to Wuthering Heights:

> "Now, Ellen, you have heard all; and I can't be prevented from going to Wuthering Heights, except by inflicting misery on two people—whereas, if you'll only not tell papa, my going need disturb the tranquillity of none. You'll not tell, will you? It will be very heartless if you do."
> "I'll make up my mind on that point by to-morrow, Miss Catherine," I replied. "It requires some study; and so I'll leave you to your rest, and go think it over."
> I thought it over aloud, in my master's presence; walking straight from her room to his, relating the whole story, with the exception of her conversations with her cousin, and any mention of Hareton (p. 268).

Though Edgar, no doubt, should know of the activities of his daughter, Nelly's methods are shown first in her promise to Cathy to consider the problem (the easy and immediate way of "smoothing over" that difficulty), second, in her immediate and unreflective revelation to Edgar, and third, in her holding back from Edgar those items that might cause her some trouble with him. Most revelatory of all, of course, is the more than satisfied manner in which she narrates the whole episode to Lockwood.

One can also contrast the superficiality of Nelly's understanding even with that of young Cathy in two passages very close together (pp. 304 and 307). Cathy, now his daughter-in-law, says in the former,

"Mr. Heathcliff, *you* have *nobody* to love you; and, however miserable you make us, we shall still have the revenge of thinking that your cruelty arises from your greater misery! You *are* miserable, are you not? Lonely, like the devil, and envious like him? *Nobody* loves you—*nobody* will cry for you, when you die! I wouldn't be you!"

The realization of cruelty as the consequence of misery is beyond Nelly who had once explained his character as due to the evil example of Hindley. To emphasize Nelly's inability to understand, immediately after the passage just quoted, Emily Brontë has /126/ Heathcliff tell Nelly of his opening of Cathy's grave, and the reader is more than ever aware of the torments he has suffered, especially when he ends, "It was a strange way of killing, not by inches, but by fractions of hairbreadths, to beguile me with the spectre of a hope, through eighteen years." To this she comments to Lockwood:

Mr. Heathcliff paused and wiped his forehead—his hair clung to it, wet with perspiration; his eyes were fixed on the red embers of the fire; the brows not contracted, but raised next the temples, diminishing the grim aspect of his countenance, but imparting a peculiar look of trouble, and a painful appearance of mental tension towards one absorbing subject. He only half addressed me, and I maintained silence—*I didn't like to hear him talk* [italics mine].

And while he had been talking, she had interrupted him with, " 'You were very wicked, Mr. Heathcliff!' I exclaimed; 'were you not ashamed to disturb the dead?' " (p. 305), quick to register conventional horror at a breach of custom, but apparently oblivious of the overwhelming torment that had caused the breach. Here, with particular intensity, the reader revolts from accepting the wholesome, normal person as a criterion of thought and behavior, and tends to accept any passion so long as it is real, and in so doing becomes his own active interpreter of the true state of affairs and is powerfully affected by the genuine insight into human emotion.

Yet he may not be allowed to forget that Nelly is a fine woman nevertheless; she is once more contrasted with Joseph when Lockwood finds both of them together on his unexpected visit in September 1802, just after, furthermore, he had encountered her cloddish successor at the Grange (see p. 324):

. . . at the door, sat my old friend, Nelly Dean, sewing and singing a song,
which was often interrupted from within, by harsh words of scorn and
intolerance, uttered in far from musical accents.

"Aw'd rayther, by the haulf, hev 'em swearing i' my lugs frough morn
tuh neeght, nur hearken yah, hahsiver!" said the tenant of the kitchen, in
answer to an unheard speech of Nelly's. "It's a blazing shaime, ut Aw
cannut oppen t' Blessed Book, bud yah set up them glories tuh sattan, un'
all t' flay- /127/ some wickedness ut iver wer born intuh t' warld. . . . O
Lord, judge 'em, fur they's norther law nur justice amang wer rullers!"

"No! Or we should be sitting in flaming fagots, I suppose," retorted the
singer. "But wisht, old man, and read your Bible like a christian, and never
mind me. This is 'Fairy Annie's Wedding'—a bonny tune—it goes to a
dance" (pp. 326-327).

With this picture of Nelly's natural attractiveness and gaiety in
mind we reach her narration of Heathcliff's end, his "queer" end,
as she calls it (p. 328).

As any reader of the novel will have guessed, Nelly was taken by
surprise at Heathcliff's death: as with all the other now dead
characters, she had supposed him sound in all ways:

"But what do you mean by a *change*, Mr. Heathcliff?" I said, alarmed at
his manner, though he was neither in danger of losing his senses, nor dying;
according to my judgment he was quite strong and healthy; and, as to his
reason, from childhood, he had a delight in dwelling on dark things, and
entertaining odd fancies. He might have had a monomania on the subject
of his departed idol; but on every other point his wits were as sound as
mine (p. 344).

Such phrases as "delight in dwelling on dark things," "monomania
on the subject of his idol" are perhaps a climax in Nelly's brushing
aside of all powerful emotion, and above all, it should be noted
that the only thing that here alarms her is Heathcliff's unwholesome
manner.

As his death approaches, Nelly finally begins to worry about
him; she fears for a short time, as the only way of explaining him,
that he must be some "ghoul, or a vampire" (p. 350) but rejects
that explanation and tries to conjure up some type of parentage
that would account for his nature, but concludes by turning her
attention aside to a serious abnormality, that he will not be able to
have a proper tombstone, since his age and true name are unknown: "We were obliged to content ourselves with the single word,
'Heathcliff.' . . . If you enter the kirkyard, you'll read on his headstone, only that, and the date of his death" (p. 350). Her final
words show how well for her own tranquillity she has settled the

whole violent tale, when in response to Lockwood's half jest that
/128/ the ghosts of Cathy and Heathcliff will be the future inhabitants of Wuthering Heights, " 'No, Mr. Lockwood,' said Nelly, shak-
ing her head. 'I believe the dead are at peace, but it is not right to
speak of them with levity' " (p. 358).

We have received the story almost entirely from Nelly, a representative of an admirable type of person, a character developed in
great detail and with great skill, no obvious technical device, but
a genuinely memorable character. In the circumstances in which
she has been forced to live, she has revealed the futility of a tolerant, common-sense attitude which is the result of a desire merely
to avoid trouble, to deny serious problems, and of a failure to grasp
genuinely the emotions of others; the futility of compromise which
is a mere improvisation from day to day in the interest of averting
"explosions," of the futility of a constant attempt to preserve surface decorum and tranquillity on the grounds that what does not
appear will not do any harm, and she has made the reader feel that
her action had been throughout the best that can be expected
of the type she represents. The reader continually decreases in
sympathy with a type that he would usually admire, as she goes
healthily and happily singing about her household duties and
amusing the babies, since her so consistently emphasized good qualities turn out to be of so little use.

Thus, constantly rejecting her explanations, the reader substi-
tutes his own, based always on the available evidence which she
supplies but does not take into account or understand, and he becomes through his own perceptions increasingly sympathetic with
the thoughts, feelings, and deeds of Heathcliff and Cathy.

The engaging of the reader actively as one who does a large part
of the work of comprehending is an important cause of the power
of the novel. As Nelly contentedly provides her superficial interpretations of motive, and contentedly recounts her inadequate
parental behavior, we are constantly directed toward feeling the
inadequacy of the wholesome, and toward sympathy with genuine
passions, no matter how destructive or violent. /129/

Questions for Discussion and Writing

1. What does a writer mean when he says that a novel has "power"? In
what way(s) is power the "memorable quality of *Wuthering Heights*"?
(page 106)

2. Why, according to Mathison, must the reader reject Nelly Dean's point of view? Do you agree? What have critics said about the reader's relation to Nelly?

3. On pages 107 and 108 Mathison explains the roles of Joseph and Zillah. Make an expanded statement about the function of minor characters in *Wuthering Heights*.

4. Find evidence to support the idea that Heathcliff has affection for Nelly Dean.

5. What are the failures of Nelly Dean, as seen by Mathison, by you, and by other critics?

6. Does Mathison find the novel biographical, sociological, psychological, or something else? What reasons would readers have for considering it biographical, sociological, or psychological?

7. On page 109 Mathison says, "By indirection, Emily Brontë has produced not a personal protest but a work of art." What does his expression, "By indirection," mean?

8. Mathison asserts that the readers recognize Nelly's "lack of understanding of the principals." (page 109) Do we? Have other critics recognized this lack?

9. Amplify Mathison's suggestion that Emily Brontë conditions her readers' attitudes.

10. Our view of Edgar Linton is tempered for us by Nelly Dean, says Mathison. Who else tempers it for us? What is Linton really like?

11. "The customary always triumphs with Nelly. Admirable feelings in Heathcliff, if strange or uncustomary, are shut out of her mind. Far from admirable attitudes in Edgar are approved without question, if they would be shared by most normal people in his station." (page 117) Find material to illustrate these statements.

12. To what extent does Mathison believe Emily Brontë foreshadows events in *Wuthering Heights?*

13. What does Mathison say about use of contrast in *Wuthering Heights?* Is contrast fundamental to the novel?

14. What materials do you find in this essay to combat the view of Ellen Dean set forth by James Hafley? What do you find that supports his thesis?

The Narrators of
Wuthering Heights

CARL R. WOODRING

Since the seminal study by C. P. Sanger in 1926, the structure of
Wuthering Heights has been further illumined by a host of laudatory critics, notably Paul M. Fulcher (1929), Lord David Cecil
(1934), Boris Ford (1939), G. D. Klingopulos (1947), Melvin R.
Watson (1949), Mark Schorer (1949), Royal A. Gettmann (1950),
Bruce McCullough (1950), Dorothy Van Ghent (1952), B. H. Leh-
man (1955), and V. S. Pritchett (1956). Reprintings of the Oxford
World's Classics edition preserve an older view in H. W. Garrod's
resolute assertions, dated 1930, that the story, suffering from "inferior technique," is in parts "uncertainly conceived" and "in
general ill constructed." Although most laudatory critics have noticed the debt owed by the structure of the novel to its use of two
presumed narrators, more remains to be said about the utility of
Lockwood and Nelly Dean.

The earlier scholar, learned in Gothic romances and tales from
Blackwood's, found in Nelly's narrative within narrative the misfortune of inherited inconvenience; the later critic, familiar with
selected masterworks, hails the use of contrasting narrators as a
wonder of creative intuition. Let us accept the method as borrowed
from inferior tales, but chosen rather than inherited. What /298/
other method could have better provided the reader with the inter-
locking of familiar details concerning two generations and a stranger's astonishment over the beginning, the middle, and the end
of Heathcliff's story? Nelly alone, Heathcliff himself as Jamesian or
Austenian register, omniscient author, a series of actors or servants

speaking independently—none of these as narrative authority could have provided the union of intimacy, intensity, interpretation, and detached admiration that Emily Brontë needed and achieved. Lockwood, the stranger, shares the reader's wonder at the characters and events; Mrs. Dean, the intimate, has long supped with wonders; stranger and intimate combine to certify the general facts.

The double narration is a convention and must be accepted as a convention. Much in *Wuthering Heights,* including characters as well as techniques, rests upon transformed conventions. Swept with the surge of demonism and quieted with purgation and repose at the end, the reader need not be disturbed because the conventions allow Nelly to linger overlong at various doors or Lockwood to report what Nelly said Zillah said the second Catherine said to Hareton. If, however, the critical reader becomes disturbed, if he demands a logic in the deviousness by which soliloquies reach him, he has no justification for exclaiming that Lockwood must have memorized Isabella's unlikely letter to Nelly verbatim. The logic he unnecessarily demands lies in this: ultimately all the words come to us from Lockwood. As after accepting the illusion of memory in a flashback, we may believe on critical reflection that the letter from Isabella as read by Nelly contained a briefer summary than Lockwood reports to us. Like his creator, Lockwood understands the value of first-person narrative; after 1784 in the events related by Nelly, he continues the story "in her own words, only a little condensed." That the events occurred, their impact makes us believe; Lockwood's intervention can account for similarities between the styles of Nelly, Isabella, and Zillah through which the events make their impact. If we /299/ hesitate to believe that Nelly remembers what Heathcliff said the Lintons said to each other some twenty-five years ago (Chapter VI), we can believe that Lockwood has supplied the appropriate words. To a protest that the author clearly thought of each scene as resting on the authority of its original narrator, the answer is that each scene does still so rest and that no justification exists for hanging critically suspended between these narrators and Lockwood, who is characterized by the author as a man who did in fact compose the book as we have it. The self-taught Nelly may mimic Joseph; so may Isabella; always it is the tenant of Thrushcross Grange who records Joseph's dialect.

Lockwood is an educated diarist from the city who records in course the remarkable events of his first two days among moors and boors. By dreaming in Cathy's paneled bed, he comes to pursue less palpable wilds. Emily Brontë may seem to allow him four days to transcribe the first nine chapters, a day for Chapter x, four weeks altogether (ill as he was) to hear and record the story through Chapter xiv, another week to report the urgency of Chapters xv through xxx, and at last the leisure of a possible three months to compose the subdued descent from Chapter xxxii to the final meditation over "the sleepers in that quiet earth." A qualification seems necessary. Without hesitation the author sacrifices strict consistency for immediate effect, but Lockwood's diary entries, as in Chapters iii, ix, x, xv, and xxxi, especially the bored remarks in the present tense, may be taken as his immediate record during illness and convalescence when he resisted the appeal of violent rusticity. We may suppose that increased understanding and physical distance from the moors greatly stimulated his memory of the narrated details and permitted lengthy insertions when the story became meaningful to him. Observe the tenses in the following passage in Chapter x:

I am too weak to read; yet I feel as if I could enjoy something interesting. Why not have up Mrs. Dean to finish her tale? I can recollect its chief incidents, as far as she had gone. Yes: I remember her hero had run off, and /300/ never been heard of for three years; and the heroine was married. I'll ring: she'll be delighted to find me capable of talking cheerfully. Mrs. Dean came.

At first Lockwood parades before us as a brittle ironist; slowly his irony mellows and finally dissolves. Quoted against himself, he has been called misanthropic. He is not. A reticent man, he comes to Thrushcross embittered because his chilly reticence has cost him the love of an attractive girl. In an unsociable mood, he nonetheless finds Heathcliff disgustingly unsociable. So gregarious is he that he soon craves conversation with his unpromising housekeeper, Mrs. Dean. If he seems inane, he suffers from the inanity his author attributes to the average London reader into whose hands her book will fall. In his introduction to the Rinehart College Edition, Mark Schorer follows Garrod in interpreting the original plan of the novel as the edification of a sophisticated and sentimental prig, Lockwood, in the natural human values of grand passion. Rather, Lockwood reacts for the normal skeptical reader in appropriate ways at each stage of the story and its unfolding theme. Within the action, he plays a more individual role. As actor, he tries to protect his "susceptible heart" (Chapter ii) from attachment to the widowed Catherine; by March (Chapter xiv), he feebly resists the fascination of her eyes because he fears a "second edition" of her mother. By such self-restraint he thinks to "extract wholesome medicines from Mrs. Dean's bitter herbs." He reveals in Chapter xxv that he has fallen, he has asked that her portrait be hung over his fireplace, but he hesitates to act precipitately lest Catherine not return his love. Here the author intends Lockwood to replace Linton in the reader's mind as the active rival of Hareton. The suspense of this rivalry is to imbue Mrs. Dean's last words in the spring: ". . . I can see no remedy, at present, unless she should marry again; and that scheme it does not come within my province to arrange" (Chapter xxx). Always the sentimentalist, Lockwood feels pain when Catherine fails to perceive the value of dining with him instead of with "clowns and misanthropists" (Chapter xxxi). In September, he reports, /301/ "I bit my lip, in spite, at having thrown away the chance I might have had" (Chapter xxxii), and at the very end he admits to grumbling at the complacent love of Catherine and Hareton. The author manipulates and tolerates Lockwood much more for structure and plot than for theme.

Prefiguring Conrad's use of Marlow, Nelly's oral language sets itself off from Lockwood's prose by such simple phrases as "really, you know, Sir" and "well, Mr. Lockwood." Again an adequate convention, productive of immediate credibility and pleasure. Verisimilitude of narration gives way, happily, before binding detail. Cathy returned from her five weeks at Thrushcross Grange a neat little lady: "I was all over flour making the Christmas cake, and it would not have done to give me a hug; and, then, she looked around for Heathcliff" (Chapter vii).

As judge, Nelly pronounces Heathcliff a "black villain" and "evil beast"; Cathy a "wild, wicked slip" who "meant no harm"; and Joseph the "wearisomest, self-righteous pharisee." Cathy, she decrees, must be "chastened into humility." As interpreter, Nelly calls Heathcliff's a cuckoo's story—although she avoids assigning such a label to the later spiritual cuckoldry. As chorus, she lays aside superstition to proclaim happiness in the tranquillity of Cathy's death-chamber. In interviews, as attorney, she asks questions the reader wants asked. As in *The Brothers Karamazov*, the intensity of the passion lends credibility to the compulsive confessions; Nelly is the natural recipient of natural and unnatural confession.

She also acts. Attentive witness, narrator, and elucidator of past events, Mrs. (that is, Miss) Dean not only plays an active role economically designed, but also commands interest as a personality considerably beyond any of Thackeray's justly admired servants. Alert, observant, prying, gossipy, slightly superstitious, bold, saucy, tolerant, motherly, she has a very suspicious array of traits. Firm at the center, her character seems conveniently amorphous at the periphery. Even more than Lockwood's, her actions and utterances /302/ fit the immediate needs of the situation before the reader; she is no Mrs. Gamp to steal either attention or consistency from the central characters. This malleability makes her seem more complex. Heathcliff must be complex; Nelly may merely seem so. Superstitious enough to foreshadow with presentiments, she is skeptic enough to acknowledge her superstition. She remains a credible and canny witness by doubting the supernaturalness of the characters and events that certainly are, she has convinced us, supernatural. With placid disapproval, she can feel and communicate the basic distinction, expounded by Heathcliff and his Cathy, between demonic love and civilized emptiness.

In Nelly, Emily Brontë ingeniously produced the exactly needed combination of servant, companion, and saucy antagonist. With personal dignity, she keeps secrets; as a respected nurse, she tattles; she intercepts letters between young culprits; she scolds; she watches pots; she dances with the ungentle gentlefolk when needed (Chapter VII). Her removal in 1783 from Wuthering Heights to Thrushcross Grange had to be conceived before composition began; perception of her wonderful capacities as a catalyst could not have been long delayed. As witness and chorus, she must take part in nearly every scene in the book. We become accustomed to her interference from the time she admits putting the waif Heathcliff on the landing to encourage his running away (Chapter IV). Soon deciding to scrub his person and manners, she plants in him the germinal suggestion that he might be an Oriental mogul, able to buy Wuthering Heights (Chapter VII). She provokes Cathy to show violence before Edgar (Chapter VIII); she unloads Hindley's gun (Chapter VIII); after her tattling to Edgar of Heathcliff's insolent acts results in an open clash, she lies to avoid further violence (Chapter XI). Yet even when she combines instigation of acts with explicit judgment of those acts, her author scrupulously prevents Nelly's actions from seeming to modify in any way either the personalities of the more important characters or the major directions of the plot. Nelly is /303/ allowed, not to advise Cathy on accepting or rejecting Edgar, but to catechize her after the acceptance (Chapter IX). Her own admissions of guilty responsibility make the reader the more ready to distribute blame among the principals. Locked inside Wuthering Heights in August 1800, she uttered and then withdrew a confession:

I seated myself in a chair, and rocked, to and fro, passing harsh judgment on my many derelictions of duty; from which, it struck me then, all the misfortunes of all my employers sprang. It was not the case, in reality, I am aware; but it was, in my imagination, that dismal night; and I thought Heathcliff himself less guilty than I (Chapter xxvii).

Most scenes in the novel receive some imprint from Nelly's character or positon. Her catalytic instigations gather strength almost imperceptibly from the many times when her actions help build portraits of herself and of the principals but otherwise merely provide a way of stating what occurred, as when she innocently supplies little Catherine with provisions for a ride to Wuthering Heights (Chapter xviii). The frequency with which her character helps to determine the nature of immediate acts helps to support the rarer occasions when she influences the action without motivation, as when her one prolonged illness makes possible the meetings between Cathy and Linton (Chapter xxiii). Occasionally, she acts with inadequate motive to gain and communicate information for her author; more often adequate motives impel her. She softens toward Heathcliff the waif because measles make him quiet and lead him to praise her for nursing him; soon, therefore, Heathcliff can deceive her by his silence at mistreatment from Hindley (Chapter iv). It is a condition of both respectability and forehandedness that she chaperon the final meeting of Heathcliff with Cathy, who is about to die in childbirth. That the unearthly lovers show awareness of her presence merely emphasizes their undiminished passion (Chapter xv). Even here Nelly is up to her usual trick: by her own actions, in character or credible for the moment, she reveals the character of others. /304/

Acknowledged as narrators and interpreters, Mrs. Dean and Lockwood have been slighted as actors in the plot. Lockwood does not merely hear the tale in a tavern in Leeds; he dreams in the paneled bed beside the ghostly window and himself threatens to interrupt the final purgation and the happy-ever-after. As Heathcliff intrudes from some netherworld, Lockwood intrudes from the city. Mrs. Dean belongs. From the time she takes Hindley's knife between her teeth, she perfects the symbols. She interweaves Heathcliff's hair with Edgar's for Catherine's locket; at the end she combs the hair of the dead Heathcliff and closes the window. /305/

Questions for Discussion and Writing

1. What critics agree (completely or in part) with H. W. Garrod? (page 298) What qualities of *Wuthering Heights* lead them to such judgments?

2. Select several of the types of narrators Woodring lists on page 299, and suggest difficulties they would raise in the presenting of Emily Brontë's story.

3. Woodring suggests some improbabilities of narration on page 299. Find more improbabilities of this nature, and decide how seriously they hurt the novel.

4. Not every critic agrees with Woodring's estimation of Lockwood and Lockwood's role in *Wuthering Heights*. What other estimations have been made? With which do you agree?

5. On page 301 Woodring says, "Here [Chapter XXV] the author intends Lockwood to replace Linton in the reader's mind as the active rival of Hareton." Do you agree with that statement? To what degree and in what ways is Lockwood involved as a character—not just a narrator—in the novel?

6. On what evidence does (or can) Woodring call Lockwood a sentimentalist? Support Woodring's assertion further, or attempt to refute it.

7. What does Woodring mean by, "Verisimilitude of narration gives way, happily, before binding detail"? (page 302) And why does he say "happily"? Do you agree? Discuss verisimilitude in *Wuthering Heights*.

8. "Nelly is the natural recipient of natural and unnatural confession," says Woodring on page 302. What does he mean by "natural" and "unnatural"? Discuss these two words in general relation to *Wuthering Heights*.

9. Woodring finds Nelly Dean amorphous (page 302) and malleable (page 303). Do you? What does Woodring mean? Have other critics seen these characteristics in Nelly Dean?

10. How canny is Nelly Dean?

11. Cite some incidents in which Nelly "acts with inadequate motive to gain and communicate information for her author . . ." (page 305)

12. Does Woodring believe Nelly not only fulfills her role (as catalyst) but transcends it? What does he conceive her total value as a character to be? With reference to other critics' opinions, estimate the characterization of Nelly Dean.

13. Contrast Woodring's and Mathison's views of Nelly.

Emily Brontë's Mr. Lockwood

GEORGE J. WORTH

The character of Mr. Lockwood, one of the two narrators of *Wuthing Heights* (the one through whose consciousness all the events of the plot are ostensibly filtered) has been the subject of much critical disparagement and disagreement. Even if it is granted that Emily Brontë's elaborate manner of placing her material before the reader is not impossibly cumbersome, Lockwood himself is generally considered something of a prig and a dullard. Dorothy Van Ghent, for instance, refers to him as "the effete, almost epicene Lockwood," and similarly slighting epithets abound in the sizable critical literature that has grown up around *Wuthering Heights*.[1]

But critics differ regarding the precise role which Lockwood plays in the novel. At one extreme, there is Mark Schorer, who sees the figure of Lockwood, the symbol of conventional emotion, as one of the chief means by which Emily Brontë's theme—unconsciously on her part, he implies—is brought home to the reader.[2] At the other, May Sinclair affirms that Lockwood is not, properly speaking, a character at all: he is purposely left a vague sketch by /315/ Emily Brontë, for "he is a mere looker-on."[3] The middle road is taken by Melvin R. Watson, who regards Lockwood as a character in his own right but without the thematic significance Mr. Schorer

Copyright 1958 by The Regents of the University of California. Reprinted from *Nineteenth-Century Fiction*. Volume XII, Number 4 (March), pp. 315 through 320, by permission of The Regents.

[1] "The Window Figure and the Two-Children Figure in *Wuthering Heights*," *Nineteenth-Century Fiction*, VII (1952), p. 190. Cf. Irene Cooper Willis, *The Brontës* (London, 1933), pp. 111-112 and 114-115; Muriel Spark and Derek Stanford, *Emily Bontë* (London, 1953), p. 246; Royal A. Gettmann, Introduction to the Modern Library edition of *Wuthering Heights* (New York, 1950), pp. xiii-xiv.

[2] "Technique as Discovery," in John W. Aldridge (ed.), *Critiques and Essays on Modern Fiction* (New York, 1952), p. 71, and "Fiction and the 'Analogical Matrix,'" *ibid.*, p. 87.

[3] *The Three Brontës* (London, 1912), p. 224.

reads into him: he is "an ordinary person from the outside world" with whom the reader can identify himself as Mr. Lockwood, and the reader, become immersed in the strange atmosphere of the Heights, Thrushcross Grange, and the bleak moors that lie between.[4]

Although there has been no scarcity of commentaries on Lockwood's personality nor of attempts to define his relationship to the material he is supposed to narrate, no critic as far as I know has taken a searching look at the manner in which Emily Brontë characterizes Lockwood or drawn from this the appropriate conclusions regarding his function in the novel. It is my thesis that she *did* intend him to stand as a clearly defined figure, and that she indicated to us, by implication rather than by explicit statement, in what light we are to regard him.

Lockwood is endowed by Miss Brontë with three leading traits, each important in helping him to fulfil his role in the novel: an ill-disguised gregariousness, a sentimental (as opposed to a passionate) view of life and love, and a clumsy and tactless garrulity.

He represents himself in the opening paragraphs of *Wuthering Heights* as a misanthrope—he has rented a house on the desolate Yorkshire moors, he says, because he regards the region as a "perfect misanthropist's heaven"—and some critics have taken his view of himself at face value. But what are the facts? He calls on his neighbor and landlord "as soon as possible after my arrival"; treated with surliness and contempt by Heathcliff on this first visit, he nevertheless resolves to come again the next day; having weakened in his determination to return, he seizes on a flimsy pretext— the servant girl is cleaning his study—to trudge four miles in threatening weather to enjoy once again the pleasantries of Heathcliff and the other inmates of the Heights; and after his /316/ return from this unfortunate second expedition, bored, lonely, and ill, he relentlessly pumps Mrs. Dean for information about Wuthering Heights, its inhabitants and their history, thereby getting for us the story of the novel.

Obviously, had Lockwood been the misanthrope he claimed to be, he would have shunned all intercourse with Heathcliff and Nelly and there could have been no novel, at least not in its present form. Emily Brontë had to create him as a sociable and more than normally curious character. If he had been genuinely contemptuous of everything outside himself, would he have bothered on his second

---

[4] "Tempest in the Soul: The Theme and Structure of *Wuthering Heights*," *Nineteenth-Century Fiction*, IV (1949), pp. 95-96.

visit to the Heights to look into Cathy's Bible, thus precipitating the nightmare-vision which introduces us to the supernatural element in *Wuthering Heights?*

Why, then, does Emily Brontë invest Lockwood with this veneer of misanthropy which so quickly peels away under the scrutiny of even a moderately observant reader? Clearly, to furnish an appropriate vantage point from which to observe, and an appropriate standard with which to compare, Heathcliff's true misanthropy. Lockwood, deluded about his own character, insists on seeing Heathcliff as something he is not, and the change in his opinion, when it comes, is as painful as it is illuminating. Since we identify ourselves temporarily with the narrator, the truth about Heathcliff's fierce nature dawns on us gradually—although probably not quite so gradually as it does on him. And Lockwood's spurious scorn for mankind and yearning for isolation furnish a pale background against which Heathcliff's violent misanthropy, when revealed, blazes with unnatural brightness.

It is interesting to observe how Lockwood's estimate of Heathcliff changes. In the first paragraph of the novel he calls him, with a wide-eyed enthusiasm that is typical of him at this stage, "A capital fellow!"

"He little imagined," he goes on, "how my heart warmed towards him when I beheld his black eyes withdraw so suspiciously under their brows, as I rode up, and when his fingers sheltered /317/ themselves, with a jealous resolution, still further up in his waistcoat, as I announced my name!" Two of a kind, obviously! Later in the opening chapter, Lockwood indulges in some analysis of the character of his taciturn host, a task for which he considers himself uniquely qualified by virtue of their similar outlook on life; needless to say, his analysis is hopelessly wide of the mark.

Possibly, some people might suspect him of a degree of underbred pride; I have a sympathetic chord within that tells me it is nothing of the sort: I know, by instinct, his reserve springs from an aversion to showy displays of feeling—to manifestations of mutual kindliness. He'll love and hate equally under cover, and esteem it a species of impertinence to be loved or hated again.

(But Lockwood is not an utter fool: he adds, "No, I'm running on too fast: I bestow my own attributes overliberally on him.") By the end of the first call he pays him, Lockwood confesses to some bewilderment concerning Heathcliff's character—"It is astonishing how sociable I feel myself when compared with him"—and after he has seen Heathcliff's savagery in its full force during his second visit to Wuthering Heights, even the vapid Lockwood can remain under no illusions regarding Heathcliff's nature or the identity in feeling between them.

Why has Lockwood sequestered himself in the remote wilds of Yorkshire? He regards himself as a man cruelly disappointed in love, and presumably he hopes to nurse his wounds and recover his equanimity in isolation. But his view of himself as a victim of passion is no more admissible than the role of misanthrope he insists on assuming, as is obvious from the paragraph in which he fatuously sets forth the history of his romance.

While enjoying a month of fine weather at the seacoast, I was thrown into the company of a most fascinating creature: a real goddess in my eyes, as long as she took no notice of me. I "never told my love" vocally; still, if looks have language, the merest idiot might have guessed I was over head and ears: she understood me at last, and looked a return—the sweetest of all imaginable looks. And what did I do? I confess it with shame—shrunk icily into myself, like a snail; at every glance retired colder and farther; till finally the poor innocent was led to doubt her own senses, and, overwhelmed /318/ with confusion at her supposed mistake, persuaded her mamma to decamp. By this curious turn of disposition, I have gained the reputation of deliberate heartlessness; how undeserved, I alone can appreciate (chap. i).

This absurdly stunted love affair and Lockwood's occasional daydreams about the pleasures of a possible romance with Catherine seem to be the extent of his capacity to feel passion—an atrophied capacity to which the superhuman love of Heathcliff and Cathy furnishes a violent contrast. Indeed, all the unruly emotions in which *Wuthering Heights* abounds seem much more strange when viewed from the vantage point of the humdrum sentimentalist who gives us the story.

In showing us Lockwood's indomitable inclination to be sociable and his tamely conventional outlook on the events of the story, Emily Brontë employs considerable irony. She lets Lockwood characterize himself, and then helps us to realize, by letting us witness his character in action, that he is not really like that at all. The incongruity between the way a man regards himself and the way he is regarded by others is, of course a perennial source of comedy, and Lockwood is the only genuinely comic figure in *Wuthering Heights*.

Lockwood's third key trait, his bumbling talkativeness, also helps him to carry out his function in the novel. In addition to branding him even more completely as a good-natured buffoon, his well-meant but inane chatter serves to draw out, more successfully than a more discreet character could have done, Heathcliff and the other members of his menage, thus furnishing the reader with valuable information about them. For instance, in chapter ii, Lockwood's dogged efforts to be ingratiating give Emily Brontë an opportunity to display Hareton and Catherine at their most churlish, and his persistent questioning of Heathcliff drags out of him an account of the relationship between these strange people. His imprudent babbling to Heathcliff of his dream also helps move the story along.

"If the little fiend had got in at the window, she probably would have /319/ strangled me! . . . I'm not going to endure the persecutions of your hospitable ancestors again. Was not the Reverend Jabes Branderham akin to you on the mother's side? And that minx, Catherine Linton, or Earnshaw, or however she was called—she must have been a changeling—wicked little soul! She told me she had been walking the earth those twenty years: a just punishment for her mortal transgressions, I've no doubt!" (chap. iii).

It is in response to this outburst that the impassioned Heathcliff, a few moments later, tears open the bedroom window and tearfully beseeches the spirit of Cathy to come to him—the first concrete indication we have that he is moved by something more than mortal impulses.

As previous critics have recognized, Lockwood is an ordinary observant man, the representative of the great body of ordinary readers, viewing an extraordinary situation much as any of us might view it. But he is more than this: he is a distinct character—a character with comic overtones—in his own right, whom Emily Brontë deliberately fashioned as she did to serve as a useful source of information and an often unconscious commentator on the series of events around which she built her novel. /320/

Questions for Discussion and Writing

1. Why does Worth use the word *ostensibly* in his first sentence?

2. Trace in detail the critical evaluations of Lockwood as a person. Is Worth's addition valuable?

3. Agree or disagree with Worth's thesis on Lockwood. If you agree, write a supporting argument; if you disagree, write a dissenting argument.

4. How have various critics of *Wuthering Heights* defined the word *misanthrope* and applied it to Lockwood?

5. Put together an explanation of the early actions of Lockwood that suggest a motive other than gregariousness. Decide whether your explanation or Worth's is more defensible.

6. Worth speaks of Lockwood's "atrophied capacity" to feel "passion." (page 319) Which synonym seems better suited to his meaning—*emotion*, or *love*? Support your answer by reference to the novel.

7. In what sense is the love of Heathcliff and Cathy "superhuman"?

8. Worth mentions Emily Brontë's use of irony in *Wuthering Heights*. Investigate irony in the novel more fully.

9. Extend Worth's comments on the use of Lockwood to "draw out" the other characters. (page 319)

10. What "comic overtones" has Lockwood, and why?

11. In his article Worth ignores Nelly Dean as narrator. Assuming his case for Lockwood is sound, write a paper on the role of Nelly Dean that will not conflict with Worth's conception of the role of Lockwood.

Wuthering Heights: the Land East of Eden

RUTH M. ADAMS

And Cain went out from the presence of the LORD, and dwelt in the land of Nod, on the east of Eden. . . .

And Lamech took unto him two wives: the name of one was Adah, and the name of the other Zillah. . . .

And Lamech said unto his wives: Adah and Zillah, here my voice; ye wives of Lamech, hearken unto my speech: For I have slain a man to my wounding, and a young man to my hurt.

If Cain shall be avenged sevenfold, truly Lamech seventy and sevenfold.

—Gen. 4 : 16, 19, 23, 24

In Chapter iii of *Wuthering Heights*, Lockwood, the victim of a heavy storm, his own ineffectuality, and the indifference of Heathcliff's household, spends a tumultuous night at the Heights, terrified by both actuality and dreams. The nightmare of the pleading child captures the reader's attention completely; but as E. K. Brown has commented, he soon forgets, if indeed he was ever aware of, ". . . the importance in the novel of that imaginary sermon of the Reverend Jabes Banderham, on the theme 'Seventy Times Seven, and the First of the Seventy-First,' "[1] which precedes the dream about Catherine. This initial nightmare is, to all intents and purposes, the first forward-moving incident in the novel. As such it establishes once and for all the fact that in *Wuthering Heights* no conventional morality prevails, that here resides a race strangely and abhorrently protected against the usual consequences of evil deeds. /58/

[1] E. K. Brown, *Rhythm in the Novel* (University of Toronto Press, 1950), p. 6.

The text of the sermon is from Gen. 4 : 24; but to understand its significance, we must recall that Cain moved to the land east of Eden as a marked man. The mark of Cain does not identify the condemned murderer. Rather it is protective: Cain is the man against whom his fellows cannot raise their hands, the man who cannot be killed without a sevenfold vengeance being visited upon his murderers. As a consequence of his fratricide, Cain becomes a man outside the usual order as he is outside the familiar community. He is not subject to the disciplines of other men. So far removed from them is he that divine ordinances cannot apply to him; and in his impunity God acquiesces.

This alien race produces in Lamech, Cain's great-great-great-grandson, another murderer who, unlike his ancestor, shows no remorse for his deed. Lamech, rather, is triumphant when he kills the young man, and in his arrogance claims an even greater degree of immunity, seventy times seven. Thus the race dwelling east of Eden can work its evils in the assurance that no conventional consequence of punishment will follow. In this land, values are reversed, familiar morality has no place, right is equated with power and passion, and regret is unknown.

Wuthering Heights and its surrounding crags and moors is a similar land. Its residents, those whose natures qualify them to live there—the Earnshaws and Heathcliff—have a similar tendency to passionate violence and a similar immunity to punishment. To introduce us to this world, Emily Brontë utilizes Lockwood's dream. In it, he accompanies Joseph through the snows, his destination not the security of Thrushcross Grange, but the dereliction and decay of Gimmerton Kirk. This is a pilgrimage, but in place of the customary symbol of peace and heavenly aspiration, a pilgrim's staff, the traveller is provided with a cudgel, the weapon of force, cruelty, and assault. The destination is not a citadel of physical or spiritual security, as in the usual pilgrimage; Gimmerton Kirk, in the physical world of Wuthering Heights, deteriorates and decays, and in the dream world houses a scene of condemnation and con- /59/ flict. As Jabes Banderham concludes his sermon with fulminations against Lockwood, the congregation turns to the attack, confusion dominates, the cudgels of the assembled pilgrims fly, and in the author's words, ". . . each man's hand was against his neighbor."[2] The church becomes the battleground, the pastor the directing general—reversals of what conventional associations might expect.

[2] Emily Brontë, *Wuthering Heights,* Rinehart Editions (New York and Toronto, 1954), p. 24.

Thus the perversion of the Heights is introduced to Lockwood and its consequence is immediate. Violence and cruelty prove contagious. Although weak and petty by nature, Lockwood is so contaminated by this display of force and malevolence that in the subsequent dream, that of the pleading Catherine, he can conceive himself as rubbing the delicate wrist of the child against the jagged edge of the broken pane, till the blood runs down. The Lockwood of the introductory chapters of *Wuthering Heights* would not have been capable of this brutality; but once caught by the environment, he adopts the behavior most appropriate. The weak man turns cruelly against the most weak, the defenseless child.

Lockwood's corruption is paralleled by that of another weak character. Isabella's experiences with Heathcliff, the person most at home in this land of violence, change her rapidly from the pettish, sulky, spoiled daughter of the Grange. She casts off the morality of that sheltered area. Viciously she delights in Heathcliff's grief at Catherine's death; and when Nellie reproaches her, speaking the conventional words that punishment lies in the hands of God, Isabella replies:

"But what misery laid on Heathcliff could content me, unless I have a hand in it? I'd rather he suffered *less,* if I might cause his sufferings, and he might *know* that I was the cause. Oh, I owe him so much. On only one condition can I hope to forgive him. It is, if I may take an eye for an eye, a tooth for a tooth; for every wrench of agony, return a wrench, reduce him to my level. As he was the first to injure, make him the first to implore pardon; and then—why then, Ellen, I might show you some generosity. But it is utterly impossible I can ever be revenged, and therefore I cannot forgive him."[3] /60/

Her recognition of Heathcliff's immunity to ordinary consequences is significant; but more than this, Isabella displays an intense vindictiveness aping that of the man she so hates. She is tainted by the atmosphere of the Heights, a change that had displayed itself earlier when only self-preservation had kept her from aiding Hindley against her husband: " '. . . I'd be glad of a retaliation that wouldn't recoil on myself; but treachery, and violence, are spears pointed at both ends—they wound those who resort to them, worse than their enemies.' " To which Hindley exclaims, " 'Treachery and violence are a just return for treachery and violence!' "[4]

Hindley, too, despite the cloudy appeal that his victimization at the hands of Heathcliff creates, lives outside God's jurisdiction.

[3] *Ibid.,* p. 190.
[4] *Ibid.,* p. 186.

Even before Heathcliff's campaign against him, Hindley moved toward his own destruction and met Nellie's protest about the salvation of his soul with the arrogant " '. . . I shall have great pleasure in sending it to perdition, to punish its Maker. . . . Here's to its hearty damnation!' "[5]

Even Joseph—Joseph of the warped Christianity, the ugly voice of religious fanaticism at the Heights—delights in prospects of violence. His stubborn devotion to the last of the Earnshaws, Hareton, does not manifest itself in attempts to combat Heathcliff's influence.

He allowed that [Hareton] was ruined, that his soul was abandoned to perdition; but then, he reflected that Heathcliff must answer for it. Hareton's blood would be required at his hands; and there lay immense consolation in that thought.[6]

The word "blood" colors this passage. The destruction of Hareton has been in terms of spirit and intellect, not body; but for the violent, revenge must be conceived in terms of blood.

And finally, Catherine and Heathcliff themselves illustrate the perverse values that prevail in *Wuthering Heights*. Catherine's dream rejects peace and serenity with the angels. /61/

". . . heaven did not seem to be my home; and I broke my heart with weeping to come back to earth; and the angels were so angry that they flung me out, into the middle of the heath on the top of Wuthering Heights, where I woke sobbing for joy."[7]

Heathcliff in his agony at her death exclaims, " 'May she wake in torment!' " assured she will be no resident of heaven.[8] And in his last days, confronted by Nellie's conventional advice to make conventional amends in this world, he explodes, " '. . . as to repenting of my injustices, I've done no injustice, and I repent of nothing. . . .' "[9]

Hareton and the younger Catherine prepare at the end of the novel to move to the Grange. Neither by race nor by capacity for evil-doing do they qualify as residents of the Heights. After temporary corruption, they choose the conventional home. The Heights will be possessed by the spirits of its proper residents, Heathcliff and Catherine.

Wuthering Heights, then, is a book without conventional ethics

[5] *Ibid.*, p. 80.
[6] *Ibid.*, p. 209.
[7] *Ibid.*, p. 84.
[8] *Ibid.*, p. 177.
[9] *Ibid.*, p. 353.

or morality.[10] Emily Brontë, aware of the adjustment such a pattern demanded of her readers, undertook to assist them from the very beginning. Thus, with Lockwood's dream of Banderham's sermon, she indicated that readers were to travel east of Eden, in the company of those alienated from God and paradoxically protected by him against the punishing consequences of their deeds. In Genesis such alienation is an awesome thing; in *Wuthering Heights* alienation becomes the norm. Heathcliff and Catherine themselves are awesome as they work, without God's interference, through only their own power, their punishments and their final reward. /62/

Questions for Discussion and Writing

1. In what way is Lockwood ineffectual in the opening chapters of *Wuthering Heights?* Why? What have critics made of Lockwood's ineffectualness at the start of the novel?

2. What is a "forward-moving incident"? (page 58) Select a few incidents from the novel, and show why they are or are not forward-moving.

3. Discuss the unconventional morality of *Wuthering Heights,* explaining the definition of it.

4. Contrast Miss Adams's discussion of the use of the Bible in *Wuthering Heights* with those of other critics.

5. Do you agree that Lockwood changes during the novel because of his environment? Do other critics?

6. Study the role of Isabella in more detail, extending Miss Adams's comments.

[10] See Dorothy Van Ghent, "The Window Figure and the Two-Children Figure in *Wuthering Heights," Nineteenth-Century Fiction,* VII (September, 1952), 189-197, for a commentary on other evidence to this point.

The Villain in
Wuthering Heights

JAMES HAFLEY

To propose, over one hundred years after its publication, that a cel-
ebrated novel has been consistently and seriously misread—so much
so that its essential meaning has not in that time been recognized
by the countless persons who have discussed it—is to assume a responsibility that almost certainly can't be satisfied within the
bounds of a single essay; nonetheless that is what I should like to
propose here about *Wuthering Heights*. The one fact upon which
my thesis rests can be simply enough stated: Ellen Dean is the villain of the piece, one of the consummate villains in English literature. Read *Wuthering Heights* in the light of that fact and it is a
new experience—the experience, I believe, which it was meant to
be but has never thus far been in its history. Yet of course since that
fact challenges a solid century of habitual response, intellectual
and emotional, demonstration of it must be rather a more complicated affair, depending ultimately upon thoughtful and "impersonal" rereading of the novel more than upon looking over the
various evidences that I want here to marshal forth. Indeed, the
evidence is so clearly to be deduced that there is a sort of outrage
involved, perhaps, in using it to arrive by induction at the all-
important point of Nelly's villainy; but let her be assumed innocent
till she has been proved guilty.

And it is no job to assume such innocence as long as we read
words other than her own. Emily Brontë's sister Charlotte thought
Nelly "a specimen of true benevolence and homely fidelity,"[1] and

Copyright 1958 by The Regents of the University of California. Reprinted
from *Nineteenth-Century Fiction*, Volume XIII, Number 3 (December), pp. 199
through 215, by permission of The Regents.

[1] "Editor's Preface" to the 1850 ed. of *W.H.*

so opened a door through which every reader has followed her. Lord David Cecil added that Nelly and Joseph "provide a standard of normality /199/ which shows up in vivid relief the thrilling strangeness of the protagonists"[2]; he found Nelly "detached and normal."[3] Others have it that she is "a norm, beside which the extremes and excesses of the other characters are measurable,"[4] that she is "used to indicate the writer's own attitude towards the protagonists, or rather towards what they stand for, at a given moment,"[5] that she is "the old family retainer . . . representing . . . the conventions of the humblest moralism," from the perspective of whose "conventional morality" the behavior of Heathcliff and Cathy is defined as "a devastating spectacle of human waste."[6] Now all of this is completely familiar,[7] and even the occasional critic who has had reservations to make about Nelly's virtual sanctity has made them without questioning her general goodness; so, although V. S. Pritchett remarks that "she is an abdurate architect of the tragedy, for if she had told Catherine that Heathcliff was listening, the great confession scene . . . would not have had its tragic climax," he nevertheless finds her "the shrewd, plain Yorkshire stuff," whereas Heathcliff is "black-hearted, the devil."[8] And though Bruce McCullough says that "as a character in whose uncertain hands the fate of the children sometimes hangs, [Ellen] forms a definite part of the action," he views her as "manifestly a sensible, matter-of-fact person, whose obvious disapproval of much that she has to tell is an added guarantee of its authenticity."[9] Richard Chase, remarking that "the Brontë novels are concerned with the neuroses of women in a man's society,"[10] doesn't make the case for Nelly Dean, perhaps the most obviously neurotic of these women.

[2] *Early Victorian Novelists* (New York, 1935), p. 185.

[3] *Ibid.*, p. 195.

[4] Muriel Spark and D. Stanford, *Emily Brontë, Her Life and Work* (London, 1953), p. 256.

[5] Martin Turnell, "Wuthering Heights," *The Dublin Review*, CCVI (March, 1940), 145.

[6] Mark Schorer, "Technique as Discovery," in *Critiques and Essays on Modern Fiction 1920-51*, ed. J. W. Aldridge (New York, 1952) , p. 70.

[7] See also, for example, Leicester Bradner, "The Growth of 'Wuthering Heights,'" *PMLA*, XLVII (March, 1933), 145; Carl H. Grabo, *The Technique of the Novel* (New York, 1928), pp. 140-41; Lawrence and E. M. Hanson, *The Four Brontës* (London, 1950), p. 234; Dorothy Van Ghent, *The English Novel: Form and Function* (New York, 1953), pp. 157, 165.

[8] "Introduction," *W.H.* (Boston, 1956), pp. x, xi.

[9] *Representative English Novelists* (New York, 1946), pp. 191, 190.

[10] "The Brontës: a Centennial Observance," *Kenyon Review*, IX (Autumn, 1947), 406.

But if we turn away from the Charlotte Brontë-inspired myth of Ellen's decency, and look simply at the novel itself as Emily Brontë designed it, I think we find an Ellen very different from the customary one. Emily Brontë had nothing to say of Nelly's role and /200/ character except in her novel—though it might be mentioned in passing that a person as fiercely reticent and aloof as Emily Brontë would no doubt have disliked such a gregarious gossip—but the novel itself says, surely, all that's needed or wanted about her; for the most part, in fact, she says it herself, and Emily Brontë thereby accomplishes a technical feat of real brilliance. Lockwood's innocence (and we should never forget poor Lockwood's making faces at the dogs) assumes a new dimension as the sounding board of Ellen's viciousness, which can be most conveniently illustrated by our noticing the instances of it as they occur in the novel.

The first mention of Ellen Dean in *Wuthering Heights*, though it doesn't involve even a mildly spectacular instance of her evildoing, nonetheless is of major importance in the establishment of her character: "I dine," says Lockwood in a parenthetical remark—but one beginning "*N.B.*"—"between twelve and one o'clock; the housekeeper, a matronly lady, taken as a fixture along with the house, could not, or would not, comprehend my request that I might be served at five."[11] To be sure, this assertion of Nelly's will can be seen as the first step in the country's education of the citified Lockwood; but it is an advance warning about her, and it invests Heathcliff's first speech—" 'Thrushcross Grange is my own, sir. . . . I should not allow any one to inconvenience me, if I could hinder it' " (chapter i)—with a meaning that grows to enormous import as the novel proceeds. If Nelly has inconvenienced Lockwood slightly, she has " 'inconvenienced' " Heathcliff to the point of tragedy; and unless Heathcliff is to be seen as either a straw man or a devil[12] he must be looked at as tragically helpless, an Othello, in Nelly's hands. Charlotte Brontë's remark about him is as true in some ways as it is false in others: Heathcliff, she wrote,

exemplified the effects which a life of continued injustice and hard usage

[11] Chapter ii; since editions of *W.H.* are so numerous, references to the novel will be to chapter number only; and they will hereafter be made parenthetically in the text.

[12] "Deprived of the satanic nimbus which enthusiastic critics have conferred on him, Heathcliff is seen as a rough perfidious lout. . . . Heathcliff as a boy is a genuine person: . . . as a man a melodramatic dummy." Spark and Stanford, pp. 255-256.

may produce on a naturally perverse, vindictive, and inexorable disposition. Carefully trained and kindly treated, the black gipsy-cub might possibly have been reared into a human being, but tyranny and ignorance made of him a mere demon.[13] /201/

Charlotte Brontë here underlines the way in which her sister's novel is related to the social novel of the 1840's, however perserve and vindictive is her own appraisal of what Heathcliff "naturally" is. The tyranny, the injustice, of which she speaks are not, as we shall see, to be blamed upon Hindley so much as upon Nelly. Probably the most irresponsible of all comments about *Wuthering Heights* was made by G. K. Chesterton, when he said that Emily Brontë's "imagination was sometimes superhuman—always inhuman. *Wuthering Heights* might have been written by an eagle."[14] And many remarks almost as grotesque have been made about the "uniqueness" of this novel. Yet the tension between Heathcliff and Nelly, as well as the reasons for that tension, certainly insist at least upon our seeing *Wuthering Heights* as one of the novels of social awareness typical of its decade.

Nelly always likes to identify herself with the Lintons, and she resents Cathy as much as she does Heathcliff. After Cathy's death she is promoted from " 'wait[ing]' " on her (chapter iv) and made Edgar's housekeeper; she tells Lockwood that " 'Hareton is the last of them [the Earnshaws], as our Miss Cathy is of us—I mean, of the Lintons' " and at the same time remarks of Heathcliff, " 'it is strange people should be so greedy, when they are alone in the world' " (chapter iv). But the real greed is that by which Nelly has advanced to her position. She had begun life by considering herself as on a par with the Earnshaws—she dined as well as played with them. Heathcliff—to whom she refers at first as "it"—was a threat to her position: " 'Mr. Earnshaw told me to wash it, and give it clean things; and let it sleep with the children' " (chapter iv). She allows Cathy to grin and spit at him, and when the children will not accept him in their bedroom, " 'I put it on the landing of the stairs, hoping it might be gone on the morrow' " (chapter iv); when she is obliged to admit to Mr. Earnshaw her having done this, she is banished from the house as punishment. Such reminders that she is not one of the Earnshaws constitute the basis for Nelly's villainy. She admits to Lockwood that she hated Heathcliff, though

[13] Letter to W. S. Williams, 14 Aug. 1848, quoted by L. and E. M. Hanson, *op. cit.,* p. 260.
[14] *The Victorian Age in Literature* (New York, 1913), p. 113.

" 'Miss Cathy and he were now very thick,' " and " 'my pinches
moved him only to draw in a breath and open his eyes, as if he
had hurt himself by accident and nobody was to blame' " (chapter
iv). (This passage quite crumples /202/ Charlotte Brontë's estimate of what Heathcliff "naturally" was!) Even after his illness,
Nelly is unable to love Heathcliff and still wonders how Mr. Earnshaw can think him worthy of favor.

The ugliest instance of Nelly's behavior towards young Heathcliff occurs in the incident with which chapter iv concludes: Hindley,
who has been periodically beating Heathcliff, hits him with an iron
weight after their argument about the horses;

"and," [says Nelly] "had I not prevented it, [Heathcliff] would have gone
just so to the master, and got full revenge by letting his condition plead
for him, intimating who had caused it. . . . I persuaded him easily to let
me lay the blame of his bruises on the horse: he minded little what tale
was told since he had what he wanted."

If the "moral valuation" with which Nelly concludes this passage
is to be taken as proof of her normality and simple goodness, then
the novel hardly deserves serious reading. Young Heathcliff's demand to have Hindley's horse seems hardly "evil" in view of the
thrashings he'd had to suffer, and actually Nelly's own corruption,
rather than his, is what her remark emphasizes. It would be difficult
to find an example of adolescent cruelty more poignant than
Nelly's behavior here offers.

Nelly blames upon old Earnshaw's liking for Heathcliff the " 'humour[ing of] his partiality' " that she calls " 'rich nourishment to
the child's pride and black tempers' " (chapter v), though by now
the real reason for Heathcliff's mood has been made clear enough
to the reader. She calls Cathy " 'wild, wicked,' " and adds that " 'she
was much too fond of Heathcliff' " (chapter v)—fonder, that is to say,
than Nelly could endure. She speaks of herself as one of Cathy's
" 'companions,' " and one who " 'would not bear slapping and
ordering,' " and the rest of chapter v offers all too much witness
that in view of Nelly's superior attitude—for she feels herself quite
justified in slapping and ordering her " 'companions' "—she is
hardly the person to speak of Joseph as a " 'pharisee.' "

" 'We don't in general take to foreigners, here, Mr. Lockwood,
unless they take to us first' " (chapter vi), says Nelly, and though she
isn't referring to her treatment of Heathcliff, the remark echoes
both that and her idea of herself as rightly belonging to the same
social level as the Earnshaws. Thus, at Hindley's return to the

/203/ Heights she is quite ready to turn against him, too, when he orders her and Joseph to quarter themselves in the back-kitchen and leave the house for the family. In revenge, she encourages the recklessness of Cathy and Heathcliff: " 'many a time I've cried to myself to watch them growing more reckless daily, and I not daring to speak a syllable, for fear of losing the small power I still retained over the unfriended creatures' " (chapter vi). Surely Emily Brontë expects the reader to see rich irony in such speeches, rather than mawkish matter-of-factness. (Compare, in the preceding chapter, Nelly's " 'I would not bear slapping and ordering: and so I let her know.' ") Since Nelly herself is telling the story to Lockwood— it is her crowning act of villainy, and Lockwood's acceptance of it at face value is the ultimate comment upon his innocence—she will of course tell it so as to present herself in the genteel and upright role she fancies; she blames herself for what has happened only at times when she can be sure of his sympathizing with her; in the crucial instances she is silent, and we must watch, rather than hear, the role she plays; or in other instances, she maneuvers herself out of the way by coy references to her ignorance, her youth, her excitement. The art of Emily Brontë (like that of, say, Ford in *The Good Soldier* or even Marquand in *Apley*) by indirection finds direction out; and we have here a classic example of the point of view that both conceals and reveals all that it informs.

After Cathy's accident and stay at the Grange, Nelly—who had earlier complained of the child's wildness and tomboy habits—now frets at " 'playing lady's maid' " (chapter vii) to the changed girl, and recalls her better treatment—that is, her treatment as an equal to her employers—in the past. It's not without revealing her own desires that she tells Heathcliff, in a famous passage, " 'Were I in your place, I would frame high notions of my birth; and the thoughts of what I was should give me courage and dignity to support the oppressions of a little farmer' " (chapter vii): like Miriam in *Sons and Lovers* Nelly has built a romantic dream for herself; unlike Miriam, she sets about realizing that ironically shabby dream, to the extent to which she can, with an unscrupulousness that puts Heathcliff's to shame. We may, in chapter vii, consider it mere narrative ruse when Ellen sneaks upstairs to hear what is going on /204/ between Cathy and Heathcliff; indeed, what else can we consider it if we're committed to Charlotte Brontë's moral Ellen Dean? It is otherwise, like all such incidents in the novel, plain-and-simple spying, however offensive that may be to our accustomed notions about her. At any rate, we have the same sort of

choice to make when, at the close of chapter vii, Lockwood remarks that Ellen has " 'no marks of the manners which I am ha-
bituated to consider peculiar to your class,' " and Ellen, after sur-
veying her accomplishments with books and languages, calls them
" 'as much as you can expect of a poor man's daughter.' " We must,
I should think, feel that Ellen can't be at once what Lockwood
describes her as being *and* "the perdurable voice of the country."[15]
If she is just simple Nelly Dean, then here again is a ruse that allows Emily Brontë to employ a wider range of language and a more
complex style than would otherwise be probable; if she is not, then
here is another strand in the neatly wrought web of her motivation throughout the novel.

Cathy's ladylike qualities send Nelly once more to Hindley's side,
and like Richardson's Pamela, but not without the author's awareness, she finds the pat excuse for condoning his behavior: " 'I had
been,' " she brings out, " ' his foster-sister, and excused his behav-
iour more readily than a stranger would' "; but of Cathy, whose
" 'foster-sister' " she had also been, she says simply, " 'I own I did
not like her, after her infancy was past; and I vexed her frequently
by trying to bring down her arrogance' " (chapter viii). What she
dislikes most about Cathy now is her being " 'full of ambition' "!

"I've had many a laugh at her perplexities and untold troubles, which she
vainly strove to hide from my mockery. That sounds ill-natured; but she
was so proud, it became really impossible to pity her distress, till she should
be chastened into more humility. She did bring herself, finally, to confess,
and confide in me; there was not a soul else that she might fashion into an
adviser" (chapter viii).

That is, I think, the sort of passage that by now can be seen as speaking for itself; again, the picture of Heathcliff chastening the Earnshaws and Lintons into humility pales beside this brutal image;
pales, even though it is given from this point of view. Before Linton's visit, Nelly evidently combs the curl out of Cathy's hair; and,
when he has arrived and Cathy quite understandably asks her to
leave—remark- /205/ ing that servants don't start to clean a room
into which a guest has just stepped—Nelly creates a scene; Cathy has
angrily pinched her, and she reminds Lockwood as she recounts the
incident, " 'I've said I did not love her, and rather relished mortify-
ing her vanity now and then' " (poor Joseph! whom Nelly so
scorns for doing the same thing in his relatively naïve fashion).

When Nelly does depart, she leaves the door open to hear what's said between Cathy and Linton; Cathy cries out, as he criticizes her, " 'I did nothing deliberately,' " and Ellen—testifying to the truth of that for the reader—encourages Linton to leave: " ' "Miss is dreadfully wayward, sir," I called. "As bad as any married child: you'd better be riding home, or else she will be sick, only to grieve us." ' " The superb tone of that speech, with the strong contrast between its first word (a servant's) and its last (a relative's), beautifully illustrates Nelly's skill as an "inconveniencer."

In chapter ix occurs the famous confession scene, Mr. Pritchett's comment upon which I have already cited. Ellen at first says that she believes Heathcliff to have gone out to the barn; later, however, when she becomes aware of his presence during Cathy's speech, she watches him leave the settle bench, tells Cathy that he is in the barn and will soon be entering the house, and only when it is too late—when her revelation will hurt Cathy without mending the situation—admits that he had overheard their conversation; she is at this point " 'rather uneasy myself,' " but when Hindley enters she says of Cathy only, " 'Oh, she is naughty!' " Joseph then reveals that Nelly has been making possible secret interviews between Cathy and Linton, and upbraids Nelly: " 'Yah gooid fur nowt, slattenly wench!' "[16] Her behavior has deserved at least that. She caps it, however, admitting that she was not a gentle nurse to Cathy, and going so far as to say that

"one day I had the misfortune, when she provoked me exceedingly, to lay the blame of [Heathcliff's] disappearance on her: where indeed it belonged, as she well knew. From that period, for several months, she ceased to hold any communication with me, save in the relation of a mere servant." /206/

Here again, act and motive are carefully aligned. Ellen's statement, at the end of this chapter, that she did not wish to leave the Heights for the Grange after Cathy's marriage, and that only Cathy's " 'lamenting' " and Earnshaw's consequent orders (she mentions as well the " 'munificent wages' " promised her by Linton) moved her to acquiesce, can be given as little weight as Joseph's statements are

---

[16] Martin Turnell notes that "there is an apparent alteration in Nelly's attitude towards Edgar Linton. The 'doll' of the earlier part of the book is the 'kind master,' the 'dear master,' of the last" (op. cit., p. 148). Nelly's attitude can be seen to alter precisely in rhythm with her realization of what the Cathy-Edgar union can do for her ambition; at first only "a servant" in relation to Edgar, she is finally his housekeeper, with a special position of familial ease and refined comfort.

traditionally given. It's obviously absurd that she had no choice but
to leave: if the action of *Wuthering Heights* is largely restricted to
the Heights and the Grange, its world is not (save as Ellen's will
circumscribes that world so terrifyingly); much more probably Edgar's reward to Ellen for her services as duenna had taken the form
of this remove to the civilized climate of the Grange; Ellen's woe at
having had to leave little Hareton is as awkward as her satisfaction
with the Grange is patent.

Settled at the Grange, Ellen behaves so that Edgar " 'many a time
spoke sternly to me about my pertness' " (chapter x). But she is from
the time of Heathcliff's return totally committed to what she considers Edgar's cause. Once again Heathcliff, in Edgar's words " 'a
runaway servant' "—and they are words certainly delightful to Ellen—dominates Cathy's consciousness;

"I determined to watch his movements. My heart invariably cleaved to the
master's, in preference to Catherine's side. . . . I wanted something to
happen which might have the effect of freeing both Wuthering Heights and
the Grange of Mr. Heathcliff, quietly; leaving us as we had been prior to
his advent. His visits were a continual nightmare to me . . ." (chapter x).

But of course Ellen is no longer connected with Wuthering
Heights, and her sense of " 'us as we had been' " extends little beyond a feeling for "me as I had been." Hindley is " 'my early play-
mate' " when Ellen sees him as she passes the Heights on a journey
to Gimmerton; and when she tries to get in touch with him, but
is faced by Heathcliff instead.

"it urged me to resolve further on mounting vigilant guard, and doing my
utmost to check the spread of such bad influence at the Grange; even
though I should wake a domestic storm, by thwarting Mrs. Linton's pleasure" (chapter xi).

Little wonder that Cathy cries at Nelly, " 'To hear you, people might
think you were the mistress! . . .You want setting down in your right
/207/ place!' " But with such a reminder of her position Nelly is
only incited to greater, and more inappropriate, action against the
"black villain" she detests. She is more than ever the mistress when
she tells Linton,

" 'Indeed, I do think it's time to arrange [Heathcliff's] visits on another
footing. There's harm in being too soft, and now it's come to this—!' And
I related the scene in the court, and, as near as I dared, the whole subsequent dispute. I fancied it could not be very prejudicial to Mrs. Linton;
unless she made it so afterwards, by assuming the defensive for her guest"
(chapter xi).

That last remark is its own comment. Nelly lies to Cathy: " 'she did not know my share in contributing to the disturbance, and I was anxious to keep her in ignorance' " (chapter xi); and she " 'took the liberty to listen' " to the mortal arguments she has caused. She is, after all, " 'convinced that the Grange had but one sensible soul in its walls, and that lodged in my body' " (chapter xii).

Ellen keeps to herself Cathy's warning that she is dying, and even deliberately antagonizes her despite " 'the doctor's injunction that she should not be crossed' " (chapter xii), by creating a false impression of Edgar's response to the situation. He is, of course, furious with Ellen when, after it is too late, he discovers Cathy's real condition; and Cathy, in her semidelirious speeches, movingly realizes something of Ellen's evil:

"I see in you, Nelly, . . . an aged woman: you have grey hair and bent shoulders. This bed is the fairy cave under Peniston Crag, and you are gathering elf-bolts to hurt our heifers; pretending, while I am near, that they are only locks of wool. That's what you'll come to fifty years hence: I know you are not so now. . . . Shake your head as you will, Nelly, *you* have helped to unsettle me. . . . Ah! Nelly has played traitor. . . . Nelly is my hidden enemy. You witch! So you do seek elf-bolts to hurt us!" (chapter xii).

This awful revelation Nelly describes as a maniac's passion; unfortunately for Emily Brontë's art, readers have more or less agreed with that description and so lost the force of one of the consummate scenes in fiction. Aware of Isabella's elopement just afterwards, Nelly says nothing, to avoid " 'confusion.' " " ' I saw nothing for it but to hold my tongue, and suffer matters to take their course.' " That is as much effect as Cathy's accusation and Edgar's fury with her have had; her villainy isn't now to be halted, though " 'I thought, myself, [Cathy] might recover, so waited on as she was.' " /208/

Telling the unsuspecting Heathcliff of Cathy's illness, Ellen " 'blamed her, as she deserved, for bringing it all on herself' " (chapter xiv). And she consents to play what she admits is a "treacherous part in my master's house' " by acting as go-between for the lovers, saying simply that after fifty refusals " 'in the long run he forced me' " to acquiesce, but giving no hint about the nature of that " 'force.' " She has thereby succeeded in preventing the possibility of Cathy's recovering. If, as I have suggested, Heathcliff is a sort of Othello, Nelly outdoes Iago at the moment when Edgar discovers Cathy and Heathcliff together:

"I heard my master mounting the stairs—the cold sweat ran from my forehead: I was horrified.

"'Are you going to listen to her ravings?' I said, passionately. 'She does
not know what she says. Will you ruin her, because she has not wit to help
herself? Get up! You could be free instantly. That is the most diabolical
deed that ever you did. We are all done for—master, mistress, and servant.'

"I wrung by hands, and cried out; and Mr. Linton hastened his step at
the noise. In the midst of my agitation, I was sincerely glad to observe
that Catherine's arms had fallen relaxed, and her head hung down.

"'She's fainted, or dead,' I thought: 'so much the better. Far better that
she should be dead, than lingering a burden and a misery-maker to all
about her'" (chapter xv).

When one considers the extent of Nelly Dean's achievement in this
passage as it measures her character, the similar one of Iago (*Othello,*
II, iii) postively yields to it for a time. It is a richly symbolic moment when, after Cathy's death, Nelly twists the lock of Heathcliff's hair with that of Edgar's and encloses them in the locket, herself the agent of their tragedy.

Nelly is now in truth the mistress of the Grange; when little
Cathy's crying disturbs Isabella, who has come to confide in Ellen,
"I rang the bell, and committed it to a servant's care'" (chapter
xvii), she says. Indeed, she has at first supposed Isabella to be "'one
of the maids,'" and cried out, "'Have done! How dare you show
your giddiness here?'" She is clearly in command. Poor Isabella,
thinking that Edgar had known of Heathcliff's visits during Cathy's
illness, cannot understand why her brother did not have him taken
into custody. And when she confesses that she enjoyed Heathcliff's
misery—"'I couldn't miss the chance of sticking in a dart: his weakness was the only time when I could taste the delight of paying
wrong for /209/ wrong'"—Nelly, who has of course always behaved
in just this way to Cathy, interrupts,

"'Fie, fie, Miss! . . .One might suppose you had never opened a Bible in
your life. If God afflict your enemies, surely that ought to suffice you. It is
both mean and presumptuous to add your torture to his!'" (chapter xvii).

"'But,'" says Nelly after another such hypocritical comment
upon the events of her story, "'you'll not want to hear my moralizing, Mr. Lockwood; you'll judge as well as I can, all these things: at
least, you'll think you will, and that's the same'" (chapter xvii):
it is almost as near as she ever comes to outright laughter at his
gullibility.

Nelly's involvement with young Cathy Linton is just as profound and sinister as that with her mother, of course; after their trip to the Heights—where Edgar had forbidden Cathy to go—

"I insisted . . . that if she revealed my negligence of his orders, he would perhaps be so angry that I should have to leave; and Cathy couldn't bear that prospect: she pledged her word, and kept it, for my sake. After all, she was a sweet little girl" (chapter xviii).

Her tone with Edgar himself is equally firm and familiar; when Joseph comes to take Linton Heathcliff to the Heights, Nelly announces his arrival to Edgar, " 'advising that he should be dismissed till next day' " (chapter xix).

Thus Nelly takes Cathy to the Heights to call on young Heathcliff despite her knowledge that Edgar would "hate" her should he discover the deception and treachery. Nelly sees almost at once that Linton Heathcliff is spiteful and dangerous, and her excuses to Mr. Lockwood for her behavior—" 'We staid till afternoon: I could not tear Miss Cathy away, before' " (chapter xxi)—are shoddier than ever in their inadequacy to justify her behavior. She is " 'fully as inclined to laugh as scold' " when she tardily discovers the letters Cathy has received, but does not acquaint the girl's father with a situation now becoming serious. Again it is the imperious—and responsible—Nelly who accepts Cathy's " 'refusal' " to forego a walk, on a rainy afternoon, and " 'unwillingly' " goes out; when Cathy jumps over the Grange wall to retrieve her hat, Ellen " 'like a fool, didn't recollect' " that she cannot return inside unless the garden door is unlocked. And when Cathy insists upon seeing Linton Heathcliff once more, /210/

"What use were anger and protestations against her silly credulity? We parted that night—hostile; but next day beheld me on the road to Wuthering Heights, by the side of my wilful young mistress's pony. I couldn't bear to witness her sorrow: to see her pale, dejected countenance, and heavy eyes; and I yielded . . ." (chapter xxi).

In view of Nelly's position and knowledge, this rings as false as any such explanation she attempts in the course of the novel. Her " 'strenuous objections' " aren't sufficiently strenuous to govern Cathy as the girl ought to be governed; once again Edgar is kept in the dark; and Cathy's unaccompanied visits to the Heights after this Nelly explains by remarking (what only a Lockwood could accept) that " 'I never considered what she did with herself after tea' " (chapter xxiii), and by confessing to a singular lack of suspicion completely out of accord with all we know of her. When she does regard the truth from which she has been so diligently averting her eyes, she goes to Edgar and tells " 'the whole story; with the exception of [Cathy's] conversations with her cousin, and any mention of Hareton' " (chapter xxiv)! She blatantly assures Edgar that he needn't worry about Cathy: " 'I'll stand her friend and counsellor to the last' " (chapter xxv). Indeed, on their next visit to the Heights, it is *Cathy* who wishes to leave, when Linton Heathcliff has fallen asleep; but " ' "we must not leave him asleep," I answered; "wait till he wakes, and be patient. You were mighty eager to set off, but your longing to see poor Linton has soon evaporated" ' " (chapter xxvi). She says little afterwards in answer to Edgar's questions about what they have been doing, " 'for I hardly knew what to hide, and what to reveal.' " Edgar assumes Linton to be of good character, " 'and I, through pardonable weakness, refrained from correcting the error' " (chapter xxvii).

On the fatal day of Cathy's capture by Heathcliff, it is Nelly herself who has arranged for Cathy's riding out beyond the Grange, and if poor Linton Heathcliff is, as he says, a traitor to Cathy in acting as bait for Heathcliff's hook, he is not nearly the traitor Nelly is. She informs Heathcliff that Linton is dying: " 'a sad thing it will be for us all, but a blessing for him' " (chapter xxvii). And she permits Cathy to accompany Heathcliff and his son to the Heights, lest he harm the boy: " 'however I disapproved, I couldn't hinder her: indeed how could she have refused him herself?' " Heathcliff's /211/ " 'glance' " she offers as reason enough for her doing nothing to prevent his keeping Cathy at the Heights; when Heathcliff goes out to speak to the servants who have come inquiring from the Grange, Nelly could, as he later tells her himself, easily open the lattice and call out for help; but she does not; and she has Lockwood by now sufficiently in command to venture this remarkable comment:

"I seated myself in a chair, and rocked, to and fro, passing harsh judgement on my many derelictions of duty; *from which,* it struck me then, *all the misfortunes of all my employers sprang* [my emphasis]. It was not the case, in reality, I am aware; but it was, in my imagination, that dismal night; and I thought Heathcliff himself less guilty than I" (chapter xvii).

This is as close as Emily Brontë could have come, without violating Ellen's character as she had created it, to insisting upon the woman's real nature; it reads almost like a plea from author to readers to be aware of her art, and perhaps suggests her own anxiety lest they too be deceived by her magnificent villain.

Even when Nelly escapes from the Heights and goes for help—as usual, it is only when help could no longer do much good—she lies: " 'I said Heathcliff forced me to go in: which was not quite true' " (chapter xxviii); and she mitigates both Linton Heathcliff's character and his father's conduct. But she has now managed things so as to be herself as comfortable as possible after Edgar's death; therefore, despite the ugly marriage of Cathy, " 'yet did I hope, and began to cheer up under the prospect of retaining my home, and my employment, and, above all, my beloved young mistress . . .' " (chapter xxix). She laughs at Heathcliff when he tells her that the dead Catherine is mystically present to him; but he warns her away from the Heights, where young Cathy is to stay: " 'I want none of your prying at my house!' " It is, however, tragically too late for such precautions.

Now Ellen Dean's story ends with chapter xxx. She has, of course, not told this long story to Lockwood without very good reason: he is gullible, he is weak, he is disposed to like her. He would, in short, make a very good "master" for her should he marry Cathy now that young Linton has died; it is her purpose to arrange his desiring such a marriage (and arrange it she does!); she concludes, " 'I can see no remedy, at present, unless [Cathy] could marry again: and that scheme it does not come within my province to arrange.' " But Lock- /212/ wood's ineffectual vanity, though it would make him useful to Nelly, is also what prevents her plan.

She sends him in chapter xxxi, with a note to Cathy—" 'the worthy woman,' " he mentions, " 'was not conscious of anything odd in her request.' " But it comes to nothing; the chapter ends with Lockwood's thinking, "What a realization of something more romantic than a fairy tale it would have been for Mrs. Linton Heathcliff, had she and I struck up an attachment, as her good nurse desired, and migrated together into the stirring atmosphere of the town!" And, he might less fatuously have added, what a realization of something even more romantic—her life's dream—for the "good nurse" herself!

When Lockwood returns for a visit to the Heights, long after his convalescence, he finds Nelly still in control of as much as she can hope for: in control of Joseph—" 'But whisht, old man, and read your Bible, like a christian, and never mind me' " (chapter xxxii) —and of Cathy—" 'She has not learnt to manage her affairs yet, and I act for her: there's nobody else' "—and of Hareton, whose marriage to Cathy is now " 'the crown of all my wishes.' " Even while Heathcliff still lived, " 'I held the mistress's post in making tea and carving' " (chapter xxxiii), and now she reigns supreme over the meager spoils of her ambition. She had never been able to gratify that ambition by a significant marriage of her own; we have it from Joseph that " 'Nelly—Nasty, ill nowt as shoo is, Thank God! *shoo* cannot stale t' sowl uh nob'dy! Shoo wer niver soa handsome, but whet a body mud look at her 'baht winking.' " She has gratified it, then, with as significant a marriage for Cathy as, barring Lockwood and his failure to come through for her, was practicable. Thus she encouraged the courtship of Cathy and Hareton: " 'I did not notice how time got on. You know, they both appeared in a measure my children' " (chapter xxxiii).

And she has seen the usurper Heathcliff join Catherine in death. Heathcliff, though he learned, too late, to try to guard against her prying, never in his life learned, as Cathy did, anything like the full horror of Ellen Dean's character; he trusted her, at the end, with his innermost secrets, to the extent to which he could articulate them—ironically confident that " 'you'll not talk of what I tell you' " (chapter xxxiii). Even after his death she continues to lie: " 'I con- /213/ cealed the fact of his having swallowed nothing for four days, fearing it might lead to trouble' "—trouble for herself, for not having reported in Gimmerton his condition and behavior. But there is an unforgettable moment in which Heathcliff, after his death, faces Ellen with the innocence that is his knowledge of her guilt; and it is too much even for her. She is arranging his corpse:

"I tried to close his eyes: to extinguish, if possible, that frightful, life-like gaze of exultation, before anyone else beheld it. They would not shut: they seemed to sneer at my attempts; and his parted lips and sharp white teeth sneered too! Taken with another fit of cowardice, I cried for Joseph. Joseph shuffled up and made a noise, but resolutely refused to meddle with him" (chapter xxxiv).

It is what Ellen has not refused to do all his life long; only in death has Heathcliff been able to resist, to escape, that "meddling"; even, in some small measure, to punish it: " 'I don't like,' " she confesses, " 'being out in the dark, now; and I don't like being left by myself in this grim house: I cannot help it.' " But she has won, nevertheless; she finishes, " 'I shall be glad when they leave it, and shift to the Grange!' " And as we last see her, she is expostulating with Mr. Lockwood for his rudeness! Surely we are meant to recognize the tragic innocence of Heathcliff and Cathy—to join Lockwood in wondering "how any one could ever imagine unquiet slumbers for the sleepers in that quiet earth."

Emily Brontë has been charged with a "failure to envisage char-

acters ethically. She has very little sense of good and evil as forma-
tive and determinative factors in the growth of personality."[17] Yet
it is precisely such a sense, totally embodied in the drama of Ellen
Dean, that constitutes one of her chief artistic resources; her moral
awareness is keen and complex enough to justify Sir Herbert Read's
remark that "she is forever perplexed by the problem of evil,"[18] and
Wuthering Heights is ultimately the dramatization of that perplex-
ity, Heathcliff and Catherine triumphing tragically over the mean
success of Nelly Dean; Hareton and Cathy coming through paradoxically both against and for that success. Anything like an explicit
analysis of the moral significance of this novel, as I have here proposed it be read, would require at least another essay; as it is, I
suspect that Swinburne was not greatly exaggerating when he wrote
of *Wuther-* /214/ *ing Heights,* "It may be true that not many will
ever take it to their hearts; it is certain that those who do like it will
like nothing very much better in the whole world of poetry or
prose."[19] /215/

Questions for Discussion and Writing

1. Agree or disagree with Hafley's thesis that Nelly Dean is the villain of
Wuthering Heights.

2. Is Nelly neurotic? What have other critics said?

3. Pass careful judgment on the phrase "gregarious gossip" (page 201) as
applied to Nelly Dean.

4. What sort of person does Hafley think Lockwood is?

5. Comment on the first piece of evidence put forth against Nelly. (page
201)

6. Where and why, according to Hafley, have readers gone astray in reading *Wuthering Heights?*

7. Search for evidence which combats Hafley's theory. Look, for example,
for indications in Nelly of a more favorable attitude toward Heathcliff.

8. Track down some of Hafley's quotations, and determine the extent to
which alternate explanations of them are possible or probable.

9. What does Hafley's evaluation of Ellen Dean do to your reading of the
novel? What, for example, does it do to the theme?

10. What assumptions about reading a novel does Hafley make?

[17] Spark and Stanford, *op. cit.,* p. 266.
[18] *Reason and Romanticism* (London, 1926), p. 180.
[19] "Emily Brontë," *The Complete Works of Algernon Charles Swinburne* (London, 1926), XIV, 54.

The Incest Theme in
Wuthering Heights

ERIC SOLOMON

According to two recent critics, much of the power of *Wuthering Heights* stems from the inevitability of the tradegy. Richard Chase considers that it is impossible to imagine such a stormy, undisciplined pair as Cathy and Heathcliff ever settling down to a normal life of domesticity.[1] Dorothy Van Ghent goes further to point out that the /80/ foster kinship "provides an imaginative reason for the unnaturalness and impossibility of their mating."[2] Might not the tragic fate that envelops the lovers be even more inevitable? Might not Heathcliff and Cathy be brother and sister?

One need not follow the dark Freudian lines of the Emily-Bramwell relationship—which have been fully explored by the author's biographers—[3] to prove Emily Brontë's familiarity with the concept of incestuous connections. Echoes of Byron and Byronism exist throughout her poems; to a writer familiar with the life of the lover of Aurora Leigh and the works of the author of *Manfred,* the incest motif would hardly be unknown. Eighteenth-century fiction certainly provided numerous examples of the theme—incest is a plot device in *Moll Flanders, Tom Jones, Humphrey Clinker,* and *Evelina,* among others.

External evidence is rarely of much value in a consideration of

Copyright 1959 by The Regents of the University of California. Reprinted from *Nineteenth-Century Fiction,* Volume XIV, Number 1 (June), pp. 80 through 83, by permission of The Regents.

[1] "The Brontës: A Centennial Observance," *The Kenyon Review,* IX (Autumn, 1947), 496.

[2] "The Window Figure and the Two-Children Figure in *Wuthering Heights,*" *Nineteenth-Century Fiction,* VII (December, 1953), p. 196.

[3] See, for example, Romer Wilson, *All Alone* (London, 1928) or Norma Crandall, *Emily Brontë: A Psychological Portrait* (Rindge, N. H., 1957).

Emily Brontë's fiction, however; nor does the dark poetry of
Wuthering Heights call for a gloss from the standpoint of logical
coherence and careful motivation. Still, Emily Brontë's technique is
not haphazard. The manipulation of time sequence and angle of
vision is carefully handled. Why, then, is there such confusion and
mystery surrounding Heathcliff's entrance on the scene?

At first glance, the discovery of Heathcliff might appear to be the
obvious way to introduce a strange child whose birth is to remain a
mystery, who may be gypsy or prince, animal or devil. Old Earnshaw travels to Liverpool, notices a child wandering the streets, and,
overcome by pity, brings the boy home with him. But this section of
the novel is strangely unsatisfactory, leaving many questions un-
resolved.

In Nelly Dean's narrative, no reason is suggested for Earnshaw's
visit to Liverpool, and this in a passage where Nelly describes not
only the distance, "sixty miles each way,"[4] and the fact that he is
going to make the journey on foot, but also the gifts—a fiddle and a
whip—to be purchased for Hindley and Cathy. These details are
presented clearly, but Nelly never so much as indicates why Earnshaw is mak- /81/ ing this arduous trip, whether in connection
with the farm, legal matters, or personal reasons.

Earnshaw returns with a mysterious dirty child whom his wife
"must e'en take as a gift of God." He gives a vague and illogical report of finding the homeless and starving child in the Liverpool
gutters. Earnshaw's rationalization of the adoption seems weak:

Not a soul knew to whom it belonged, he said, and his money and time,
being both limited, he thought it better to take it home with him, at once,
than run into vain expenses there; because he was determined he would
not leave it as he found it.

Even in an eighteenth-century provincial slum, the waif must have
had *some* protector. Mrs. Earnshaw considers her husband to be
mad, and the narrator, tart Nelly Dean, expresses doubts through
her manner of recounting the tale. She informs Lockwood that Earnshaw "*tried* to explain the matter; but he was *really* half dead with
fatigue ... all that I could make out ... was a *tale* of his seeing it ..."

The brief picture of Mrs. Earnshaw presented here would certainly supply an added motive for concealment of a child who could
possibly be Earnshaw's illegitimate offspring. She "was ready to fling

    [4] All citations to *Wuthering Heights* refer to Chapter IV of Emily Brontë,
Wuthering Heights (Oxford, 1931) [The Shakespeare Head Brontë]. Italics in
passages quoted are mine.

it out of doors"; she grumbles and berates the exhausted traveler. How would such a woman have reacted to any honest admission of sinful adultery?[5] Earnshaw could only bring a by-blow into the family by devious means, as long as his wife was still alive.

In addition, Heathcliff soon becomes Earnshaw's favorite, more cherished than his own children, an unnatural occurrence surely— unless this is a natural child. Nelly has her suspicions. Earnshaw, she comments, "took to the child *strangely*," this "poor fatherless child, as *he* called him." Hindley, for his part, sees Heathcliff "as a usurper of his parent's affections."

There can be no doubt that Emily Brontë casts a vague incestuous aura over the entire plot of *Wuthering Heights*. Heathcliff marries his lost love's sister-in-law; his wife's son marries her brother's daugh- /82/ ter; Cathy's daughter marries *her* brother's son. An unconsciously incestuous love between the two leading characters would not run counter to the tone of a novel filled with violent and savage scenes, such as the sadistic rubbing of a wrist over a broken window-pane, Cathy's fierce delirium, or the sight of Heathcliff smashing his bloody head against a tree.

Certainly *Wuthering Heights* can be read without any such theory of Heathcliff's birth. Yet this view supplies an answer to some of the novel's ambiguities. If Heathcliff and Cathy were—even unknowingly—brother and sister, they obviously never could marry on earth, however violent their passion might be. Despite her powerful vision of moral decay, Emily Brontë could not overthrow all traditional canons of taste. Again, Heathcliff, as Earnshaw's real son, would have an increased motivation for his bitter insistence that Wuthering Heights must belong to him.

Above all, the tragedy of *Wuthering Heights* is increased in intensity and inevitability if Heathcliff and Cathy are seen not only as the products of their own wilfully destructive natures, but as the victims of a fate beyond their control. When Cathy cries out that she is Heathcliff, does she mean that they are of one flesh as well as one spirit? /83/

[5] It might be objected at this point that Earnshaw hardly seems the type of man who would have a clandestine affair to conceal. One can, however, derive Emily Brontë's belief in heredity from the strong family resemblences displayed by her characters. The second generation of Heathcliffs and Lintons markedly show the parents' characteristics. Since Cathy and Hindley, Earnshaw's legitimate children, display the wild and drunken natures that their author assigns them, might not this indicate something about her view of the parent, something not incommensurate with siring an illegitimate child?

Questions for Discussion and Writing

1. "Might not Heathcliff and Cathy be brother and sister?" (page 81) Using interpretations by other critics, give your answer to Eric Solomon's question.

2. Eric Solomon avers that "The manipulation of time sequence and angle of vision is carefully handled." (page 81) What does he mean by "manipulation of time sequence" and "angle of vision"? Do you agree with Solomon's statement? Do other critics of the novel agree with it?

3. Find one or two answers to Solomon's question: "Why . . . is there such confusion and mystery surrounding Heathcliff's entrance on the scene?" (page 81)

4. What is "vague and illogical" (page 82) about Earnshaw's account of finding Heathcliff? Solomon mentions two things; do you agree with him? Are there more?

5. In his footnote on page 82, Solomon describes Cathy and Hindley as having "wild and drunken natures." What does he mean by "drunken" here? Do you accept the word as applicable to both characters?

6. What do you think of Solomon's "added motive" (page 82)—that is, that the character of Mrs. Earnshaw supports the idea of her husband's concealing the identity of Heathcliff?

7. On page 83, Solomon says that his theory "supplies an answer to some of the novel's ambiguities." What instances of this does he supply? Are they convincing? Can you find other ambiguities that are resolved by the proposed theory concerning Heathcliff's birth?

8. Contrast what Eric Solomon finds "inevitable" in *Wuthering Heights* with the findings of other critics.

9. What does Solomon think is the theme of *Wuthering Heights?* Is this an unusual or usual analysis of the theme?

Lockwood's Dreams and the Exegesis of *Wuthering Heights*

EDGAR F. SHANNON, JR.

I

Few novels have a more vivid, even bizarre, introduction than *Wuthering Heights*. At once prologue and *raison d'être* for the primary narrative, the first three chapters, presenting Lockwood's rude reception at the Heights, reach a climax in his extraordinary dreams in the panelled-bed. Until recently these two dreams attracted little critical attention. The first, in which Lockwood, accompanied by Joseph, braves the snow to Gimmerton Church, hears the Reverend Jabes Branderham preach the sermon "Seventy Times Seven and the First of the Seventy-First," and endures the staves of the congregation, Edith M. Fenton dismissed as "an inconsequential medley"; and E. K. Brown merely noticed as having a "mysterious meaning."[1] The second, or nightmare, in which Lockwood saws the wrist of the elder Catherine's childish shade against the broken glass of the windowpane and deafens his ears to her pleas for admittance until his frenzied scream restores him to consciousness, interested Miss Fenton only for its divergence from the dreams of Gothic romance. Lately, however, Ruth M. Adams in "Wuthering Heights: the Land East of Eden" has postulated a theory of the novel upon Lock-

[1] "The Spirit of *Wuthering Heights* as Distinguished from That of Gothic Romance," *Washington University Studies*, VIII (Humanistic Series, No. 1, 1920), 108; *Rhythm in the Novel* (Toronto, 1950), p. 6.

wood's first dream.[2] Yet, in founding her commentary upon one dream, she makes the same mistake as Dorothy Van Ghent, who explicates the book in terms of the nightmare alone; for the two dreams are inextricably linked.[3] In /**95**/ both action and import they are integral to each other and to a full understanding of *Wuthering Heights*.

Ironically for Miss Adams's interpretation of the first dream, the land east of Eden is the land of Nod; and she asserts that the text of the sermon is Gen. 4:24, "If Cain shall be avenged sevenfold, truly Lamech seventy and sevenfold"—a verse that has no relevance whatever to Branderham's pious discourse. Actually, both its title and substance derived from Matt. 18:21-22:

> Then came Peter to him, and said, Lord, how oft shall my brother sin against me, and I forgive him? till seven times?
>
> Jesus said unto him, I say not unto three, Until seven times: but, Until seventy times seven.

Lockwood himself pointedly identifies this reference. He suddenly realizes in the dream that, instead of returning to Thrushcross Grange, he and Joseph are "journeying to hear the famous Jabes Branderham preach from the text—'Seventy Times Seven'; and either Joseph, the preacher, or I had committed the 'First of the Seventy-First,' and were [*sic*] to be publicly exposed and excommunicated" (p. 27).[4] Branderham's sermon is "divided into *four hundred and ninety* parts [the product of seventy times seven] . . . each discussing a separate sin." Moreover, Lockwood includes the hypothetical brother of Peter's question when he says, ". . . it seemed necessary the brother should sin different sins on every occasion . . . odd transgressions that I never imagined previously." The first of the seventy-first is the first of the category of unforgivable sins; and when the preacher reaches the first of the seventy-first, Lockwood rises and denounces him "as the sinner of the sin that no Christian need pardon" (p. 28). Protesting forbearance and forgiveness for four hundred and ninety heads of discourse, the dreamer declares, " 'The four hundred and ninety first is too much. Fellow-martyrs, have at him! Drag him down, and crush him to atoms, that the place which knows him may know him no more!' " But Branderham turns the charge against his accuser:

[2] *NCF* (June, 1958), pp. 58-62.

[3] "On *Wuthering Heights*," in *The English Novel: Form and Function* (New York, 1953), pp. 153-170.

[4] Parenthetical page references are to the Modern Library College Edition of *Wuthering Heights*, ed. Royal A. Gettmann (New York, 1950).

"*Thou art the man!*" cried Jabes, after a solemn pause, leaning over his cushion. "Seventy times seven times didst thou gapingly contort thy visage —seventy /96/ times seven did I take counsel with my soul—Lo, this is human weakness: this also may be absolved! The First of the Seventy-First is come. Brethren, execute upon him the judgment written."

When the congregation set upon Lockwood with their staves, he awakens to discover the source of their rattling blows and Branderham's rapping of the pulpit is a fir branch and cones striking the lattice window.

The second dream follows immediately as Lockwood, sinking back into slumber and imagining himself breaking the window to reach out and deflect the "importunate branch," is seized by Cathy's icy fingers. Mrs. Van Ghent bases her case for the symbolism of the nightmare upon a supposed inadequacy of determinants for it and for Lockwood's cruelty to the dream child.[5] But, to gain the reader's acceptance, Emily Brontë prepares consistently for this culmination to Lockwood's initial experiences at Wuthering Heights. In addition to the obvious contributions of his reading of Cathy's books (with their marginal complaints against the tyranny of Hindley and Joseph and the concluding prospect of "a scamper on the moors" [p. 25]) and the insistent branch—the chief representative and presentative elements of both dreams—there is ample "stuff" for the "manifest content" of the nightmare, a credible background of atmosphere and mood to produce it.[6] In Lockwood's hearing, for instance, the second Catherine taunts Joseph with her progress in witchcraft: she credits the death of the red cow and his rheumatism to her powers in the "Black Art" and threatens to model him in wax and clay (p. 18). She retorts to Hareton's refusal to accompany Lockwood home in the snowstorm, "Then I hope his ghost will haunt you . . ." (p. 20). When Zillah surreptitiously shows Lockwood into the proscribed chamber containing the panelled-bed, she speaks of the "queer goings on" (p. 22) in the house during her employment there. As he dozes in the bed, before he dreams in earnest, the white letters of the first Catherine's name "started from the dark as vivid as spectres—the air swarmed with Catherines" (p. 23). /97/

[5] *The English Novel: Form and Function*, pp. 160-161.
[6] See Sigmund Freud, *Dream Psychology: Psychoanalysis for Beginners* (New York, 1921), p. 14, for the distinction between "manifest" and "latent content." Although the latent content of Lockwood's dreams may be pertinent to a study of his personality, it has no bearing upon the central development of the novel. The sexual symbolism of his lacking a staff and the breaking of the window-membrane with attendant blood, pain, and terror is obvious.

In two successive visits to Wuthering Heights, Lockwood, gregarious and affable, is the object of rebuffs and indignities. Detained by the snowfall, he is refused both a guide to the Grange and a bed in the house. During each of his calls ferocious dogs attack him; and on the second occasion, while Gnasher and Wolf pin him to the ground, Heathcliff and Hareton laugh at his predicament. His nose bleeds, and Zillah finally checks the gore by dashing a pint of freezing water down his neck. He goes to bed cold, dizzy, nauseated, and, not surprisingly, in a "bad temper" (pp. 21, 23, 26). His two dreams, though immediately induced by his reading and the rapping branch, emotionally derive from the events of the past two days; and the assault of Branderham's congregation provides a penultimate instance of violence to Lockwood's person.

In this dream, having "no weapon to raise in self-defense" (p. 28), he begins grappling with Joseph for his staff. Despite the conspiracy of critics to present him as a milksop, Lockwood habitually reacts swiftly and responds aggressively to abuse. When the bitch flies at him on his first visit, he flings her back, interposes a table between himself and the swarm of curs, and holds off his principal assailants with a poker (p. 8). Thinking that a derogatory remark of Joseph's to young Catherine is meant for him, he is "sufficiently enraged" to step "towards the aged rascal with an intention of kicking him out of the door" (pp. 17-18). Discovering that Heathcliff will not allow Hareton to be his guide in the snow, he snatches the lantern by which Joseph is milking and starts off alone. When the dogs pull him down and stand over him, he trembles, not in fear but in rage, and shouts imprecations at them and at Heathcliff until Zillah intervenes.

Lockwood's frantic attempt in the nightmare to break Cathy's grip by cutting her wrist on the broken glass "till the blood ran down and soaked the bedclothes" (pp. 29-30) is not, then, as Mrs. Van Ghent maintains, mere gratuitous cruelty, psychologically unmotivated.[7] He had already shown himself capable of giving pain and had "gained a reputation of deliberate heartlessness" (p. 7) when he disdained and discomfited the young lady at the sea coast who had finally returned his visual advances. But his barbarity to the child grows out of the first dream and is an ultimate act of self-assertion and self- /98/ preservation—the final terrified retaliation of the dreamer for the physical and emotional outrages he has sustained.

Clearly, there is little foundation for Mrs. Van Ghent's contention

[7] Van Ghent, p. 160.

that the very lack of motivation for Lockwood's action substantiates the symbolic quality of the nightmare as a revelation of autonomous darkness in the psychic depths of the human soul, even in the soul of a character who "more successfully than anyone else in the book, has shut out the powers of darkness."[8] Rather, the dream is symptomatic of the careful causality that governs the central action of the novel. When Lockwood contends that people in remote regions "*do* live more in earnest, more in themselves, and less in surface, change, and frivolous external things" than city dwellers, Nelly replies, "Oh! here we are the same as anywhere else, when you get to know us" (pp. 72, 73). This exchange embodies the novelist's claim for the scope of the representation. Lockwood demonstrates in little what occurs in gigantic proportions in Heathcliff. The cruelty in the nightmare indicates that all men—sophisticate as well as boor—react vehemently to exacerbation of nerves and negation of sympathy. Repelled, even Lockwood's well-bred gestures toward social intercourse overnight degenerate into brutality.

II

The two dreams which conclude Lockwood's misadventures in the first three chapters of *Wuthering Heights* not only help to authenticate Nelly Dean's tempestuous tale; they alert the reader to the ethical eye of the storm. In spite of an aura of quaint absurdity, Branderham's sermon, "Seventy Times Seven and the First of the Seventy-First," correctly interpreted, advances the idea of an unpardonable sin beyond the ordinary scale of human wrongs. The nightmare connects this notion with the elder Catherine when the ghost-child cries, "I've been a waif for twenty years (p. 30)!" In early English law "waif" (ME *waive*) was the term for a female outlaw, and the suggestion immediately arises that, like the wandering Jew, Cathy has been condemned to wander the earth, homeless and friendless, an outcast from society, for some heinous crime committed during her lifetime. Lockwood overtly links the implications of the two dreams as they apply to Cathy when he blusters to Heathcliff, /99/

"If the little fiend had got in at the window, she probably would have strangled me! . . . she must have been a changeling—wicked little soul! She told me she had been walking the earth those twenty years: a just punishment for her mortal transgressions, I've no doubt!" (pp. 31-32).

Lockwood's denunciation focuses attention on the thematic prob-

[8] *Ibid.*, p. 161.

lem of the novel—the nature of Cathy's offense. With the tradition of the Gothic novel in the background, one thinks easily of dark sins of passion—murder, incest, adultery; and Lockwood's first dream encourages the probability of the last. Branderham's words to Lockwood, " *'Thou art the man!'* " are the words of Nathan the prophet when he delivers God's rebuke to David for appropriating Bathsheba, the wife of Uriah the Hittite (II Sam. 12: 7). The action of the novel discloses an adulterous situation between Heathcliff and Cathy; but Emily Brontë disappoints simple expectancy and translates the ethical conflict from a physical to a spiritual level. There is no breach of the Ten Commandments, of the statutory code of church and state. Not to be satisfied with domestic morality, she expands her theme to universal significance—the destructive consequences of thwarted love.

The "central moral assertion in *Wuthering Heights*," as Richard Chase has said, is "Cathy's failure to fulfill her mission; which was, clearly, to marry Heathcliff."[9] Put the other way about, her sin is marrying Edgar Linton, when she loves Heathcliff with a love that springs from a natural and elemental affinity between them. Heathcliff, she tells Nelly, is " 'more myself than I am. Whatever our souls are made of, his and mine are the same; and Linton's is as different as a moonbeam from lightning, or frost from fire' " (p. 95). A page later she continues:

"My great miseries in this world have been Heathcliff's miseries, and I watched and felt each from the beginning: my great thought in living is himself. If all else perished, and *he* remained, *I* should continue to be; and if all else remained, and he were annihilated, the universe would turn to a mighty stranger: I should not seem a part of it. My love for Linton is like the foliage in the woods: time will change it, I'm well aware, as winter changes the trees. My love for Heathcliff resembles the eternal rocks beneath: a source of little visible delight, but necessary. Nelly, I *am* Heathcliff! He's always, always in my mind: not as a pleasure, any more than I am always a pleasure to myself, but as my own being. So don't talk of our separation . . ." (pp. 96-97). /**100**/

As a child, the severest punishment that her elders could invent "was to keep her separate from" Heathcliff (p. 49); and in their last passionate interview she declares, " 'I only wish us never to be parted' " (p. 187).

Cathy's two dreams, with her accompanying comments, underscore the nature of her culpability and relate directly to the waif of

[9] "The Brontës, or, Myth Domesticated," in *Forms of Modern Fiction*, ed. William Van O'Connor (Minneapolis, 1948), p. 114.

Lockwood's nightmare. In the first, heaven seems so uncongenial
that the angels, angry with her weeping to be back on earth, fling
her "out into the middle of the heath on the top of Wuthering
Heights; where" she awakes "sobbing for joy. . . . I've no more
business to marry Edgar Linton,'" she says, "'than I have to be in
heaven . . .'" (p. 94). In the second, a kind of semiconscious hal-
lucination rather than a genuine dream, she thinks herself a child
again, at the time immediately after her father's death, when Hindley forced her to sleep for the first time apart from Heathcliff. As
her consciousness clears, she remembers that she is "'Mrs. Linton,
the lady of Thrushcross Grange, and the wife of a stranger: an exile,
and outcast, thenceforth, from what had been my world'" (p. 148).
Here Lockwood's parenthetical remark concerning the dream-
child's identifying herself as Catherine Linton—"'why did I think
of *Linton*? I had read Earnshaw twenty times for Linton'" (p. 29)
—appears significant. Also on the night when Cathy recounts her
first dream to Nelly, and Heathcliff runs away before he can overhear her declaration of love for him, a violent thunderstorm
splits a tree at the corner of the house and damages the east chim-
ney-stack. It is nature's adumbration of this calamitous severance
of selves.

After Cathy's marriage to Edgar, when Heathcliff returns, she
compounds her guilt and completes the separation through deliberate self-destruction. The conflict between Edgar and Heathcliff
crystallizes her will to die: "'. . . I'll try to break their hearts by breaking my own,'" she determines (p. 138). And on the day of her death
Heathcliff fixes her responsibility:

"You teach me now how cruel you've been—cruel and false. *Why* did
you despise me? *Why* did you betray your own heart, Cathy? I have not one
word of comfort. You deserve this. You have killed yourself. Yes, you may
kiss me, and cry; and wring out my kisses and tears: they'll blight you—
they'll damn you. You loved me—then what *right* had you to leave me?
What right—answer me—for the poor fancy you felt for Linton? Because
misery and degrada- /101/ tion, and death, and nothing that God or Satan
could inflict would have parted us, *you,* of your own will, did it. I have
not broken your heart—*you* have broken it; and in breaking it, you have
broken mine" (p. 189).

Catherine recognizes that death will not alleviate her own longing
for Heathcliff. When she thinks of burial in Gimmerton churchyard, she says, "I'll not lie there by myself: they may bury me twelve
feet deep, and throw the church down over me, but I won't rest till
you are with me" (p. 149). "I shall not be at peace" (p. 187).

Again external nature punctuates the disruption of soul-mates. The evening of Cathy's burial

the weather broke: the wind shifted from south to north-east, and brought rain first, and then sleet and snow. On the morrow one could hardly imagine that there had been three weeks of summer: the primroses and crocuses were hidden under wintry drifts; the larks were silent, the young leaves of the early trees smitten and blackened (p. 199).

III

As Melvin R. Watson argues in his cogent exposition of the relationship of love and hate in *Wuthering Heights*, the fury of Heathcliff's revenge is the equal and opposite reaction to the intensity of his love.[10] His cruelty is a function of Catherine's in foiling their union. The younger Catherine effectively traces the origin of his inveteracy:

"Mr. Heathcliff, *you* have *nobody* to love you; and, however miserable you make us, we shall still have the revenge of thinking that your cruelty arises from your greater misery. You *are* miserable, are you not? Lonely, like the devil, and envious like him?" (p. 338).

From the instant of Cathy's death, Heathcliff's strain and suffering are excruciating. As he foresaw, life without her is like undergoing " 'the torments of hell' " (p. 187). He implores her to haunt him:

"I know that ghosts *have* wandered on earth. Be with me always—take any form—drive me mad! only *do* not leave me in this abyss, where I cannot find you! Oh, God! it is unutterable! I *cannot* live without my life! I *cannot* live without my soul (p. 197)!"

On the night of her burial, when he has very nearly exhumed her, he suddenly feels her presence near him, not in the coffin " 'but on /102/ the earth' " (p. 341). Refilling the grave and hurrying to the Heights, he is confident that he will discover her in their old room with the panelled-bed. The peak of his ruthlessness, in which he kicks Hindley insensible and wounds Isabella with a knife, occurs when they temporarily bar his access; and when he reaches the chamber, as he later divulges to Nelly:

"I looked round impatiently—I felt her by me—I could *almost* see her, and yet I *could not!* I ought to have sweat blood then, from the anguish of my yearning—from the fervour of my supplications to have but one glimpse! I had not one. She showed herself, as she often was in life, a

[10] "Tempest in the Soul: the Theme and Structure of *Wuthering Heights*," *NCF*, IV (Sept. 1949), 87-100.

devil to me! And, since then, sometimes more and sometimes less, I've been the sport of that intolerable torture! Infernal! Keeping my nerves at such a stretch, that, if they had not resembled catgut, they would long ago have relaxed to . . . feebleness. . . . When I sat in the house . . . it seemed that on going out I should meet her; when I walked on the moors I should meet her coming in. When I went from home, I hastened to return: she *must* be somewhere at the Heights, I was certain! And when I slept in her chamber—I was beaten out of that. I couldn't lie there; for the moment I closed my eyes, she was either outside the window, or sliding back the panels, or entering the room, or even resting her darling head on the same pillow as she did when a child; and I must open my lids to see. And so I opened and closed them a hundred times a night—to be always disappointed!" (pp. 341-342).

Lockwood, though ruffled and vindictive from his nightmare, testifies to the " 'anguish' " and " 'agony' " with which Heathcliff, in an " 'incontrollable passion of tears,' " entreats the dream-spectre to appear and enter at the lattice (pp. 33-34).

Heathcliff's cruelty, like Lockwood's to the dream-child, stems from isolation and misery. Heathcliff is the victim instead of the originator of evil. Within the ethical context of the novel, he is paradoxically accurate when, near death, he replies to Nelly's exhortation to penitence, " '. . . as to repenting of my injustices, I've done no injustice, and I repent of nothing' " (p. 395). His whole life has been a struggle against inimical forces to maintain his identity and to achieve his overwhelming human need for fulfillment in love. Hareton, whom he has tried to warp as he himself was debased by Hindley, he eventually describes as " 'the ghost of my immortal love; of my wild endeavours to hold my right; my degradation, my pride, my happiness, and my anguish' " (p. 384). And of Cathy he says, " 'The entire world is a dreadful collection of memoranda that she did exist, and that I have lost her!' " (p. 384). /103/

Manifestly, it is dubious to account for Heathcliff primarily as an archetypal embodiment of destructive primitive energy or of elemental darkness in the human soul.[11] Although a reluctant host, he provides Lockwood with a glass of wine, tea, and dinner on separate occasions; and during the narrator's illness he sends him a brace of grouse and chats amiably at his "bedside a good hour" (p. 106). Furthermore, it seems both unhistorical and uncritical to read *The Heart of Darkness* into *Wuthering Heights*. In the terms of Emily Brontë's moral equation there is no autonomous evil in the universe. Wrong issues only from the occlusion of love; hate as a corollary of

[11] See Van Ghent, pp. 154, 159, 161, 163-165, 170.

love is a central irony of human existence. And if Cathy is responsible for the malevolence that convulses the world of Wuthering
Heights, she is also the means at last of alleviating it. The sight of
her unchanged features, which Heathcliff finally obtains when
the sexton is digging Edgar Linton's grave, and his provision for
their juxtaposition with the sides of their coffins removed at his
death (p. 339), afford his first relief from torment in eighteen
years. That night he is "tranquil" and dreams of "sleeping the last
sleep" beside Cathy, with his "heart stopped and . . . [his]
cheek frozen against hers" (p. 340). " 'Now, since I've seen her,' "
he explains to Nelly, " 'I'm pacified—a little' " (p. 342).

As a result, a change comes over him in which he takes "so little
interest in . . . daily life, that . . . [he] can hardly remember to eat
and drink" (p. 383). " 'I have to remind myself to breathe—almost
to remind my heart to beat!' " he declares. " 'And it is like bending
back a stiff spring: it is by compulsion that I do the slightest act
not prompted by one thought; and by compulsion that I notice
anything alive or dead, which is not associated with one universal
idea' "—eventual union with Cathy (pp. 384-385). Although he now
controls all the property of the Earnshaws and the Lintons and,
having Hareton and young Catherine in his legal and physical
power at Wuthering Heights, can wreak upon them whatever
diabolical vengeance he chooses, he remarks to Nelly, " 'I don't
care for striking; I can't take the trouble to raise my hand. . . . I have
lost the faculty of enjoying their destruction, and I am too idle to
destroy for nothing" (pp. 382-383). At this point his desire for revenge has not merely flagged; it /104/ has not simply died out, exhausted by its very extravagance.[12] His hate has been a reflex of his
frustration, and his only gratification previously has been to bring
misfortune and pain to those who have balked his self-realization
with Cathy. Now that he is able to visualize her (" 'I am surrounded with her image!' " [p. 383]; " 'I am within sight of my
heaven. I have my eyes on it: hardly three feet to sever me!' "
[p. 389]; ". . . it seemed exactly that he gazed at something within
two yards' distance" [p. 392]) and is confident of the consummation

---

[12] Cf. Watson, p. 90, ". . . for seventeen long years . . . he works out the venom
which has accumulated in his soul. As soon as part of the venom is removed
and the day of happiness begins to dawn, he no longer has the will to keep up
his torturing"; Van Ghent, p. 156, ". . . Heathcliff's cruel energies flag and decay";
Mark Schorer, *Wuthering Heights* (Rinehart Edition, New York, 1955), p. xiii,
". . . the time of the novel is carried on long enough to show Heathcliff at last
an emptied man, burned out by his fever ragings, exhausted and will-less, his
passion meaningless at last."

that he has so constantly wished for, the pleasure derived from this prospect supersedes the barren solace of retaliation. Although Heathcliff disclaims magnanimity in ceasing to persecute the second generation, the fact of his remission offers further evidence that he is not innately demonic and that hate is subservient to love. Fascinated by his omnipresent vision of Cathy and consumed with the ardor of anticipation, Heathcliff no longer wishes to disrupt the happiness of others. He watches the rapprochement of Hareton and Catherine without interference: " 'I can give them no attention, any more' " (p. 384). Hareton, through his admiration for Heathcliff, and young Catherine, through her love for her father and her sickly husband, Linton Heathcliff, now dead, have survived the blast of Heathcliff's malice; and its withdrawal from the atmosphere allows their incipient sympathy for one another to flower. This rebirth of love begins on Easter Monday; and if Cathy has been the betrayer of Heathcliff, her daughter is the redeemer of Hareton.

IV

Heathcliff's death in the panelled-bed gives symmetry and emphasis to the novel; and Mrs. Van Ghent is apt in alluding to the lattice window—which barred the dream-child's entrance and which swings open beside Heathcliff's corpse—as indicative of the dual aspect of reality. As she points out, the plethora of windows, doors, walls, and locks in the novel have a metaphoric as well as a literal /105/ value. Again and again they not only interfere with physical movement but serve as external reminders of dammed up impulses and distorted emotions. Also especially skillful is the rhythmic device of the gate, which Emily Brontë uses to represent the estrangement prevailing at Wuthering Heights at the opening of the book—when, as in Lockwood's first dream, "every man's hand was against his neighbour" (p. 28)—and the harmony eventually attained. When Lockwood pays his first call at the Heights, the chained gate shows "no sympathising movement" to Heathcliff's inhospitable command, "walk in"; and Lockwood's horse is "fairly pushing the barrier" before his landlord unfastens it (p. 4). The next day, arriving at the gate with the first snowflakes and unable to unchain it, Lockwood leaps the impediment in order to reach the front door of the house, where, as he writes, " 'I . . . knocked vainly for admittance, till my knuckles tingled and the dogs howled' " (p. 11). After his illness, when he rides to the Heights to inform Heathcliff of his decision to vacate the Grange, the "jealous gate" is still fastened; but in contrast to the snowstorm before, the day, though frosty, is calm and bright, and the front door stands open (p. 352). When he returns for the last time in September, he sees Wuthering Heights in the light of a " 'splendid moon,' " just risen: " 'I had neither to climb the gate nor to knock—it yielded to my hand. That is an improvement, I thought.' " "Both doors and lattices" are open, though the evening is cool enough for a "fine, red fire" on the hearth (p. 362).

This treatment of the gate confirms the novelist's figurative intent and the validity of Mrs. Van Ghent's interest in the "window figure" in *Wuthering Heights*. Yet it is gravely misleading to explain the windowpane in the panelled-bed as a symbol of demarcation between the human and the demonic, a reminder of the powers of darkness that exist "autonomously, not only in the 'outsideness' of external nature, . . . but also within, . . . in the soul."[13] Referring to the image (which actually occurs twice [pp. 66-67, 213]) of the "fiend" looking out of the windows of Heathcliff's eyes and their refusal to close in death, Mrs. Van Ghent says, "the 'fiend' has now got 'out,' leaving the window open"—like the literal open lattice of the bed; and she implies that the fiend has escaped to amalgamate with the dark "other- /106/ ness" of external nature, "the world of the animals and the elements."[14] But there seems to be no dichotomy in the novel between the human and the external worlds. The thunderstorm and the shift in weather at crucial points in the tragedy reflect outdoor nature in tune with human conditions. Instead of being a counter for an absolute demonism, the fiend (or fiends), which both Nelly and Isabella discover lurking behind Heathcliff's eyes, is a metaphoric representation of his loneliness and suffering. As he nears death and is able to concentrate upon the visual image of Catherine, the novel insists upon the alteration in his eyes. Preoccupation with love instead of loss has completely changed his expression. In the last chapter, young Catherine, telling Hareton of a morning encounter with Heathcliff, asserts, " '. . . he looked so different from his usual look that I stopped a moment to stare at him.' " He appears to her " 'almost bright and cheerful. No, *almost* nothing—*very much* excited, and wild and glad!' " (p. 387). During his final weeks Nelly attests the " 'joyful glitter in his eyes, that altered the aspect of his whole face' " (p. 387), " 'the appearance of joy under his black brows' " (p. 388), the " 'unearthly vision' " of his stare (p. 392), and the " 'raptured . . . expression of his countenance' " (p. 392). When he dies, then, no "fiend" remains to get out. The "gaze of exultation" in his un-

[13] Van Ghent, p. 161.
[14] *Ibid.*, pp. 163, 170.

closed eyes and his "'girning,'" as Joseph says, "'at death'" (p. 397) portray the triumph of his release. The lattice "flapping to and fro" echoes a persistent folk belief that the window of a dead person's room must be opened to allow egress for the soul. If the window in the panelled-bed is indeed a reminder of dual aspects of reality, it signifies the barrier between two planes of existence—the physical and the spiritual, the temporal and the eternal. The world into which Heathcliff's essence has fled is not one of dark "otherness," in which he will blend with elemental and animal powers; it is a world of light, "that glorious world" (p. 188) which Cathy had contemplated through the open window before her death, where she and Heathcliff will be united.

Although the *personae* of *Wuthering Heights* repeatedly use the terms "heaven" and "hell" to describe recognizable states of experience, reward and punishment have no place in Emily Brontë's eschatology.[15] The years of travail that the novel records are sufficient ex- /107/ piation for wrong. Nelly Dean, for once abandoning trite ideas, seems to express the author's view when she says, apropos of the elder Catherine's death,

"I see a repose that neither earth nor hell can break, and I feel an assurance of the endless and shadowless hereafter—the Eternity they have entered—where life is boundless in its duration, and love in its sympathy, and joy in its fulness" (p. 194).

Like many of Nelly's remarks, this statement when uttered, invites qualification: Lockwood's introductory nightmare and Cathy's assertion (pp. 149, 187) that she will not be at peace without Heathcliff provide earnest for her restlessness as a sprite. Lockwood, questioned as to his opinion, foregoes comment upon Mrs. Dean's "heterodox" notion. At the conclusion of the novel, however, despite the reports of Joseph and the little boy and a general belief in the parish that Heathcliff's and Cathy's ghosts walk, Nelly declares, "'I believe the dead are at peace'" (p. 399)—an affirmation which reminds the reader of her earlier conviction and commands Lockwood's final assent. Looking at the graves of Edgar, Heathcliff, and Cathy, he wonders "how any one could ever imagine unquiet slumbers for the sleepers in that quiet earth" (p. 400).

[15] There is a family kinship between the attitudes of Emily and Charlotte Brontë. Helen Burns, speaking to Jane Eyre of death, cannot believe that God will allow man to degenerate into a fiend as a punishment for sins: "No; I cannot believe that: I hold another creed; which no one ever taught me, and which I seldom mention; but in which I delight, and to which I cling: for it extends hope to all: it makes Eternity a rest—a mighty home, not a terror and an abyss" (ch. vi).

V

While Heathcliff and Cathy—owing to her dereliction—are able to find oneness and peace only in the disembodied condition of death (a surrogate union in their children is diseased and barren), the second pair of lovers, Hareton and his Catherine, attain concord in life. Their importance to the resolution of the novel and Lockwood's final words concerning them need stressing. " '*They* are afraid of nothing,' " he mutters, as he watches them returning from a moonlight walk on the moors. " 'Together they would brave Satan and all his legions' " (p. 399). And so they could, since in Miss Brontë's view, evil, personified in Satan, derives solely from separation—from the denial of sympathy and love.

Admittedly, *Wuthering Heights* is a difficult book; for in a manner /108/ particularly acceptable to modern taste, Emily Brontë, by excluding herself from the narration, disdains the office of moral commentator. If her technique abjures didacticism, however, to describe the novel as "non-ethical" or a story in which "perverse values . . . prevail" is to traduce the substance of her work.[16] Like all great novelists, she is concerned with the paradoxes of existence. By presenting her action against the judgments of Lockwood and Nelly she challenges the adequacy of conventional codes and theological dogma to explain and to govern the behavior of man. Lockwood's dreams, with their overtones of unforgivable sin, introduce her search for a definition of evil—a quest that results in a paradigm of love. Instead of prescriptive morality, she offers a transcendent ethic. Love, in her metaphysics, is the primary law of human nature and the paramount principle of her universe. Adhered to, it is at once the source of joy and harmony; rejected or subverted, it becomes the fountainhead of enmity and strife. /109/

Questions for Discussion and Writing

1. In what ways are the first three chapters of *Wuthering Heights* "at once prologue and *raison d'être* for the primary narrative"? (page 95)

2. Contrast Edgar Shannon's comments on the motivation of Lockwood's dreams with those of Dorothy Van Ghent. What have other critics made of the purpose of these dreams in the novel?

3. Do you find critics who refer to Lockwood as "a milksop," as Shannon says on page 98? If so, determine what evidence is presented to support

[16] Van Ghent, p. 169; Adams, *NCF*, XIII, 61.

the charge against the narrator, and compare such evidence with Shannon's defense of him.

4. Agree or disagree with Shannon's statement that "careful causality . . . governs the central action of the novel." (page 99) What have other critics said to support or contradict this assertion?

5. Explain what Shannon means by "Lockwood demonstrates in little what occurs in gigantic proportions in Heathcliff." (page 99) With the help of other critical comments, discuss the changes in Lockwood during the course of the novel.

6. Edgar Shannon speaks of "the ethical eye of the storm." (page 99) What does he mean by "ethical," "eye," and "storm"?

7. Do you agree that "the nature of Cathy's offense" (page 100) is the thematic problem of the novel? Do modern critics support or contradict your contention?

8. Does Shannon consider the violent thunderstorm which he mentions on page 101 a symbol of something? Of what? What other symbols does he find in the novel?

9. Shannon speaks of Heathcliff's fixing of Cathy's responsibility. What does he make of responsibility as a theme in *Wuthering Heights?* How important is responsibility in the novel?

10. What, according to Shannon, motivates cruelty in *Wuthering Heights?* Discuss other critical commentary on the reasons for cruel actions in the novel.

11. Contrast Dorothy Van Ghent's and Edgar Shannon's evaluations of the nature of Heathcliff.

12. Do critics agree or disagree with Shannon's belief that, "In the terms of Emily Brontë's moral equation there is no autonomous evil in the universe"? (page 104)

13. What does Shannon say of the revenge motif in *Wuthering Heights?* What do other critics say?

14. Shannon says, "Heathcliff's death in the panelled-bed gives symmetry and emphasis to the novel." (page 105) How? Using other criticism and your reading of the novel, discuss symmetry and emphasis in *Wuthering Heights.*

15. What is Heathcliff's problem, as Shannon sees it? Do other critics agree with him?

16. Shannon says that "reward and punishment have no place in Emily Brontë's eschatology." (page 107) Explain what he means. Is there general agreement among critics on this point?

17. Why does Shannon say that *Wuthering Heights* is a difficult book? (page 108) Do you agree?

18. What does "paradox of existence" (page 109) mean? Present some such paradoxes suggested in *Wuthering Heights*.

19. This essay attempts to understand the novel through its dreams; Robert McKibben attempts a similar understanding by studying references to books mentioned in the novel. Do the two articles serve to support each other at any point—for example, in their presentation of the younger Catherine? Do they in any places conflict? What conclusions about the study of a novel can you draw from these two articles?

Wuthering Heights: Narrators, Audience, and Message

ALLAN R. BRICK

Although there exist valid interpretations of the individual narrators of *Wuthering Heights,* there is nowhere an adequate explanation of their total function. No one has properly shown why the reader enters *Wuthering Heights* under the auspices of Lockwood, is then given over to Nelly Dean, then briefly to Isabella Linton, and then, though he still listens to Nelly, is cast into a maze of conflicting sympathies with Heathcliff and young Cathy Linton, only to be returned to Lockwood at the end. It is not satisfactory to explain away this unique and complicated stratification as simply conventional or as a mechanical device necessary for plot.[1] Rather, it is important to understand how Emily Brontë's narrative form is deeply interfused with her essential message.

Perhaps the best entry into this problem can be made through a comparison—merely analogical—with Coleridge's *The Rime of the Ancient Mariner.* Immediately striking is the similarity between Brontë's Lockwood and Coleridge's Wedding Guest, who, while not the *Rime's* direct narrator, is the personified audience, as indeed Lockwood him-, /80/ self becomes after the third chapter of *Wuthering Heights.* The idea of a Wedding Guest suggests a man fully occupied in the temporal world of social amusement and self-indulgence, a thorough specimen of sophistication; and thus it is all such men—specifically the urbane reader himself—who are stopped at the threshold of the Bridegroom's house. The entrance of the ultra-civilized Lockwood into Wuthering Heights and his preliminary attempts to enjoy its atmosphere are of course more voli-

From *College English,* XXI, 2 (November, 1959), 80-86.

[1] Carl R. Woodring, "The Narrators of *Wuthering Heights,*" *Nineteenth-Century Fiction,* XI (Mar. 1957), 299, 302, so explains it.

tional than the Wedding Guest's agreement to listen to the Mariner;
yet this Wedding Guest is especially chosen out of a group of three—
presumably because he in particular not only needs to but is *willing* to listen to the Mariner's message. And by the time Lockwood
reaches some awareness of the sort of den he has entered—when he
has been set upon by dogs (Ch. II) and has spent his night in
the oak-enclosed bed—he is every bit as reluctant, as horrified, and
as enthralled as Coleridge's personified audience.

Of course, Lockwood is immediately ridiculous as compared with
the Wedding Guest, who retains his dignity, even though he is at
first pulled away from proper attention by trivia and sentiment.
Such topsy-turvy valuation is for Lockwood the dominant theme;
and sentimentality—*i.e.,* responding not to actual facts but leaping
to familiar stock conclusions brought along from 'society' and silly
novels—is the keynote. Lockwood begins, without irony (or with
only as much as such a *poseur* could muster), by affirming that
Wuthering Heights is "a perfect misanthropist's Heaven—and Mr.
Heathcliff and I are such a suitable pair to divide the desolation
between us. A capital fellow!" (Rinehart Edition, 1950, p. 1).
Such preconceptions—especially Lockwood's notion of Heathcliff
as a normal romantic hero and of the strange girl with "the most
exquisite little face" as romantic heroine—are progressively shattered, if not so much for Lockwood, then certainly for the reader
who has been allied with him. Lockwood holds to them tenaciously.
On his second visit he sits down and attempts small talk with the
"amiable hostess." Not succeeding with his compliments of the dogs,
he tries again:

> "Ah, your favourites are among these!" I continued, turning to an ob-
> scure cushion full of something like cats.
> "A strange choice of favorites," she observed scornfully.
> Unluckily, it was a heap of dead rabbits. (p. 9)

Lockwood has come from a society where anything lying on a par-
lor cushion *would* be cats. Unable to see or to see that he is unable,
he fights off puzzlement. Though admitting that Heathcliff's behavior reveals "a genuine bad nature" and feeling "no longer . . .
inclined to call Heathcliff a capital fellow," he insists that the inhabitants of Wuthering Heights "could not every day sit so grim
and taciturn, and it was impossible, however ill-tempered they
might be, that the universal scowl they wore was their everyday
countenance" (p. 11). Intrepidly, Lockwood rattles off one misinterpretation after another about the identity of the people in

Wuthering Heights and their (he presumes) normal relations with each other, discovering progressively that the girl is not Mrs. Heathcliff, that she is not married to Hareton, and that Hareton is not Heathcliff's son. Finally he comes to a dim awareness, if not an admission, that he has stepped into a land and a dwelling which are thoroughly incomprehensible, where none of his mundane methods of perception will apply.

Lockwood's inability to make out the inside of Wuthering Heights is matched by his puzzled scrutiny of its exterior, where the landmarks and dangerous pitfalls have been concealed by snow:

No one uttering a word of sociable conversation, I approached a window to ex- /81/ amine the weather. A sorrowful sight I saw: dark night coming down prematurely, and sky and hills mingled in one bitter whirl of wind and suffocating snow. (p. 13)

Such imagery not only suggests the equivocating fog of *Macbeth*[2] and Conrad's later use of white mist in *Heart of Darkness,* but also bears out the analogy with Coleridge's *Rime,* in which mist, snow, and ice are the primary conditions for the storm at the beginning of the voyage and for the appearance of the Albatross. Lockwood, like the Mariner—or, more exactly, like the Wedding Guest who is now identified with the Mariner—is in a situation where the shapes of men nor beasts and the location of dangers cannot be kenned through the mist and snow. Brontë extends the image elaborately at the end of Chapter III where Lockwood receives the guidance that he had been denied the night before.

But before Lockwood comes out of the jaws of Wuthering Heights he receives a shock which, for the moment at least, divests him of all sophistication and pretense, and forces him—and the reader with him —to pay horrified attention. It is a shock severe enough to give him, belatedly, the humble credulity of the Wedding Guest, who had felt immediately the skinny hand and glittering eye and who, by the beginning of Coleridge's Part IV, was ready to believe the Mariner a ghost.

---

[2] If one might compare Heathcliff, the usurping, fate-defying despot of the castle of Wuthering Heights, with Macbeth, it seems natural to see Lockwood as the naive Duncan who, arriving at Dunsinane, says, "This castle hath a pleasant seat"; or perhaps as the equally gullible and endangered Banquo who, judging by the temple-haunting martlet, agrees with Duncan. Both Duncan and Banquo are normal, cheerful aristocrats who react insistently in preconstituted patterns no matter how ominous the situation; their mistakes, like Lockwood's, lie in not seeing—in being *unwilling* to see—that the presence of Macbeth has dissolved and reconstituted all the old facts into thoroughly unique entities and combinations.

When Zillah leads Lockwood upstairs and places him in the chamber about which "her master had an odd notion," and when he, having fastened the door, then closes himself within the oaken bed-closet, he makes his deepest penetration into Wuthering Heights—and, it might be said, into himself. There, puzzling over the writings scratched upon the paint, and over the Testament and diary of Catherine Earnshaw, and focusing finally on the cover of "Seventy Times Seven, and the First of the Seventy-First: A Pious Discourse delivered by the Reverend Jabes Branderham, in the Chapel of Gimmerden Sough," Lockwood falls asleep and dreams:

I thought it was morning; and I had set out on my way home, with Joseph for a guide. The snow lay yards deep in our road; and, as we floundered on, my companion wearied me with constant reproaches that I had not brought a pilgrim's staff: telling me that I could never get into the house without one. (p. 22)

Lockwood soon discovers that the house Joseph refers to is not the Grange but is Gimmerden Chapel, which they presently enter, joining "a full and attentive congregation" to hear Jabes Branderham preach a prodigious sermon of "four hundred and ninety parts," each part "discussing a separate sin." These sins "were of the most curious character—odd transgressions that I never imagined previously." Finally, bored and discomfited to the point of rage, Lockwood rises and calls upon his "fellow martyrs" to join him in dragging Jabes from the pulpit. But thereupon the whole assembly rushes upon Lockwood, "exalting their pilgrim's staves," though "in the confluence of the multitude, several clubs crossed; blows, aimed at me, fell on other sconces" (p. 24). This is evidently a symbolical statement to the effect that the congregation (which is so attentive to Jabes and which assaults first Lockwood and then, by that means, themselves) represents Emily Brontë's read- /82/ ers, who must purge from themselves all sophisticated, sentimental, and pretentious elements—all Lockwood—before entering the sanctuary of Truth. Her message is precisely that of Carlyle:

There is something great in the moment when a man first strips himself of adventitious wrappages; and sees indeed that he is naked, and, as Swift has it, "a forked straddling animal with bandy legs"; yet also a Spirit, and unutterable Mystery of Mysteries. (*Sartor Resartus*, I, viii)[3]

Lockwood, a humble captive with his sconce battered by the pil-

[3] Kathleen Tillotson, *Novels of the Eighteen-Forties* (1954), pp. 150-156, attributes the abrupt turn of English novelists in the eighteen-forties to introspection, self-projection, and symbolism largely to the influence of Carlyle.

grim staves, is now prepared for the ultimate discovery; thus the dream batterings become the real tappings of a branch, and the branch, seized through the window, becomes an ice-cold hand. Lockwood's terrified rubbing of the attached wrist "to and fro till the blood ran down and soaked the bedclothes" (p. 25), his escape from the hand by false promise, and his piling of books in a high pyramid against it, all juxtaposed with Heathcliff's wild plunge on to the bed and cry at the window for Cathy's return, constitute Brontë's statement about how little reality the Victorian gentleman wants in his life, how little truth in his fiction. More important: these actions constitute her violent divestment from the reader of Lockwood. Having with growing discomfort and humiliation identified himself with Lockwood up to this point, the reader becomes revolted by Lockwood's cowardice and cruelty, and casts him aside, anxious that the new focus be directly upon Heathcliff.

At the end of Chapter III Lockwood escapes from his ordeal, flees back to civilization:

Benumbed to my very heart, I dragged upstairs, whence, after putting on dry clothes, and pacing to and fro thirty or forty minutes, to restore the animal heat, I am adjourned to my study, feeble as a kitten, almost too much so to enjoy the cheerful fire and smoking coffee which the servant has prepared for my refreshment. (p. 32)

The strange shift to the present tense conspires with that in mood to show that as participants both Lockwood and the reader's own sophistication are now dissolved. Far more than Lockwood the reader has himself been humbled and will now desist from imposing clichés upon unique reality, will now undergo, far more than Lockwood, four months' docile attention to Nelly Dean.

Coleridge's dramatic form for *The Rime of the Ancient Mariner* was, as was true of many of his poems, an adaptation of the German idealism he had derived through Schelling from Kant. When he moved his narrative point of view from the Wedding Guest to a combination of the Wedding Guest (and the reader) with the Mariner, and ultimately to the Two Voices which speak over the entranced Mariner in Part VI, he was dramatizing his theory of perception: "know thyself" (*Biographia Literaria,* ed. Shawcross, 1907, I, 173). For Coleridge, the self consisted of the subject and object egos, the I and the Me—the portion of the self which perceives and that which is perceived. Ultimate knowledge could be sought only by a penetration into the consciousness, by which means the subject self would become an object, and I a Me to be perceived and explored into; such perception of the I as a Me would necessitate the emergence of a more essential and profound subject-perceiver, which would itself become a perceived Me at the next stage.

It may however be shown . . . that even when the Objective is assumed as the first, we yet can never pass beyond the principle of self-consciousness. Should we attempt it, we must be driven back from ground to ground, each of which would cease to be a Ground the moment we pressed on it. We must be whirled down the gulf of an in- /83/ finite series. But this would make our reason baffle the end and purpose of all reason, namely, unity and system. Or we must break off the series arbitrarily, and affirm an absolute something that is in and of itself at once cause and effect (*causa sui*), subject and object, or rather the absolute identity of both. (*Biog. Lit.*, I, 187)

It was at this point that logic posited and religious faith affirmed the *Ding-an-sich,* or Kantian Apperception. At the final stage of the inward journey, all object-self dropped away: "We begin with the I KNOW MYSELF, in order to end with the absolute I AM. We proceed from the SELF, in order to lose and find all self in God" (*Biog. Lit.*, I, 186). Such was the conversion experience for the Mariner, and for the Wedding Guest through him, and the reader through the Wedding Guest. But such is not the experience for Lockwood, who never achieves the ultimate level of self-effacement.

When Brontë's primary narrator is prostrated to listen to Nelly Dean, his case is essentially that of subject-ego becoming object-ego as a new subject-ego emerges, and thus similar to that of the Wedding-Guest-become-Mariner (stage two for Coleridge) prostrated before the Two Voices. Nelly Dean is a far more essential and profound perceiving subject than Lockwood, is a perceiver far closer to a full understanding of the mysteries of Wuthering Heights. And yet even she is not the ultimate I. As her story unfolds, the reader feels an increasing need to draw away from the cheerful Mrs. Dean—to get his own view of her views. Gradually, he learns that his new alter-ego, though a far better person than Lockwood, is actually *imperceptive* because of her "desire merely to avoid trouble, to deny serious problems, and . . . [her] failure to grasp genuinely the emotions of others."[4] Ultimate understanding lies as far beyond Nelly as *her* understanding lay beyond Lockwood's.

Although Brontë never really strips away Nelly to provide any more profound subject-narrator, she does—in moving ever closer to

[4] John K. Mathison, "Nelly Dean and the Power of *Wuthering Heights,*" *Nineteenth Century Fiction*, XI (Sept. 1956), 129.

the central core of meaning—provide ever more vivid and more sustained glimpses of Heathcliff and Catherine, the characters who
commune directly with Truth. For a reader to make a leap of
faith from Nelly Dean's platform of sensible understanding to an
acceptance of and participation in the central power would be the
ultimate fusion of subject with object egos. Some readers make the
leap entirely; some remain with Nelly; but others, bewildered by
the necessity of giving up conventional standards, flounder in between.

As such readers, becoming increasingly discontented with Nelly
Dean's interpretations, are moved closer to the core of the book,
they are tempted to cast about for someone to identify themselves
with. Early, they began to sympathize with Heathcliff and Catherine—and yet were held back, and held themselves back, from
these central figures. Now, suddenly, Isabella Linton, known before
only as the dreadful little girl who begged her papa to put the boy
Heathcliff in the cellar (p. 51), becomes an important partici-
pant-narrator. She becomes another Lockwood, though far more
complex, whose upper-class priggishness, narrowness, and appalling
sentimentality must be exploded at the threshold of Wuthering
Heights. Like Lockwood, who began by thinking Heathcliff "a
capital fellow," Isabella finds him an irresistible hero; stubbornly,
despite all warnings, she imposes the Byronic clichés upon him,
closing her eyes to actual facts and behaving like her idea of a
heroine. Though Isabella's pain and involvement are far greater,
her initiation at the Heights is like Lockwood's. Prepared by seeing
Heathcliff hang her spaniel, she crosses the threshold to re- /84/
ceive one stunning blow after another. All preconceptions stripped
away, she writes back to Nelly: "How did you contrive to preserve
the common sympathies of human nature when you resided here? I
cannot recognize any sentiment which those around share with me.
. . . Is Mr. Heathcliff a man?" (p. 144).

Linton Heathcliff and then young Cathy Linton, ultimate recipient of the reader's sympathies, undergo similar initiations. The
petted, repulsively-spoiled Linton is snatched out of the Grange
and thrust into the Heights for the rudest awakening of all. Before leaving, he asks, "And what is my father like? . . . Is he as young
and handsome as uncle?" Nelly answers, "He's as young . . . , but he
has black hair, and eyes; and looks sterner. . . . He'll not seem to you
so gentle and kind at first" (p. 218). The petted, pleasantly-spoiled
Cathy is drawn inevitably to the Heights, and tries, before her marriage, to impose her pathetic little preconceptions. On her first visit,

after her dogs are bitten by the Heights dogs, she cavalierly reenacts Lockwood's own first entrance. Nelly tells her:

"Well, Miss Cathy, if you were aware whose house this is, you'd be glad enough to get out."

"It's *your* father's isn't it?" she said, turning to Hareton.

"Nay," he replied, looking down, and blushing bashfully.

He could not stand a steady gaze from her eyes, though they were just his own.

"Whose then—your master's?" she asked.

He coloured deeper, with a different feeling, muttered an oath, and turned away.

"Who is his master?" continued the tiresome girl, appealing to me. "He talked about 'our house,' and 'our folk.' I thought he had been the owner's son. And he never said, Miss: he should have done, shouldn't he, if he's a servant? . . ."

"I'll see thee damned, before I be *thy* servant!" growled the lad. (pp. 206-207)

But by this time the end, the way out, is in sight. Though transformed, Cathy does not lose her dignity and poise, does not capitulate entirely to the power of Heathcliff. This is true largely because Heathcliff himself is withdrawing—with Catherine Earnshaw—from the reader's focus; having his devotion elsewhere, he no longer remains complete despot within the Heights. Still, Heathcliff is Brontë's essential hero, and the central power of the book lies not in young Cathy—who is merely a step on the journey back from noumenal reality to mundane levels of consciousness. Far from being the value-centre—*i.e.*, the valued "calm" after the unfortunate "storm"—the romance between Cathy and Hareton is merely a sentimental aftermath. Indeed, the only reason Heathcliff, enraged by the evident affection between the lovers, does not "tear Catherine in pieces" is that he sees in her eyes the archetypal Catherine Earnshaw and realizes that this new physical presence is negligible (p. 340).

As Lockwood was the first step in, he becomes the final step out of Wuthering Heights. Is he transformed? Has he received the message for which Jabes Branderham prepared him? No—no more than such a mundane point of view can ever achieve ultimate understanding. Speculating about Cathy as his own personal heroine, he reproduces from the beginning chapters his first thoughts about her mother, and thus remains as foppish and as sentimental as ever. When he learns from Nelly that Wuthering Heights is to be closed up, he comments inanely, "For the use of such ghosts as choose to inhabit it." And she reproves him: "No, Mr. Lockwood . . . I believe the dead are at peace: but it is not right to speak of them with levity" (p. 358). Lockwood's final benediction reveals his incapacity for insight:

I lingered round them, under the benign sky; watched the moths fluttering among the heath and hare-bells; listened to the soft wind breathing through the grass; and wondered how anyone could ever imagine unquiet slumbers, for the sleepers in that quiet earth. (p. 358) /85/

Although this sentence has been marveled at, along with the last chapters in general, for ambiguity of tone,[5] its meaning now seems clear enough. The sophisticated Lockwood of course *would* wonder "how any one could ever imagine unquiet slumbers." But the reader, returning from *his* journey, knows with the little shepherd boy: "They's Heathcliff, and a woman, yonder, under t' nab, . . . un' Aw darnut pass 'em" (p. 357). The reader *is* converted, like Coleridge's Wedding Guest, who, when the Mariner left him,

> Turned from the bridegroom's door.
> He went like one that hath been stunned,
> And is of sense forlorn:
> A sadder and a wiser man,
> He rose the morrow morn. /86/

Questions for Discussion and Writing

1. Agree or disagree with Allan Brick's statements of the function of Lockwood in the novel. What have other critics said about the role of Lockwood?

2. How, according to Brick, is *Wuthering Heights* unified? Do other critics agree with him?

3. Brick finds a chain of cause and effect in the novel. With the use of your reading of the novel and its criticism, show relationship between cause and effect and motivation of the characters.

4. What does Brick mean by "subject-ego becoming object-ego as a new subject-ego emerges"? (page 84) Relate this to point of view in the novel.

5. If Nelly Dean is not "the ultimate I," who is? (page 84) What special problems in point of view did Emily Brontë face in writing *Wuthering Heights*? How did she attempt to solve her problems? Did she succeed?

---

[5] See G. D. Klingopulos, "The Novel as Dramatic Poem (II): 'Wuthering Heights,'" *Scrutiny*, XIV (1947), 271-272.

6. ". . . the romance between Cathy and Hareton is merely a sentimental aftermath." (page 85) Comment, using other critics to help you.

7. What do you think of Brick's reason for Heathcliff's not tearing Catherine to pieces? (page 85) Can you suggest some other reasons, based on other analyses of the story?

8. Brick believes that Lockwood's "final benediction" shows him to be completely unchanged from what he was at the beginning of the novel, in that he misunderstands what has happened to Heathcliff and Catherine. What other interpretations of this passage have you encountered? Which seems most plausible?

9. Brick does a rather thorough job on Lockwood's function as narrator (though you may want to look for still more evidence to support his idea), but he is brief in his comments on Nelly Dean. Can you support his contentions concerning her? Or does further study convince you that Brick is brief here because he is weak? Other critics may help you decide, but use as much of the novel itself as you can in preparing your answer.

The Image of the Book in
Wuthering Heights

ROBERT C. McKIBBEN

Recent critics, reacting against earlier evaluations, have tended to treat *Wuthering Heights* as an art product of a very high order, a work of genius in execution as well as in vision. These commentators have attempted to resolve technical and thematic questions and to clarify the rapport between the two.[1] One of the most successful of them, Dorothy Van Ghent, has effectively demonstrated the relationship between two "figures" in the novel and her conception of its central problem. To cite the opening sentences of her article:

Wuthering Heights exists for the mind as a tension between two kinds of reality, a restrictive reality of civilized manners and codes, and the anonymous unregenerate reality of natural energies. The poetic structure which, in Emily Brontë's novel, associates these two kinds of reality is a structure of variations on the possibility of a break-through from one mode of being into the other.[2]

Like the majority of her predecessors, Mrs. Van Ghent has emphasized the most ambiguous dramatization of this tension in the /159/ book, the attraction between Catherine and Heathcliff. Yet Emily Brontë did not wish to leave her reader to puzzle an ultimate

[1] Aside from Mrs. Van Ghent see especially Boris Ford, "*Wuthering Heights*," *Scrutiny*, VII (1939). 375-389; G. D. Klingopulos, "The Novel as Dramatic Poem (II): 'Wuthering Heights,' " *Scrutiny*, XIV (1947), 269-286; Mark Schorer, "Fiction and the Matrix of Analogy," *Kenyon Review*, XI (1949), 539-560; and Melvin R. Watson, "Tempest in the Soul: The Theme and Structure of *Wuthering Heights*," *NCF*, IV (1949), 87-100.

[2] Van Ghent, "The Window Figure and the Two-Children Figure in *Wuthering Heights*," *NCF*, VII (1952), 189-190.

tension: she consciously strove to assert the triumph of society in the love of the second Catherine and Hareton. A qualitative difference between the two couples must be recognized, although, as Klingopulos has observed, this is not necessarily to imply the presence of a moral judgment: Catherine and Heathcliff take their existence outside the framework of manners and codes: but at the same time a parallelism is unmistakable. If the problem of escape or "breaking-through" functions in terms of certain poetic figures, the theme of reconciliation must be operative in other images. In fact, just as the window figure is primarily identified with the more tempestuous lovers, so the image of the book is the reflection of the stabilizing love of Cathy and Hareton.

The world of the novel is divided into the two rival camps of Edgar and Heathcliff, Thrushcross Grange and Wuthering Heights. It is not surprising, then, that books which appear in the narrative are found in either one or the other of these camps and that, consequently, they operate in different ways and call forth attitudes which are fundamentally in opposition. A more detailed examination of the role of the book image in each environment should serve to illustrate the means of this contention.

The atmosphere of the Heights is dominated by suffering, and the nature of this suffering is to propagate itself. One soul in torment can find relief only in the reproduction of its agony in those around it. A forceful will initiates the process, and the tortured victim becomes in his turn the agent of torture. " 'The tyrant grinds down his slaves and they don't turn against him: they crush those beneath them,' " states Heathcliff (chap. xi). It is important to note that the desire for revenge is willed into actuality, for in the pursuit of perverse ends the will itself is perverted. Thus Isabella, caught in the unremitting psychology of the Heights, says of Heathcliff, " 'I'd rather he suffered *less*, if I might cause his sufferings and he might *know* that I was the cause' " (chap. xvii). But there is no peace in eternal vengeance, no solution in obeying the demands of this spontaneous reaction. The self-injury involved in serving its purposes may be more damaging than the original wrongs of others. As Isabella again comments, " 'treachery and /160/ violence are spears pointed at both ends: they wound those who resort to them worse than their enemies' " (chap. xvii).

Catherine Heathcliff is the first to directly introduce the image of the book into the narrative. Early in the novel (chap. ii) she avails herself of "a long, dark book" in order to exorcise Joseph, the spectre of warped Christianity. In the episode immediately following (chap. iii) Lockwood stumbles upon Catherine Earnshaw's library, which acts as link between reality and his significant nightmare. He remarks that it is " 'select' " and has been " 'thought not altogether for a legitimate purpose,' " for Catherine has filled the blank spaces in her books with her own observations. In her diary the book also plays a meaningful role: in the hands of Joseph it is an instrument of oppression, the symbol of arbitrary constraint; in the hands of the two children it is a means of rebellious protest. Catherine declares that she hates a good book and casts a volume into the dog kennel; Heathcliff follows her lead. His attitude towards the book is confirmed when, later in the same chapter, he orders the reading Catherine Heathcliff to " 'Put your trash away and find something to do.' " Bearing these instances in mind, one may proceed to some generalization concerning the function of the image in the environment of the Heights.

In a domain governed by indomitable will engaged in the task of realizing through action the terms of its reality, all objects are regarded as means to that task. In greater or lesser degree, then, depending upon the scope of individual ambition, the examples cited represent a misuse of the image, a subordination of the book to will. If it cannot be made to be the servant of the will, it is banished, ignored, or even destroyed. In a gesture which at once is an affirmation of the uselessness of the book and a revolt against illtreatment Catherine tosses away *Th' Helmet o' Salvation*. And Catherine Heathcliff tells Lockwood that " 'Mr. Heathcliff never reads; so he took it into his head to destroy my books' " (chap. xxxi). It is not a coincidence that the image which reflects the widening ground between the divergent paths chosen by Heathcliff and Catherine Earnshaw is again that of the book. As Catherine tends towards the world of the other household, she comes to accept that which is the very foundation of the security of Thrushcross Grange. Ellen Dean gives this description of Heathcliff in the period after the death of old Mr. Earnshaw: /161/

"In the first place, he had by that time lost the benefit of his early education: continual hard work, begun soon and concluded late, had extinguished any curiosity he once possessed in pursuit of knowledge, and any love for books or learning. . . . He struggled long to keep up an equality with Catherine in her studies, and yielded with poignant though silent regret . . ." (chap. viii).

The atmosphere of Thrushcross Grange is one of normalcy and convention; but since convention is merely an accepted method of simplifying reality, and since this simplification usually involves a modification or avoidance of the more unpleasant aspects of life, the Lintons, as they are portrayed by the outcast Heathcliff, exist in a polite and petty play-world. The vision of Edgar and Isabella battling for possession of a lap dog, "a heap of warm hair" (Chap. VI), a prize so little desired that it is eventually refused by both, can only arouse contempt in a proud and unregenerate nature which equates battle with life itself.

The book image, insofar as it represents a civilizing force and a bulwark of that convention which seeks to cover naked experience, is the core of the Grange. When with Heathcliff's return domestic strife becomes the rule in his home, Edgar increases the frequency of his visits to his books: the tranquillity of the Grange is upset by the wild energy of the Heights, and he is personally threatened by those forces which his early education failed to take into account. Ellen tells Catherine that he is continually in the library " 'since he has no other society' " (chap. xii). The book becomes the natural heritage of the second Catherine and is closely identified with her. Her father takes her training upon himself, introduces her to reading, and permits her to share his sanctuary. " 'She learned rapidly and eagerly,' " comments Ellen, " 'and did honour to his teaching' " (chap. xviii). By the time of Edgar's final illness it can be asserted that "the library, where her father stopped a short time daily . . . and his chamber, had become her whole world" (chap. xxvii).

If the domain of Heathcliff illustrates an attempt to create a reality, then Thrushcross Grange under Edgar Linton reflects a shrinking from reality, a denial of aggressive will. There, escape from the conditions of an unpleasant status quo is effected by means of withdrawal, and refuge is found in the book. Heathcliff and Catherine may be said to exist solely in terms of active voli- /162/ tion; Edgar derives his requirements for life from passive retreat. The book is used to sustain a shallow view of the world, a view rendered false by its omissions, and in this way the image is again misused. When young Catherine first makes the acquaintance of a seemingly inoffensive Heathcliff, her father undertakes to enlighten her as to his true character:

She appeared so deeply impressed and shocked at this new view of human nature—excluded from all her studies and all her ideas till now—that Mr. Edgar deemed it unnecessary to pursue the subject. He merely added—
"You will know hereafter, darling, why I wish to avoid his house and family: now return to your old employments and amusements, and think no more about them" (chap. xxi).

Isabella too indulges in this characteristic misuse of the image (chap. xvii). It is apparent that such a limitation of awareness through the medium of the book may involve dangers greater than those to be feared from the aspects of life which are denied. The book becomes an excuse for weakness; its misuse is confirmed when Ellen states that Edgar " 'shut himself up among books that he never opened' " (chap. xii). In his flight from that experience not admitted by convention, he ends by ignoring the civilizing factor; his "philosophical resignation" is a false peace.

Another approach to the analysis of the role of the image is afforded by the situations of the two Catherines. These heroines are raised in opposite environments but find that each must face her destiny in the domain of the other. When Heathcliff returns, Mrs. Catherine Linton reacts violently to her position. In the throes of her self-induced illness she is told that her husband is " 'among his books,' " and she cries, " 'What in the name of all that feels has he to do with *books*, when I am dying' " (chap. xii). This is the appeal of the totally involved, those who live in the realm of passionate consciousness and willful action, to the reclusive; and the mind of Catherine for a time strays back to her childhood when she realizes that the Lintons are alien to her and exemplify a completely foreign mode of perception. As his wife slowly regains her health, Edgar uses the logical instrument to bring her into his household again, the book. But the gulf between their sensibilities cannot now be bridged, and his gesture is futile: /163/

A book lay spread on the sill before her, and the scarcely perceptible wind fluttered its leaves at intervals. I believe Linton had laid it there: for she never endeavoured to divert herself with reading, or occupation of any kind, and he would spend many an hour in trying to entice her attention to some subject which had formerly been her amusement (chap. xv).

As Edgar tries unsuccessfully to reconcile the spirit of the Heights to that of his own sphere, so his daughter, using the same means, essays the same feat. For her Wuthering Heights exercises an unavoidable attraction, and the presence there of young Linton is only another inducement to the creation of a new harmony between the houses. Her first efforts to send Linton some books are thwarted by Ellen, but difficulties are overcome, and she is soon able to visit the Heights regularly. Her marriage to Heathcliff's son is, however, destined to end unhappily, for in order to assimilate past into present and create a confident future, she must descend into and emerge from the reality of Wuthering Heights. Edgar failed to win

Cathy's mother to the cause of an image of withdrawal; now Cathy will have her books, those same images of an unreal security, confiscated. After she enters the camp of Heathcliff, the image predominates, a climax is attained, and the book reappears as reconciliation.

From her lifelong haven Catherine Heathcliff is thrust into a vortex of abnormal emotion. Her faith in herself has never been forged, and Zillah asks, " 'what will all her learning and her daintiness do for her now?' " (chap. xxx). The death of her pitiful husband breaks her only link to her former home: it is the death of all sense of purpose in her life. She suddenly awakes, as did her mother before her, to find herself in an adverse world which threatens the very basis of her identity. " 'I feel like death!' " she cries (chap. xxx). Shaken by her experience, she (in unconscious imitation of her father) withdraws. In her heart she erects a shrine to the illusion of her girlhood, the illusion represented by the book. When Hareton appropriates some volumes that she has found, she complains to Lockwood: " 'Those books, both prose and verse, were consecrated to me by other associations; and I hate to see them debased and profaned in his mouth!' " (chap. xxxi). The cold drives her into the midst of the society of the Heights, but she adopts the rude manners of the household /164/ only insofar as they serve her to keep the present from desecrating her spiritual retreat into the past: not being able to enforce self-exile, she wishes to exile the world. " 'Mr. Hareton,' " she informs the company, " 'and the whole set of you, will be good enough to understand that I reject any pretence at kindness you have the hypocrisy to offer! I despise you, and will have nothing to say to any of you!' " (chap. xxx). It is the ultimate sterility of this attitude which she recognizes when she tells Hareton she is " 'stalled.' "

It is significant that she addresses this confession to Hareton, as if she were already aware that he is to be her salvation just as she is to be his. Heathcliff has formed Hindley's son into a replica of his own youthful degradation and humiliation, which Ellen pictures in the following terms:

"Then personal appearance sympathised with mental deterioration: he acquired a slouching gait and ignoble look; his naturally reserved disposition was exaggerated into an almost idiotic excess of unsociable moroseness; and he took a grim pleasure, apparently, in exciting the aversion rather than the esteem of his few acquaintance" (chap. viii).

It has already been noted that Heathcliff's rejection of the book was a cause of his gradual estrangement from Catherine Earnshaw, and it is here seen as the reason for his physical deterioration as well. He has carefully inculcated this hatred in Hareton (chap. xxxi). Nevertheless, there is a strain of quality in the boy which even the machinations of Heathcliff cannot alter. Ellen's description of Hareton can be compared to the one of his evil mentor just cited:

"I could scarcely refrain from smiling at this antipathy to the poor fellow: who was a well-made, athletic youth, good-looking in features, and stout and healthy, but attired in garments befitting his daily occupations of working on the farm. . . . Still, I thought I could detect in his physiognomy a mind owning better qualities than his father ever possessed. Good things lost amid a wilderness of weeds, to be sure . . . yet, notwithstanding, evidence of a wealthy soil, that might yield luxuriant crops under other and favourable circumstances" (chap. xviii).

Heathcliff acknowledges the superiority of Hareton only to credit himself with its eternal subjugation. But this is not to be the case, for Hareton has within him the seeds of transformation.

Mrs. Van Ghent, as has been seen, refers to the novel as "a ten- /165/ sion between two kinds of reality." It is obvious that both Cathy and Hareton are victims of that tension, each representing a kind of reality. Each is the incarnate ideal of the heroes in opposition, Edgar and Heathcliff; each is a product of a certain misuse of the book. But unlike those who molded them, they conceive of the limitations of their positions and move to counteract absolute stagnation. Only together, mutually aiding one another, can they struggle free of influences which have made them prey to conscious or unconscious misunderstanding. The value of Catherine's inheritance, striving to disassociate itself from false purposes, discovers its proper subject in Hareton; and he, recognizing his own potentialities and needs in it, takes it for his proper object. This value, which resolves an apparently inevitable and insurmountable tension, is, quite logically, expressed by the image of the book.

Hareton is stimulated by his contact with Catherine to desire education, and he tries to make himself agreeable when she begins to frequent the kitchen. There she discovers some volumes which Hareton helps her to reach: "That was a great advance for the lad. She didn't thank him; still, he felt gratified that she had accepted his assistance . . ." (chap. xxx). This is the initial hint of cooperation between the two, and although the event does not conclude happily, it is a portent of times to come. The characteristic misuse of the book at Thrushcross Grange stands between Catherine and her surroundings; but a second and decisive encounter of the two young people and the book is to dissolve the final barrier.

Hareton steals Catherine's small library, and she views this as a threat to the truest level of her identity: " 'And he wants *me* to sink into a dunce, meantime' " (chap. xxxi). She and he argue; the resources of suffering and pride are marshalled and sent into action. In a climactic gesture Hareton, the slave of the psychology of the Heights repeating its distinctive misuse of the image, throws the books into the fire. The conflagration would appear to depict the victory of the ungoverned will over moderation and forgiveness: the image of a possible reconciliation is consumed; discord and brutality triumph.

In 1842, while a student of M. Heger in Brussels, Emily Brontë wrote, as an exercise, a number of short essays in French. One of these curious productions is a philosophical piece on the nature of /166/ creation entitled "The Butterfly."[3] In it the first-person protagonist wanders on a summer day through a peaceful wood, but in the processes of nature she can see only an insane mutual destruction. Within a flower she finds "an ugly caterpillar," a symbol of human activity upon the earth, which can only derive its sustenance from annihilation; and she arrives at an unavoidable question: "why was man created? He torments, he kills, he devours; he suffers, dies, is devoured—that's his whole story" (p. 18). From this cycle there is seemingly no escape. She throws flower and insect to the ground and tramples them. But just as she does so, a butterfly, "a symbol of the world to come," flutters before her eyes; and the truth is revealed: "this globe is the embyro of a new heaven and of a new earth whose meagerest beauty infinitely surpasses mortal imagination"; and the greater conclusion is inferred:

God is the God of justice and mercy; then, assuredly each pain that he inflicts on his creatures, be they human or animal, rational or irrational, each suffering of our unhappy nature is only a seed for that divine harvest which will be gathered when sin having spent its last drop of poison, death having thrown its last dart, both will expire on the funeral pyre of a universe in flame, and will leave their former victims to an eternal realm of happiness and glory (pp. 18-19).

It is through suffering that evil is eventually purged and happiness made possible. A general conflagration separates the two worlds of pain and bliss, a conflagration in which sin and death are forever consumed. So in *Wuthering Heights,* when the prime mover of evil is exhausted, when Heathcliff suffers his *crise de volonté,* the image of the book, abused by two extremes of reality, is

---

[3] Emily Brontë, *Five Essays Written in French* (El Paso, 1948), pp. 17-19.

fed to the flames; and out of the microcosmic conflagration arises an existence of stability and peace, the ideal of the novel realized in the unheroic terms of Cathy and Hareton, who find in their natures and experience the possibility of reconciliation within the framework of society and who accept the conditions of man's limitations.

It has already been noted that *Wuthering Heights* does not invoke an omnipotent point of view representing some absolute concept of morality; however, a mode of justice does function in the novel, and it is the same justice which is at work in "The But-/167/ terfly"; but here the apocalyptic character of the destructive fire is set within one world, only types of reality being differentiated. The collapse of the reality of the Heights takes place immediately after Hareton has consigned the volumes to the blaze. Heathcliff appears and for the first time his resolution falters: " 'It will be odd if I thwart myself' " (chap. xxxi). The fire has returned things to themselves, to the paradise of normalcy: Cathy and Hareton are ready to resume their rightful places, evil is spent. In this new life founded upon acceptance, operating as reconciliation, the book fulfills its proper duty.

When Lockwood returns to the Heights after an absence of nearly a year, he is greeted by its summer aspect, by the sight of the lovers united by the book. Catherine Earnshaw strove in her way to provide an environment for Heathcliff and herself; indeed, this was a principal reason for her marriage to Edgar; but she overestimated the power of her will, the efficacy of her love, and by so doing misjudged the nature of life itself. " 'I thought,' " she exclaims during her spiritual breakdown, " 'though everybody hated and despised each other, they could not avoid loving me' " (chap. xii). Her crisis results in self-discovery, for she perceives that she has attempted what cannot be realized in this world, but only in some world beyond. In order to meet her challenge Heathcliff must disassociate his love from the desire for revenge, and in order to do this he must undermine the very basis of his identity, itself the creation of a thwarted will. No bond in this life can join such lovers. But Cathy Heathcliff is able to accomplish what the first Catherine could not: she places her love not within a self-created environment, the glorification of the will, but within human society, the modification of the will; and Hareton in his turn endows her existence with purpose. The bond which joins them is imaged by the book. " 'The intimacy thus commenced, grew rapidly,' " Ellen reports, "though it encountered temporary interruptions. Earnshaw was not to be civilized with a wish, and my young lady was no philosopher, and no paragon of patience; but both their minds tending to the same point— one loving and desiring to esteem, and the other loving and desiring to be esteemed—they contrived in the end to reach it" (chap. xxxii).

Throughout the novel Ellen Dean has remained the calm in the eye of the hurricane. Secure and unassailable in her limited uni- /168/ verse, she demonstrates the strengths and weaknesses of convention. She does not hesitate to credit the cause of her stability: " 'I have undergone sharp discipline, which has taught me wisdom; and then, I have read more than you would fancy, Mr. Lockwood. You could not open a book in this library that I have not looked into, and got something out of also . . .' " (chap. vii). She refers to the library at Thrushcross Grange, the same library from which new books arrive after Hareton's destructive act. And from these books comes a world of eternal summer where the individual is reconciled to himself and to reality. Catherine and Hareton both attain their true natures and resolve their animosities to others. This was Emily Brontë's conception of the effectiveness of the book and its rightful use. In another of her French essays, "Lettre d'un frère à un frère," the library is the scene of renunciation and forgiveness, and in one of the Gondal poems, which has been related to the theme of the Palace of Instruction in that imaginary country, she writes;

> All day I've toiled, but not with pain
> In learning's golden mine;
> And now at eventide again
> The moonbeams softly shine.
>
> .   .   .
>
> True to myself, and true to all,
> May I be healthful still,
> And turn away from passion's call
> And curb my own wild will.[4] /169/

Questions for Discussion and Writing

1. Robert McKibben mentions Dorothy Van Ghent's criticism of *Wuthering Heights* twice, and even quotes Mrs. Van Ghent's opening sen-

[4] C. W. Hatfield (ed.), *The Complete Poems of Emily Jane Brontë* (New York, 1941), p. 35.

tences (page 159). Do the two scholars conflict in their readings of the
novel? If so, in what respects? (With which critic do you agree?) If not,
what does Mr. McKibben add to Mrs. Van Ghent's interpretation and
analysis? Is his a significant addition?

2. McKibben speaks of the contrasts in *Wuthering Heights*. To what
extent does he believe the novel is based on contrast? What do other
critics make of contrast in *Wuthering Heights?*

3. How does McKibben define the environment of *Wuthering Heights?*
Compare and contrast his definition with those of other critics.

4. The first sentence of the second paragraph on page 161 is difficult to
understand at first reading. When you are sure of its meaning, especially
in relation to the rest of the paragraph, put the sentence into your own
words, and state its explicit relationship to McKibben's central idea.

5. McKibben says that each Catherine "must face her destiny in the
domain of the other." (page 163) He applies this statement to his own
purposes; can you find other applications? The other critics will supply
you with some, but try to draw a few from your own reading as well.

6. What would David Cecil say to the above statement? Would he entirely agree that the younger Catherine, living at Wuthering Heights, is
in a domain which is the opposite of her own nature? (Note on the following page that McKibben calls the Heights "an adverse world.")

7. What role, according to McKibben, does suffering play in *Wuthering
Heights?* Does he consider it a theme in the novel? Is suffering an important element in *Wuthering Heights?* What is the general critical comment on suffering in the novel?

8. What does McKibben mean when he speaks of "the book image" in
Wuthering Heights? Do you agree that books are a sustained image
throughout the novel? What attention has been paid to the books in other
critical articles?

9. Account for the similarity of metaphor between Edgar Shannon's "the
ethical eye of the storm" (see his article, page 99) and Robert McKibben's
"the calm in the eye of the hurricane." (page 168) Why are the two critics
led to such similarity of expression? Does the novel itself lead one to such
metaphors?

10. One may conclude from this article that McKibben finds the younger
Catherine and Hareton superior to the mother and Heathcliff—do you
agree? Support or modify this idea. Many other scholars wholeheartedly
propose the reverse idea—that the older couple is superior to the younger.
Present the two contrasting ideas fully; then see if you can reconcile them
to any degree.

Topics for Research

The purpose of the following lists is not to exhaust the possibilities for research in *Wuthering Heights,* but to suggest the kinds of approaches that may be made to the novel. The first list, which suggests topics which can be pursued entirely within this text, is divided into medium (1000-1500 words) and long (more than 1500 words). Such division is to some extent arbitrary; the student may well change the length of many topics in either list, according to the extent to which he pursues his problem, and his ability to write concisely. The second list presents topics which will take the student beyond the confines of this text. In addition to the obvious use of such topics in upper-class courses, it is hoped that they may serve as a basis for library exercises for students learning the methods of research.

Medium Topics

1. *Wuthering Heights* as a realistic novel.
2. *Wuthering Heights* as a dramatic novel.
3. *Wuthering Heights* as a novel of violence.
4. *Wuthering Heights* as a pastoral.
5. *Wuthering Heights* as a tragedy.
6. Supernatural elements in *Wuthering Heights.*
7. The motif of extremity and excessivism in *Wuthering Heights.*
8. The weather of *Wuthering Heights.*
9. Emily Brontë's use of background.
10. Animal imagery in *Wuthering Heights.*
11. The incest theme in *Wuthering Heights.*
12. Heredity as a factor in Emily Brontë's novel.
13. The villain of *Wuthering Heights.*
14. The function of the narrators.
15. The role of Lockwood.
16. Lockwood's comments at the conclusion of the novel.
17. A study of Lockwood's dreams.
18. A study of Catherine's dreams.
19. The two Catherines: comparison and contrast.
20. The role of the second Catherine.
21. The role of Hareton.
22. The role of Edgar Linton.
23. The role of Isabella.

24. *Wuthering Heights* and the problem of probability.
25. Emily Brontë's handling of passage of time.
26. Comic elements in *Wuthering Heights*.
27. Emily Brontë's prose style.
28. Emily Brontë's definition of love.
29. Flaws in *Wuthering Heights*.

Long Topics

1. *Wuthering Heights* as a novel of revenge.
2. *Wuthering Heights* as a novel of contrasts.
3. *Wuthering Heights* as a psychological novel.
4. *Wuthering Heights* as a poem.
5. The imagery of *Wuthering Heights*.
6. Emily Brontë's use of irony.
7. Realism and romance in *Wuthering Heights*.
8. The function of dreams in *Wuthering Heights*.
9. Atmosphere in *Wuthering Heights*.
10. The landscape of *Wuthering Heights*.
11. The role of nature in *Wuthering Heights*.
12. Purpose of violence in *Wuthering Heights*.
13. Tyranny as a motif in *Wuthering Heights*.
14. *Wuthering Heights:* a definition of degeneration.
15. Character motivation in *Wuthering Heights*.
16. Morality in *Wuthering Heights*.
17. Heathcliff as a focal point of differing ways of considering human personality by Emily Brontë's characters.
18. Attitude toward death in *Wuthering Heights*.
19. Point of view in *Wuthering Heights*.
20. The structure of *Wuthering Heights*.
21. A history of criticism of Emily Brontë's novel.
22. The unity of *Wuthering Heights*.

Topics Requiring Research Outside This Volume

1. Emily Brontë and the tradition of the Victorian novel.
2. Victorian England as mirrored and commented upon in *Wuthering Heights*.
3. *Wuthering Heights* and its contemporary audience.
4. Autobiographical elements in *Wuthering Heights*.
5. *Angria* and *Gondal:* dry runs for *Wuthering Heights?*
6. The claims for Branwell and/or Charlotte as co-authors.
7. A comparison of *Wuthering Heights* and *Jane Eyre*.
8. A comparison of Emily Brontë and Jane Austen.
9. The handling of protagonists in *Wuthering Heights, An American Tragedy,* and *A Farewell to Arms*.
10. The handling of protagonists in *Wuthering Heights, Vanity Fair,* and *Great Expectations*.

11. The handling of protagonists in *Wuthering Heights, Moll Flanders,* and *Tristram Shandy.*
12. The supernatural contrasted in *Wuthering Heights, The Scarlet Letter,* and *The Turn of the Screw.*
13. *Wuthering Heights* and the poetry of Emily Brontë.
14. *Wuthering Heights* and the tradition of the ghost story.
15. Heathcliff and the daemonic tradition.
16. Heathcliff as a Byronic figure.
17. Emily Brontë and contemporary religion.
18. Emily Brontë's use of the novel.
19. The enduring popularity of *Wuthering Heights.*
20. The influence of *Wuthering Heights* on modern fiction.

Bibliography: Emily Brontë and *Wuthering Heights*

Aiken, Ralph. "Wild-Heart: An Appreciation of Emily Jane Brontë," *South Atlantic Quarterly*, XXXIV (1935), 202-210.

Allen, Walter. *The English Novel*. London, 1954; New York, 1958.

Allot, Miriam. "*Wuthering Heights*': the Rejection of Heathcliff?" *Essays in Criticism*, VIII, 1 (January 1958), 27-47.

Bald, Marjory A. *Women Novelists of the Nineteenth Century*. Cambridge, England, 1923.

Bataille, George. "Emily Brontë et la mal," *La Littérature et Le Mal* (1957).

Bentley, Phyllis. *The Brontës*. Denver, 1947.

Blondel, Jacques. "Emily Brontë: Recentes Explorations," *Etudes Anglaises*, XI, 4 (October-December 1958), 323-330.

Bloomfield, Louis. "Review of *Wuthering Heights*," *Time and Tide* (March 1948).

Bradner, Leicester. "Growth of *Wuthering Heights*," *Publications of the Modern Language Association*, XLVIII (March 1932), 129-146.

Brown, E. K. *Rhythm in the Novel*. Toronto, 1956.

Crandall, Norma. *Emily Brontë: a Psychological Portrait*. Rindge, New Hampshire, 1957.

Dean, Christopher. "Joseph's Speech in *Wuthering Heights*," *Notes and Queries*, VII, 2 (February 1960), 73-76.

Debri-Bridel, Jacques. *Le Secret d'Emily Brontë*. Paris, 1950.

Dodds, M. H. "Heathcliff's Country," *Modern Language Review*, XXXIX (1944), 116-129.

Dugas, J. H. "The Literary Reputation of the Brontës, 1846-1951," *Dissertation Abstracts*, XII (1952), 61-62.

Escombe, Lucienne. *Emily Brontë et ses dèmons*. Paris, 1941.

Evans, Margiad. "Byron and Emily Brontë," *Life and Letters*, LVII (1948), 193-216.

Fenton, Edith M. "The Spirit of *Wuthering Heights* as Distinguished from That of Gothic Romance," *Washington University Studies*, VII (Humanistic Series, No. 1, 1920), 108.

Ford, Boris. "*Wuthering Heights*," *Scrutiny*, VII, 4 (March 1939), 375-389.

Forster, E. M. *Aspects of the Novel*. New York, 1927.

Fotheringham, James. "The Work of Emily Brontë and the Brontë Problem," *Transactions of the Brontë Society* (June 1900), 107-134.

Gettmann, Royal A. Introduction to *Wuthering Heights*. Modern Library College Edition. New York, 1943.

Goldstone, Herbert. "*Wuthering Heights* Revisited," *English Journal,* XLVIII, 4 (April 1959), 175-195.

Hatfield, C. W. *The Complete Poems of Emily Jane Brontë*. New York, 1941.

Hawkes, Jacquetta. "Haworth Moors," *Spectator,* CXC (May 15, 1953), 600.

Hinkley, Laura L. *Charlotte and Emily*. New York, 1945.

Justus, James. "Beyond Gothicism: *Wuthering Heights* and an American Tradition," *Tennessee Studies In Literature,* V (1960), 25-33.

Kavanagh, C. S. *Symbolism of* Wuthering Heights. 1929.

Klingopulos, G. D. "The Novel as Dramatic Poem (II): '*Wuthering Heights*,'" *Scrutiny,* XIV, 4 (September 1947), 269-286.

Law, Alice. *Patrick Branwell Brontë*. London, 1923.

Lewis, C. Day. *Notable Images of Virtue*. Toronto, 1954.

Lucas, Peter. *Introduction to the Psychology of* Wuthering Heights. 1943.

MacCarthy, B. G. "Emily Brontë," *Studies,* XXXIX (1951), 15-30.

Macaulay, Rose. Introduction to *Wuthering Heights*. Modern Library Edition. New York, n.d.

Mackay, Angus. "Emily Brontë," *Westminster Review,* CL (August 1898), 203.

Maeterlinck, Maurice. *Wisdom and Destiny*. Tr. by Alfred Sutro. New York, 1914.

Maurer, K. W. "The Poetry of Emily Brontë," *Anglia,* LXI (1937), 443-448.

Moore, Geoffrey. Foreword to *Wuthering Heights*. Signet Classics Edition. New York, 1959.

Moore, Virginia. *The Life and Eager Death of Emily Brontë*. London, 1936.

Morgan, Charles. "Emily Brontë," *The Great Victorians*. Ed. H. J. and Hugh Massingham. New York, 1932.

Nicoll, W. R. "Emily Brontë," *British Weekly* (October 1908).

Pritchett, V. S. Introduction to *Wuthering Heights*. Riverside Edition. Boston, 1956.

Ratchford, Fannie Elizabeth. *The Brontë's Web of Childhood*. New York, 1941.

Read, Herbert. *Reason and Romanticism*. London, 1926.

Robinson, A. Mary F. (Madame Duclaux) *Emily Brontë*. New York, 1883.

Saintsbury, George. *The English Novel*. London and New York, 1913.

Schorer, Mark. "Fiction and the Matrix of Analogy," *Kenyon Review,* XI, 4 (September 1949), 544-550.

Shorter, Clement. *The Brontës: Life and Letters*. London, 1908.

Simpson, Charles. *Emily Brontë*. New York, 1929.

Sinclair, May. *The Three Brontës*. Boston and New York, 1912.

————. "Who Wrote *Wuthering Heights?*" *Bookman*, LVI (May 1924), 97-98.

Smith, J. C. "Emily Brontë: A Reconsideration," *Essays and Studies*, V (1914), 132-152.

Spark, Muriel, and Derek Stanford. *Emily Brontë*. London, 1953.

Spurgeon, Caroline Frances Eleanor. *Mysticism in English Literature*. Cambridge and New York, 1913.

Stephen, Leslie. *Hours in a Library*. New York, 1879.

Swinburne, A. C. "Emily Brontë," *Miscellanies*. London and New York, 1911.

Symons, Arthur. *Dramatis Personae*. Indianapolis and New York, 1925.

————. *Emily Brontë*. New York, 1906. Reprinted in *Figures of Several Centuries*. New York, 1916.

Taine, Hippolyte A. *History of the English Novel*. 1909.

Traversi, Derek. "The Brontë Sisters and *Wuthering Heights*," *Dickens to Hardy;* Vol. VI of *The Pelican Guide to English Literature*. Hammonds-Worth, Middlesex, England, 1958.

Turnell, M. "*Wuthering Heights*," *Dublin Review*, CCVI (January 1940), 134-149.

Van Ghent, Dorothy. "The Window Figure and the Two-Children Figure in *Wuthering Heights*," *Nineteenth-Century Fiction*, VII (December 1953), 189-197.

Wagenknecht, Edward. "The Greatness of *Wuthering Heights*," *Cavalcade of the English Novel*. New York, 1954.

Walker, Hugh. *The Literature of the Victorian Era*. Cambridge, 1910.

Watson, Melvin R. "*Wuthering Heights* and the Critics," *The Trollopian*, III (1948), 243-263.

————. "Form and Substance in the Brontë Novels," *From Jane Austen to Joseph Conrad*. Ed. Robert C. Rathburn and Martin Steinmann, Jr. Minneapolis, 1958.

West, Rebecca. *The Great Victorians*. New York, 1932.

Willy, Margaret. "Emily Brontë: Poet and Mystic," *English*, VI (1946), 117-122.

Wilson, Romer. *All Alone, the Life and Private History of Emily Jane Brontë*. London, 1928.

Wise, Thomas James, and J. A. Symington. *The Brontës: Their Lives, Friendships, and Correspondence*. Oxford, 1932.

Notes on the Critics

RUTH M. ADAMS is an assistant professor of English at the University of Rochester. She studied at Adelphi, Columbia, and Radcliffe. Her major concerns are Victorian biography and novel, and the short story. Among her writings are articles on Gissing and Scott.

EARNEST A. BAKER was a noted English librarian and man of letters, the first director of the University of London School of Librarianship, 1919-1934. In addition to the monumental *History of the English Novel*, he compiled several anthologies.

EDWARD FREDERIC BENSON, British novelist, essayist, and biographer, graduated from Cambridge and was an honorary fellow of Magdalen College. He is the brother of the well-known poet and scholar, A. C. Benson. One of his earliest novels, *Dodo* (1893), was an outstanding popular success, but he is now best remembered for his biographies, which include *Charlotte Brontë, Queen Victoria,* and *The Kaiser and English Relatives.*

ALLAN R. BRICK took his B.A. at Haverford and his Ph.D. at Yale. He has taught at Dartmouth, and is now assistant professor of English at Goucher College.

LORD DAVID CECIL, a distinguished British literary critic and historian, is Goldsmiths' Professor of English Literature at Oxford. Among his many books are *The Stricken Deer* (a biography of William Cowper); *Hardy, the Novelist; Melbourne;* and *The Fine Art of Reading.*

RICHARD CHASE is a New Englander who received his B.A. from Dartmouth and his Ph.D. from Columbia, where he is presently teaching. He is the author of many articles in literary journals, and has published the following works of criticism: *Quest for Myth, Herman Melville, Emily Dickinson, Walt Whitman Reconsidered,* and *The American Novel and Its Tradition.*

JAMES HAFLEY is an associate professor of English at Catholic University. He has written a study of Virginia Woolf entitled *The Glass Roof.*

ARNOLD KETTLE is Senior Lecturer in English Literature at the University of Leeds.

JOHN K. MATHISON is an associate professor of English at the University of Wyoming. Although a specialist in nineteenth-century fiction, he has written substantial articles on Gerard Manley Hopkins and William Wordsworth.

BRUCE MCCULLOUGH, emeritus professor of English at New York University, has also taught at Grinnell College, the University of Pennsylvania, the University of Akron, and the University of Chattanooga. His specialty is prose fiction.

ROBERT C. MCKIBBEN teaches English at the University of New Hampshire.

VICTOR SAWDON PRITCHETT is a British author and critic, the current Director of the *New Statesman and Nation*. In addition to several articles, his publications include *The Spanish Virgin, Shirley Sanz, Nothing Like Leather, Dead Man Leading, You Make Your Own Life, In My Good Books, It May Never Happen, The Spanish Temper,* and *Collected Stories.*

MARK SCHORER is Chairman of the Department of English of the University of California at Berkeley. He has written introductions to several English novels, is the author of many articles in literary journals, and has published several scholarly books on English literature.

EDGAR E. SHANNON, JR., a noted student of Victorian literature, is the President of the University of Virginia.

ERIC SOLOMON teaches English at the Ohio State University.

MRS. DOROTHY VAN GHENT has taught, among other places, at the University of Kansas, the University of Vermont, and Brandeis University. She has published significantly in the literary journals, and is currently at work on a book on the Continental novel.

MELVIN R. WATSON is an associate professor of English at the Louisiana State University. He has taught at Queens College (North Carolina) and at Mary Washington College. Besides interest in the Brontës, he has concerned himself with Keats, Shelley, and the neo-classical period.

CARL R. WOODRING is an associate professor of English at the University of Wisconsin. He has held Ford and Guggenheim Fellowships. Nineteenth-century English literature is his field of special study.

VIRGINIA WOOLF, the daughter of the eminent English critic Sir Leslie Stephen, is considered by some to be the most important of modern English novelists. Her chief works are *The Voyage Out, Night and Day, Jacob's Room, Mrs. Dalloway, To the Lighthouse,* and *The Waves.*

GEORGE J. WORTH, an assistant professor of English at the University of Kansas, was born in Vienna, Austria, and educated at the University of Chicago, University College (London), and the University of Illinois. His main literary interests are theory and history of prose fiction and Victorian literature. He has written on Conrad, Carlyle, and Thackeray.